THE CHANGING SHAPE OF WO

The Changing Shape of Work

Edited by

Richard K. Brown
Emeritus Professor of Sociology
University of Durham

Contributors

Sheila Allen, Huw Beynon, Harriet Bradley,
Richard Brown, Robert MacDonald, Lydia Morris,
Ian Roberts, Stephen Taylor

First published in Great Britain 1997 by
MACMILLAN PRESS LTD
Houndmills, Basingstoke, Hampshire RG21 6XS and London
Companies and representatives throughout the world

A catalogue record for this book is available from the British Library.

ISBN 0–333–67814–1 hardback
ISBN 0–333–67815–X paperback

First published in the United States of America 1997 by
ST. MARTIN'S PRESS, INC.,
Scholarly and Reference Division,
175 Fifth Avenue, New York, N.Y. 10010

ISBN 0–312–17251–6

Library of Congress Cataloging-in-Publication Data
The changing shape of work / edited by Richard K. Brown ;
contributors, Sheila Allen . . . [et al.].
p. cm.
Based on papers presented to Section N (Sociology and Social
Policy) of the British Association for the Advancement of Science at
a meeting in 1995.
Includes bibliographical references and index.
ISBN 0–312–17251–6
1. Work—Sociological aspects—Congresses. I. Brown, Richard K.,
1933– . II. Allen, Sheila. III. British Association for the
Advancement of Science. Section N (Sociology and Social Policy)
HD4904.C4535 1997
306.3'6—dc20   96–46174
                                                                          CIP

This book is printed on paper suitable for recycling and made from fully managed and
sustained forest sources.

10   9   8   7   6   5   4
06   05   04   03   02   01   00

Printed and bound in Great Britain by
Antony Rowe Ltd, Chippenham, Wiltshire

Contents

List of Tables		vi
Preface		vii
Notes on the Contributors		ix
1	Introduction: Work and Employment in the 1990s *Richard Brown*	1
2	The Changing Practices of Work *Huw Beynon*	20
3	What is Work for? The Right to Work and the Right to be Idle *Sheila Allen*	54
4	Flexibility and Security: Contradictions in the Contemporary Labour Market *Richard Brown*	69
5	Gender and Change in Employment: Feminization and its Effects *Harriet Bradley*	87
6	Informal Working, Survival Strategies and the Idea of an 'Underclass' *Robert MacDonald*	103
7	Economic Change and Domestic Life *Lydia Morris*	125
8	The Culture of Ownership and the Ownership of Culture *Ian Roberts*	150
9	'Empowerment' or 'Degradation'? Total Quality Management and the Service Sector *Stephen Taylor*	171
Bibliography		203
Subject Index		218
Author Index		223

List of Tables

2.1   Changing Patterns of Employment in the UK
1979–95 ('000s)   22

2.2   Changing Patterns of Gender Employment
1979–95 ('000s)   25

2.3   Changes in Weekly Earnings 1979–95 (in 1995
prices)   28

2.4   Labour Force Changes 1979–95 ('000s)   31

2.5   Changing Labour Contracts 1979–95 ('000s)   34

2.6   State Sector Employment 1982–92 ('000s)   39

2.7   Economic Activity Rates 1975–93
(percentages)   44

5.1   Employees' Attitudes to Employment   94

5.2   Time Taken Out of the Labour Market to Bring
up Children   95

5.3   Percentages of Women and Men Wishing for
Promotion at Work, by Age (Full-time Workers
Only)   98

6.1   The Status of Young Adults in 1995 who were
Involved in Enterprise in 1989   107

Preface

The chapters in this book are based on papers presented to Section N (Sociology and Social Policy) of the British Association for the Advancement of Science at its Annual Festival in 1995 held in the University of Newcastle upon Tyne. As President of the Section for that year I organized its programme for one day of the Festival on the theme of 'The Changing Shape of Work'. The day concluded with a panel discussion which involved all the contributors to this volume, and some of the points and arguments made during that discussion have been incorporated in the Introduction to this book.

I would like to thank all the contributors to this book both for agreeing to present papers to the British Association meeting and for subsequently preparing their contributions for publication. I am also very grateful to John Cooper, Recorder of Section N, and to Robin Humphries, Local Secretary to the Section in 1995, for all their advice and support in arranging and carrying out the programme for the 'President's Day'.

Basil Blackwell is gratefully acknowledged for permission to include Chapter 8 by Lydia Morris which originally appeared in *The International Journal of Urban and Regional Research*, Vol. 18, 1994, under the title 'Informal aspects of social divisions'.

Richard K. Brown

Notes on the Contributors

Sheila Allen is Research Professor of Sociology and University Advisor on Equal Opportunities, and Director of the Work and Gender Research Unit, in the University of Bradford. Her main areas of research are the sociology of work, ethnic and race relations, and the sociology of gender divisions. She has published extensively in these areas and is currently writing a book for Oxford University Press on 'Feminist Contributions to Sociology'. In addition to articles in books and journals her recent publications include *Homeworking – myths and realities*, with Carol Wolkowitz (Macmillan, 1987) and *Women in Business: perspectives on women entrepreneurs*, edited with Carole Truman (Routledge, 1993).

Huw Beynon is Professor of Sociology in the University of Manchester where he has also been Research Dean of the Graduate School of Economic, Social and Legal Studies. He has undertaken research and published extensively on many aspects of work and industry including the motor industry (*Working for Ford*, Penguin, second edition 1984), chemicals (*Living with Capitalism* (with Theo Nichols), Routledge, 1977), and steel and coal (*A Tale of Two Industries*, Open University Press, 1991, and *A Place called Teesside*, Edinburgh University Press, 1994 (both with Ray Hudson & David Sadler)). The first volume of his study of the Durham miners, *Masters and Servants* (with Terry Austrin, Rivers Oram Press) was published in 1994.

Harriet Bradley is Lecturer in Sociology at Bristol University and was previously Reader in Sociology at Sunderland University. Her most recent publication is *Fractured Identities: changing patterns of inequality* (Polity Press, 1996) and she is currently writing a book based on her research project on women, work and trade unions, which provided the material for the paper in this volume.

Richard Brown is Emeritus Professor of Sociology in the University of Durham. His research interests are in the sociology of work and employment, and he was the founding editor of the British Sociological Association journal, *Work, Employment and Society*. His recent publications include *Understanding Industrial Organisations. Theoretical perspectives in industrial sociology* (Routledge, 1992).

Robert MacDonald is Senior Lecturer in Sociology in the University of Teesside, and researches and writes about youth and about changing cultures of work. In addition to many articles he is the author of *Risky Business? Youth and the enterprise culture*, with Frank Coffield, (Falmer Press, 1991).

Lydia Morris is Professor of Sociology at the University of Essex. She has a long-standing interest in the social effects of economic decline, and particularly in unemployment and gender relations. Her publications include: *The Workings of the Household* (Polity Press, 1990); *Dangerous Classes. The underclass and social citizenship* (Routledge, 1994); and *Social Divisions. Economic decline and social structural change* (UCL Press, 1995).

Ian Roberts is Lecturer in Sociology in the University of Durham, where he has researched and taught for over ten years. He has worked for Durham University Business School researching industrial relations in small firms, and his publications include *Craft, Class and Control* (Edinburgh University Press, 1993), a study of the changing nature of the community and the labour process in the shipbuilding industry. He is currently undertaking research into the changing relationships between skilled and unskilled workers in the construction and engineering industries.

Steve Taylor is Lecturer in Sociology in the University of Teesside. He studied at the Universities of Nottingham Trent and Warwick, and recently completed a Ph.D. thesis, *Work and Autonomy. Case studies of clerical work*, in the Department of Sociology and Social Policy in the University of Durham. His current research interests include emotion and organizations, labour process theory, and the 'culture' of work.

1 Introduction: Work and Employment in the 1990s

WORK AND EMPLOYMENT

This is a book about work. Thus it is about those activities which are 'central to our material existence, to our place in the world and in fact to every aspect of human life' as Sheila Allen puts it in Chapter 3. In a world in which the changing patterns of employment in Europe and beyond, and the continuing recalcitrant high levels of unemployment, are matters of everyday comment by politicians, in the media and elsewhere, it may seem unnecessary to make this point. Yet among sociologists the study of work and employment has become much less fashionable than it was twenty to thirty years ago. Consumption (admittedly previously greatly neglected) is claimed to be more important than production as a source of identity. Questions of cultural change, or the ways in which the social world is constituted through discourse, are seen as more interesting than the operation of labour markets or the nature of the labour process. However, the availability of opportunities for employment, and the conditions under which people are employed, still have more impact on most individuals' life chances than many other more fashionable concerns. Work and employment structure our lives and shape inequalities of condition and opportunity to a greater extent than most if not all other areas of social life.

Such a generalization about a declining interest in work and employment is sweeping, of course, and subject to considerable reservations and exceptions. The contributors to this book can be counted among these many exceptions. All of them would, I think, agree about the centrality of the changing shape of work to any understanding of contemporary society. They have certainly focused on the study of work and employment throughout their own working lives as students, researchers and teachers. They, and many others, have contributed to the substantial knowledge and understanding of work in Britain, and elsewhere in the world, which sociologists

1

in this country have garnered over the last half century. In consequence this area of enquiry continues to be one with a great richness of research findings, and of concepts and theoretical perspectives, which have been subjected to extensive discussion and critical refinement; a wealth of material and ideas which is reflected in the contributions to this volume.

The papers which formed the starting point for this book were first presented to a meeting of the Sociology and Social Policy Section of the British Association for the Advancement of Science in 1995. That meeting took place in Newcastle upon Tyne a month after the fiftieth anniversary of the end of the Second World War. During the half century which has followed the War the 'shape' of work in Britain, and in many other parts of the world, changed dramatically. During the past two decades the pace of change seems to have increased and its direction altered in certain important respects. The purpose of this book is to explore these changes, especially the more recent ones, and to identify their significance and implications. In tackling this brief the contributors have not only been able to draw on many years' study of work and employment but also on their own detailed empirical research in a variety of locations.

As was appropriate for a meeting held in that region many, though by no means all, of these locations were in the North-East of England. This area of the country has had a distinctive economic and social history and the question arises as to how far patterns of work and employment in the region are different and unlikely to be replicated in other parts of the country. Whilst a definitive answer to this question would require more comparative research recent trends in the region's economy and patterns of employment have been towards reductions in the differences from the rest of the country (Evans et al., 1995). The changes and processes discussed in the contributions to this volume can certainly be paralleled in many other parts of the UK. Although local labour markets in many parts of Britain continue to have specific and distinctive characteristics, they cannot be insulated from national and international influences. Processes of globalization, which are discussed further below, are increasingly subjecting all of them to similar pressures so that the trend is towards greater homogeneity, nationally and internationally.

To discuss the changing shape of **work** is often seen as identical with and limited to discussion of **employment**, that is work for which payment is received as an employee or by someone who is self-employed. Employment is undoubtedly the dominant framework within which the production and distribution of goods and services takes place in societies like our own, both in quantitative terms of volume and value, and symbolically. It is important to emphasize, however, that much work takes place in other contexts, notably the household and the voluntary sector, and not in return for payment or any direct material reward. Indeed, as feminists and others have rightly reminded us in recent years, without the enormous volume and unremitting cycle of domestic labour the formal economy of jobs and pay packets would cease to function; the essential daily and generational reproduction of the labour force is almost entirely dependent on such work.

This distinction between 'work' and 'employment' is now widely and generally accepted amongst sociologists of work. Nevertheless the bulk of their research and writing continues to be devoted to employment, and it is easy for this to obscure the significance of other forms of work. The changing shape of **employment** receives most attention in this volume, but as is acknowledged here and in later contributions it is only one context for work. More specifically the book does include important studies of 'informal' and voluntary work by Robert MacDonald (Chapter 6), and of the connections between employment and unemployment and the organization of the household by Lydia Morris (Chapter 7).

THE HISTORICAL CONTEXT

The reliance on employment as the way in which most individuals and families in our society secure their livelihoods dates from the late 18th and early 19th centuries when the economic and social structure of Britain was transformed by the early stages of industrialization. The nature of the work in which employees and the self-employed have been engaged, and the pattern of social relations of which their employment formed a part, have, however, changed in major ways since that initial transformation, and the pace and extent of the changes have not diminished in recent decades.

Perhaps the most fundamental continuing long-term change has been the shifts in the numbers employed between the main sectors of economic activity. Intrinsic to the initial stages of the process of industrialization is the growth of employment in extractive and manufacturing industry at the expense of employment in agriculture. The contemporary distributions between sectors vary in different highly industrialized societies in interesting and significant ways: markedly higher proportions still employed in manufacturing in Germany, for example, than in most other European societies. In all cases, however, the later stages of industrialization, sometimes labelled 'post-industrialism', have seen a further decline in employment in the primary sector, a decline in employment in manufacturing and an increase in the tertiary, service sector.

In such societies the effective demand for goods may continue to rise but capital investment, increasing mechanization and greater productivity mean that it can be satisfied with fewer employed in manufacturing. The demand for services of all kinds – transport and communications, government and administration, health, education and welfare, financial services, wholesale and retail distribution, leisure facilities, personal services and so on – continues to grow, and cannot all be met by increases in productivity. In Britain fewer than two per cent are now employed in agriculture, forestry and fishing, and the proportion employed in manufacturing had fallen to around 18 per cent in 1995 from nearly 40 per cent 25 years earlier, and for much of the past century (DfEE 1996, p. 12; Brown 1984, pp. 136–7; and see Table 2.1).

This long-term secular trend is often seen as necessarily involving a change in the nature of the work people do from manual to non-manual occupations. Such a change has certainly occurred: only 42 per cent of all employees, self-employed and unemployed in Britain were classified as manual workers in the 1991 Census (half of all males and fewer than a third of all females) in contrast to a situation where nearly three-quarters of all employees were manual workers in 1911 and more than 54 per cent in 1971. The shift from manual to non-manual work, however, has also occurred *within* sectors and is not solely attributable to the growth of the service industries. Thirty nine per cent of those employed in manufacturing in 1994, for example, were in non-manual work (managerial, professional, technical, clerical and sales occupations); and, as it always has done, the service sector includes substantial proportions engaged in manual work, much of it seen as relatively low skilled, and low paid (OPCS/GROS 1994, Table 17; Brown 1984, p. 141; DfEE 1996, p. 14).

These relatively long-term shifts in the contexts in which people work and the nature of the work they do have been accompanied by important changes in the locations for work (from the household and small workshop to employers' premises). The nature of employment relations has also changed: when most employers were small in terms of the numbers employed relations between employer and employee were personal and particularistic (though not for that reason necessarily any less exploitative or oppressive). There were some important early exceptions (for example, the railways, the post office, government) where employment relations were impersonal and bureaucratic. The last hundred years, however, have seen employment dominated by large increasingly impersonal and bureaucratic organizations with hundreds or thousands of employees, a trend which has perhaps been halted and even partially reversed in recent years. In 1993, however, whilst a majority of all businesses in the UK (more than three million out of a total of three and a half million) had between 0 and 4 employees, nearly half of all employees were in organizations employing one hundred or more people, and more than a third in organizations of more than 500 employees (DfEE 1996, p. 18).

There are certain other trends which are almost equally long-term. Over the past century there has been a continuing increase in the proportion of the economically active population (employed and unemployed) who are women (see Harriet Bradley's discussion in Chapter 5, and Table 2.2 below). Census figures show this as rising from less than 30 per cent in 1911 to over 36 per cent in 1971 and nearly 43 per cent in 1991; it is currently close to a half. An increasing proportion of the women who are economically active are married or cohabiting (more than three quarters in 1991); and an increasing proportion of married women are economically active (Brown 1984, p. 141; OPCS/GROS 1993, Tables 91 and 92). Associated with this growth in married women's employment has been the absolute and relative increase in the number of part-time jobs, most of them filled by women (see Chapter 2, and Table 2.5).

These quantitative changes in the gender distribution of employment – a crucial part, but only a part, of what is meant by the 'feminization' of the labour force – should not be allowed to obscure some regrettably persistent qualitative differences in the occupational distributions of men and women. Despite legislative and other commitments to equal opportunity most women are occupationally 'segregated' from men. More than three quarters of them work in one of four occupational categories: professional occupations related to health, welfare and education; clerical work; selling; and catering, cleaning, hairdressing, etc.; and such occupational categories remain dominated by women, whilst they are greatly under-represented in many other, male dominated, occupations. There also continues to be evidence of a 'glass ceiling'; women are vertically as well as horizontally segregated. Qualifications can sometimes be used effectively as a lever to overcome this discrimination but women remain under-represented in posts of greater seniority and responsibility (and rewards) (Crompton and Sanderson 1992).

During the past twenty to twenty-five years the pattern of employment which became established after the end of the Second World War, and only altered relatively slowly as these long-term trends had their effect, has been subjected to considerable and largely unanticipated changes.

First, and most notable, has been the re-emergence of large scale unemployment as a seemingly permanent feature of the employment landscape. For nearly three decades after 1945 the number officially unemployed remained below (and mostly well below) a million and the unemployment rate rarely exceeded, and was often well below, the three per cent which Beveridge (1944, p. 21) suggested was the lowest level at which frictional unemployment could normally be held. Since the mid-1970s, however, the number registered as unemployed has never dropped below a million, and has been well over double that, or more, most of the time, despite numerous changes in the ways in which the unemployed were counted

(Showler and Sinfield, 1981; Ashton 1986; Table 2.4 below). Recorded unemployment has been particularly high at the two ends of the age range, for young workers aged 16 to 25 and for those aged 55 or over. Indeed the difficulties older male workers have experienced over the past two decades in obtaining paid work has contributed to a significant withdrawal of many of them from the ranks of the economically active, through early retirement, long-term sickness and so on (see Table 2.7 below).

Secondly, the long-term trend for the number and proportion of those who are self-employed to decline has been reversed; the number rose from just over two million in the UK in 1976 to well over three million in 1993 (HMSO, 1994, Table 5.3; and Table 2.4 below). Partly this reflects strong ideological and material support from government for self-employment and small businesses, and for the virtues of enterprise generally; partly it must be seen as an, often rather desperate, response to unemployment (as is discussed further in Chapter 6).

Thirdly, the immediate post-war years saw the growth in the absolute and relative size of the public sector as a consequence of the growth of central and local government, the nationalization of the utilities and other basic industries, and the creation of the National Health Service and the welfare state. Since 1979 this has been reversed through the privatization of the publicly owned industries, many of which made major cuts in the numbers employed both before and after they were sold off (see Chapter 2 and Table 2.6). Many services which remain publicly provided are now in the hands of 'agencies' with an arms-length relationship to government or operate with greater financial and managerial autonomy, as in the case of Grant Maintained schools.

Fourthly, whereas trade union membership had fluctuated widely in the inter-war period, it grew markedly in the postwar years up to 1980, eventually including more than half of those employed, nearly 13 million in total in Britain. The declining numbers employed in extractive and manufacturing industry, and in the public sector, the increase in unemployment, and the explicitly anti-trade union policies pursued by the government since 1979, have all contributed to a fall in the size of the union movement and the proportion of employees who are members (less than 35 per cent in the UK in 1993) (Brown 1984, p. 177; HMSO 1994, Table 5.24). These quantitative changes have been accompanied by significant changes in the patterns of collective bargaining and negotiation which are now increasingly enterprise- or plant-based rather than national in scope (Millward et al., 1992).

Finally, as Huw Beynon discusses further in Chapter 2, there has been the growth of what have come to be labelled 'non-standard' or 'non-regular' forms of employment, a trend which reverses the tendency to de-casualize employment in the earlier part of the post-war period. 'Non-standard' forms of employment are jobs which are *not* full-time and permanent (that is contracted for an indefinite duration), such as part-time working, freelance working, homeworking, subcontracting, fixed term contracts and the employment of 'temporary' workers either directly or via an agency.

As we have seen part-time employment has grown considerably in the past two decades; although it is clearly not 'standard' in that it is not full-time, many, though by no means all, part-time jobs are relatively permanent and their occupants part of the 'core' workforce of the organization in which they are employed. Similarly self-employment varies from highly paid professional workers whose services are always in demand, or employers with securely established businesses, to those who struggle to set up on their own as an alternative to unemployment.

It is the growth of the other forms of 'non-standard' employment, of what is perhaps more appropriately – and certainly more vividly – labelled 'precarious' employment (Allen and Henry 1996), which is of greater significance as an indication of fundamental changes in the shape of paid work. It is difficult to demonstrate unambiguously the absolute and relative increase of those engaged on such 'precarious' non-standard employment contracts (see, for example, Hakim 1987, 1990; Beatson 1995). One of the boldest estimates is that by Hutton (1995, 1996) who has suggested that 30 per cent of adult workers are in insecure forms of employment. Such an estimate would have to include those in jobs which are nominally of indefinite duration but recognized by their occupants to be insecure, but it is probably a better reflection of the extent of insecurity of employment than narrower definitions provide.

Thus, the past two decades have seen marked changes in the labour market and the pattern of employment relations. Some long-term trends – the decline of manufacturing, the growth of non-manual work, of women's employment, and of part-time work – have been accelerated. But other aspects of the pattern of employment which emerged in Britain after 1945 have been radically and suddenly reversed. The outstanding characteristics of the labour market have become flexibility and insecurity (see Chapters 2 and 4), and the demands for flexibility, enterprise and responsiveness to the market have also transformed employment relations within organizations (as is discussed by Ian Roberts and Steve Taylor in Chapters 8 and 9 respectively).

GLOBALIZATION?

The genesis of these changes is complex. In the case of Britain the most obvious starting point might seem to be the election in 1979 of a Conservative government under Margaret Thatcher which had the explicit intention of changing many of the labour market characteristics of the previous three decades. Certainly the 1980s saw the end to any attempt at a tri-partite corporatist management of the economy, the dismantling of various forms of employment protection, and the weakening of the ability of trade unions to protect their members, all in the context of a massive increase in unemployment which in itself inevitably altered the balance of power between capital and labour in a major way. These changes were accompanied by the advocacy of, and some material support for, enterprise and labour market flexibility, which were seen by the government as essential if Britain was to break out of its pattern of long-term economic decline. They were also accompanied by the privatization of previously nationalized industries, and the exposure of as much as possible of the public sector which remained to the 'disciplines' of the market through the creation of 'agencies', compulsory competitive tendering, internal markets, and so on.

Yet, as a number of commentators have remarked, the beginnings of this process can be traced back to 1976, and the demands of the IMF (International Monetary Fund), if not to 1973, and the first oil price rise. Similar developments can be observed in most if not all advanced capitalist societies, and although some of them, such as the USA under Reagan, have had right wing governments with a similar ideological stance to that of the Thatcher governments, others, such as France under Mitterand, have been forced to follow similar policies although at least nominally left-wing governments were in power. Whilst the particular decisions made and policies pursued by the Conservative governments in Britain in the 1980s and 1990s certainly had an effect – and alternative policies *could* have been pursued – they must be set in a wider context.

One way in which this wider context can be characterized is by reference to the notion of globalization. This refers to the removal of technical and political barriers between national economies so that the world approaches being one unified market and national and regional economies and industries are subject to unrestrained international competition.

The British economy has been part of a 'world system' for several centuries, and at many times, for example during the 1930s, changes in the pattern of world trade had a decisive influence on levels of employment and prosperity. 'Globalization', however, implies something more than this. There has been the liberalization of trade which was initiated in the immediate post-War years, partly as a response to the protectionism of the thirties, and has subsequently been extended and strengthened as for example during the recent renegotiation of the GATT (General Agreement on Tariffs and Trade). Secondly, since the early 1980s there has been a big increase in the freedom to move financial capital across national borders to wherever it can secure the highest rate of return, so that national economic policy has become much more closely constrained by the demands of these markets. Thirdly, transnational corporations (TNCs) now dominate world trade and, in particular, are responsible for much higher levels of foreign direct investment. Securing such investment is important for the 'success' of most national economies, and thus governments adjust their policies – for example, on taxation, industrial relations, the regulation of working conditions and of the environment – in order to compete successfully with other societies in attracting it (Leys 1996). The development of means of transport and communication, combined with the fragmentation of processes of production, have made it much more easily and cheaply possible to locate operations almost anywhere in the world in order to take advantage of the availability of cheaper labour, land, capital and/or other resources, and of financial inducements such as lower rates of tax.

It would be wrong, however, to see 'globalization' as some sort of inevitable process arising from the working out of immutable economic laws. The liberalization of trade and deregulation of financial markets are the result, at least in part, of political decisions, and their effects can be modified by political choices on the part of individual governments, or perhaps more effectively nations acting in concert, as for example in the European Union. Further, there are some commentators who question the impact of globalization; they point out, for example, that large areas of any national economy, particularly in the service sector, are not subject to any effective competition from outside the country concerned.

An alternative way of characterizing the current context for work is to see the contemporary phase of capitalist development as 'post-Fordist' (or 'neo-Fordist'). Fordism refers to the pattern of production and consumption which supposedly characterized the decades immediately after the Second World War, though as the term implies it can be referred back to Henry Ford's successful innovations in 1913: the mass production of motor cars using an assembly line, and the creation of a mass market for them in the decades which followed. It denotes an economy in which standardized goods are mass produced for sale to a mass market, and economic policies, such as Keynesianism, and state supported welfare measures, provide the necessary relatively stable demand. Its decline is seen variously as due to the satiation of such markets, the increasing problems arising from government management of the economy – inflation, industrial conflict, loss of competitiveness – and the opportunities offered by new computer based technologies for changes in patterns of production, and in the labour processes and division of labour associated with them.

Thus a 'post- or neo-Fordist' economy is dominated by production which is much more 'flexible' and 'specialized', able to produce a greater variety of goods and services in response to the changing demands of highly differentiated markets. Such flexibility has been made possible, it is argued, at least in part by developments in computer based technologies, which permit much more rapid changes in the use being made of multi-purpose machinery and equipment. However, it also requires developments in the organization and control of the labour process to secure both 'functional' flexibility (the movement of a more highly skilled and responsible workforce between different tasks as production requirements dictate) and 'numerical' flexibility (the possibility of changing the size of the workforce in response to changes in the level of demand) (for further discussion see Allen and Massey, 1988, esp. Ch. 4).

These ideas have aroused considerable controversy as to their empirical relevance and theoretical status. The notions of Fordism and post-Fordism only imply that economies are *dominated* by a particular organization of production and consumption, not that all economic activities are organized in the specified way. The historical adequacy of even this claim has been questioned in relation to Fordism as regards most societies with the possible exception of the USA; and there is a growing body of evidence that flexible specialization and the flexible firm are to be found relatively rarely in the clear-cut forms suggested by the strongest advocates of 'neo-Fordism' (see, for example, A. Pollert 1991).

Equally disputed is whether the presumed changes are really inherent in the development of capitalism in its current stage, or merely one possibility among others so that economic and political choices and decisions remain significant. In addition, it can be argued that developments which are being claimed as new and significant, such as more flexible use of labour, are merely the re-emergence in a new context and in new terms of possibilities which have always been present and often exploited within capitalist economies over the last two hundred years.

What is clear, however, is that the present context for 'work', and especially paid work, is in important respects different from anything previously experienced. Technological changes alone, particularly those associated with micro-electronics and information technology, would have ensured this, but they have been accompanied by changes in the international division of labour and in patterns of world trade which have had massive repercussions on national economies. These developments have contributed to making the 'shape' of paid work in Britain significantly different now from what was taken for granted even twenty years ago.

THEMES AND ISSUES

In the chapters which follow this Introduction the changed context for work and employment in Britain, as in other highly industrialized societies, is the background for the detailed discussion and exploration of particular aspects of the organization and distribution of work, and their implications for other areas of social life.

Thus in Chapter 2 Huw Beynon looks in greater detail at many of the changes in the labour force outlined above and goes on to illustrate what they mean in terms of the experience of work. He emphasizes the impact which changes in the nature and distribution of employment have had on individuals and the communities where they live, and provides graphic illustrations of the insecurity and stress which is the lot of so many of those who have paid work at the present time, whilst others face involuntary economic inactivity, particularly unemployment and early retirement. The role of the state is crucially important in understanding these changes not only through policies like privatization but also through its withdrawal from the labour market leaving deregulation and 'moral turbulence'.

Sheila Allen, in Chapter 3, emphasizes the importance of work, especially but not only paid work, for individuals as a source of identity and meaning, as well as in providing access to life's necessities and, for some, luxuries as well. Whereas involuntary unemployment always tends to have unwelcome consequences, materially, psychologically and socially, 'the right to be idle' – leisure – should accompany 'the right to work' for everyone, as it could do in the modern world if opportunities for employment were organized and distributed differently.

In Chapter 4 Richard Brown pursues a similar theme: the ways in which the contemporary labour market fails to meet the demands of most employees and potential employees for work which is secure, and the mostly deleterious consequences of this uncertainty for the employment relationship and the economy more generally. Given the current context, it may be difficult to change this situation, but even within one country there are political choices which could be made and which would make a difference.

In Chapter 5 Harriet Bradley looks at one of the major developments in the organization and distribution of paid work, the so-called 'feminization' of employment. She subjects this notion to critical examination in the light of the findings of her own research on male and female employees in five industries and finds that while the structures of male power within organizations remain 'fairly intact', there is evidence among women of growing commitment to employment, rising aspirations and increasing levels of economic activity, the latter leading in many cases to dual earner households and the stresses which follow from this pattern of living.

A different aspect of the distribution of opportunities for paid work is explored by Robert MacDonald in Chapter 6, but he too finds strong commitments to paid work. In Teesside, an area of persistent high levels of unemployment, those who are unemployed continue to try to engage with the world of work – through setting up their own small businesses, doing voluntary work, and/or working 'informally' ('on the fiddle') whilst claiming benefit. The prevalence of such survival strategies leads him to question the pejorative labelling of these workers as a dependent 'underclass'; rather they have a strong 'work ethic' and are forced by their circumstances to engage in such 'disorganized, insecure, risky, casualized and poor work'.

Lydia Morris's contribution, Chapter 7, also derives from research carried out on Teesside, in her case in Hartlepool. She investigated how different patterns of employment within households relate to other aspects of household organization, and to the relations between households and kin and neighbours. The pattern she uncovered was complex and is explored in detail and with great care. The chapter demonstrates the importance of looking at the interrelations of 'household strategies', labour market circumstances, and location in social networks. It also emphasizes the constraints on the 'choices' especially of the unemployed and insecurely employed derived from both 'the gendered practices of everyday life and the institutional arrangements of the state and the labour market'.

The remaining two chapters are concerned more directly with the organization of work within the workplace. In Chapter 8 Ian Roberts outlines how contemporary management thought has seized on the notion of culture as a key to transforming work organizations in management's interests, and then goes on to explore the implications of this for training in the construction and engineering industries. Whereas the traditional apprenticeship transmitted skills and a workplace culture which 'belonged' to the workforce collectively, the contemporary pattern of training individuals in specific, fragmented competencies does not provide socialization into skilled identities, nor all the knowledge and experience needed to exercise these 'skills' effectively in the workplace itself.

The discourse of contemporary management is also the starting point for Steve Taylor's contribution, Chapter 9, in his case the notion and practice of Total Quality Management (TQM). Drawing on his own researches in an airline ticket office and a bank he details the demands made on employees by TQM and the ways in which they respond to them. The combinations of techniques of surveillance and sanctions for performance available to management provide them with powerful means of control over employee behaviour, including the emotional labour demanded by TQM. Nevertheless there remains scope for employees to negotiate within the employment relationship and to resist managerial demands.

The contributions provide detailed accounts and illustrations of the ways in which the shape of work has been changed in the past two decades. A major theme which runs through most chapters is the growing instability of employment in

relation to both the labour market – how long will the job last?
– and the workplace – what do management expect and what
means will they use to secure it? The pressures to produce
more, of higher quality, at lower cost, and to be responsive to
changing market requirements, have led to demands for increased flexibility, numerical and functional, and more intensive working. The sort of stability which characterized patterns
of employment in the first three decades after 1945 has been
lost and most people's experience of paid work and expectations regarding future employment are now very different
from what they were less than a generation ago.

One way of characterizing these changes has been to regard
them as a 'feminization' of employment: the types of jobs
(service sector work rather than manufacturing), conditions
of employment (part-time, insecure), rewards (poor pay, few
benefits) and levels of union organization (low) which have
long been typical of women's work are now being experienced
by many men as well. The aspects of 'feminization' which
meant a growth in employment opportunities for women,
and especially opportunities to undertake more skilled and
responsible work, may be seen as positive for them and
inevitably *relatively* disadvantageous for men; 'feminization' as
a more general change in the character of employment brings
a deterioration in the quality of working life for men with no
benefit to women. It can be argued that there are some positive aspects to such changes: part-time work, for example,
could allow men to achieve a more satisfactory balance
between their obligations to employers and those to the family
and domestic economy; but the cost of this in terms of a
reduced income could be very high. Indeed, most working
class women have never had a choice but to accept jobs on
these inferior terms because of economic need, and the
absence of affordable – or any – child care.

Questions of the relationship between the changing shape
of paid work and the class structure, or inequality more generally, are important ones which cannot be pursued in detail
here. Much of the evidence, however, suggests an increasing
polarization between the relatively privileged and relatively
deprived. The starkest example of this is the contrast between
those in well rewarded occupations, who find themselves
working ever longer hours under ever greater stress, and the

unemployed with minimal incomes and enforced idleness. In between may be found those whose jobs are equally demanding in terms of long hours and intensity of work, but far less well rewarded. A more rational distribution of paid work and its rewards could be to everyone's advantage.

Polarization is built into the notion of flexibility: a 'core' workforce provides functional flexibility and is rewarded by security of employment and relatively good pay and benefits; the 'periphery' of employees provides numerical flexibility and can be offered inferior 'non-standard' conditions of employment. Unemployment increases the degree of polarization, whether it derives from pressures for flexibility or other causes. Those suffering long-term or recurrent unemployment by that fact alone have diminishing chances of obtaining a job, especially work which is relatively well paid and secure. Their social and spatial concentration and segregation from the employed (see Chapter 7) further reduce their chances of finding paid work. In the light of this well known feature of the labour market the efforts of the unemployed to establish their own businesses, undertake voluntary work and/or work 'on the side' have an obvious rationale (see Chapter 6).

The relationship between the changing shape of paid work, other sorts of work, and other aspects of people's lives is a theme which runs through many of the contributions to this book. As Morris's contribution (Chapter 7) makes very clear the relations between employment/unemployment and domestic organization are subtle and complex. What her work suggests, and this is echoed elsewhere in the book, is a further tendency to polarization: dual earner 'work rich' households at one extreme, and both partners unemployed 'work poor' households at the other.

The problems of the latter are both obvious and, in the absence of measures to expand demand in the labour market, relatively intractable. As MacDonald's research suggests the remedies available to and sought by the unemployed, like self-employment, may bring further stress, and little material help (see Chapter 6). The problems of the former may be less obvious. Who is to take care of the young, and of the elderly? What are the consequences for individuals and families, and for society generally, of too many people having too much stressful work and insufficient leisure and time for recuperation? In both types of household, as indeed in many of those with a more mixed pattern, the logic of the situation demands changes in the distribution of domestic work and responsibilities, and of opportunities for leisure, between partners. In contemporary Britain the old pattern of male breadwinner/ female homemaker is inappropriate, but it is not yet clear how far new patterns are emerging.

A number of other important questions remain unanswered, some of them possibly at the moment unanswerable. The present period of instability with regard to work and employment represents a significant change from the first three decades after the Second World War. Is this a situation which will continue indefinitely into the future or merely a period of transition at the end of which we can expect to move into another period of relative stability, albeit one which will almost certainly not be a return to anything like the 1950s and 1960s? In contrast to how it appeared to many at the time, it is now possible to see the post-war decades as an exceptional interlude in our experience of capitalist economies. We have returned to conditions of alternating boom and recession, and of high though fluctuating levels of unemployment, which were typical of most of the period from the end of the 18th century to the Second World War.

An answer to the question of whether the current instability will continue depends at least in part on the answer to two other questions: how far is it possible for individuals, collectivities or the state to take effective action to determine the future? In so far as such action is possible will it be taken?

The last two decades have seen a widespread acceptance of the argument that 'there is no alternative': no alternative to largely unregulated capitalism, no possibility of resisting the demands of the market, individually, collectively or nationally. The collapse of the Soviet bloc and of the 'state socialist' alternative has provided reinforcement for such arguments. Contemporary politics in Britain and other highly industrialized societies mostly fails to offer clear alternatives; the major parties fight to occupy the centre ground. Nevertheless a careful examination of the policies and practices of different *capitalist* societies will reveal important differences between them as to how their political economies work, as has been pointed out very clearly by Hutton (1995); and there are possibilities which are outside even this range. Bringing about change may be difficult but it is not intrinsically impossible. Normal politics remains, with the dual tasks of envisaging alternative futures and mobilizing politically to try to realize whichever is desired.

Finally, the contributions to this volume emphasize and illustrate the continuing importance of work and employment in people's lives. The 'leisure society', which has been forecast in the past as technological developments (automation; micro-electronic technology) appeared to promise a work-free future, has not arrived. Though a different more equitable distribution of available work, and income, might be seen to be an improvement compared with the current polarized situation, it would still mean most people spending a lot of their time working. There is much work which will continue to demand human labour power for the foreseeable future. Indeed, the potential demand is even greater if the resources could be mobilized to pay for it, notably in the caring occupations, and in health and education. Further, the 'work ethic' appears to remain strong for all except a discouraged minority. For most of us it remains desirable as well as necessary to have a job. The sort of work, especially paid work, we are able to undertake will considerably constrain our style of life, but it will also have less tangible consequences for our sense of identity, our relations with others and our place in society. Thus exploring how the shape of work is changing remains an essential step towards a more general understanding of our contemporary world.

2 The Changing Practices of Work

Over the past ten years, I have spent a lot of time talking with people about their work: more precisely about their jobs and their employers. What has been striking about these discussions is the force with which people identify significant changes that have taken place in their working lives. Repeatedly I have listened to people recounting how 'things have changed completely these last ten years'; 'compared with how things were ten or fifteen years ago I would say the situation is completely different'; some have spoken with dramatic effect about how they 'wouldn't have believed possible' the kind of changes that have taken place. In this, of course, there is some exaggeration and there has been further distortion as sociologists and business commentators have occasionally amplified these accounts. Many things have changed only slightly and within change there is always continuity, but it does seem that at this moment the social organization of western economies is going through a period of quite significant disturbance.

In reflecting upon these matters I have increasingly thought about upon how they have been expressed in my own life. In the town where I was brought up in South Wales, the 'jobs' available were clearly outlined and understood. There were 'jobs' in the steel works and in the coal mines. Boys who left school at fifteen or sixteen went into either of these workplaces and became coal miners or steel workers. Those with academic qualifications became apprentices and were prepared for jobs as skilled maintenance workers in these industries. All of them understood their job to involve a powerful occupational identity and to be a 'job for life'. At that time (the late fifties) the steel works in the town employed over 13,000 workers and the coal mines 3,000. Nationally these industries between them employed one and a quarter million workers. There were comparatively few manual jobs for women. The girls who left school at fifteen worked as machinists in the one garment factory in the town; alternative employment was offered in local shops and, for those with some academic qualifications, in the local 'council offices'. The strong expectation was that young women would marry and not return to employment.

During this period, those who passed examinations and went to University looked forward to employment in management or in one of the professions. Their world mirrored the world of manual work in two main respects: it was regarded as a long term commitment, often based in the public sector; and it was strongly marked by gender. For the men these were jobs for life with a strong occupational identity and the security of a pension. In the professions, as with manual work, women tended to be segregated into particular activities (like school teaching) and generally experienced marriage and childbearing as major obstacles to career advancement.

While this place where I grew up was different in some respects from others (for example textile belts where women had employment in the mills throughout their lives) it helps to highlight certain characteristics of a set of social arrangements which have been variously identified as welfare statism, Fordism, and 'smoke stack' industrialism. These terms have been developed in response to changes which have been seen to produce their opposite in Thatcherism or anti-statism, post-Fordism and post-industrialism (see, for example, Piore and Sabel, 1984; Allen and Massey, 1988). They reflect upon the dramatic change that has taken place in the composition and organization of work and employment across the UK which can be seen most dramatically in the changes in the coal and steel industries. Once the centre of a state managed 'smoke-stack' economy, today they are privately owned and with a combined labour force of less than 40,000 reduced to just 3 per cent of their post-war strength. In my town, the coal mines have closed and less than a thousand people are now employed in the steel works.

DE-INDUSTRIALIZATION: FROM MANUFACTURE TO SERVICES

In 1979 just over seven million people were employed in manufacturing industries in the UK; in 1995, the figure had reduced to three and three quarter millions (see Table 2.1). The scale of employment decline is extended if we add the experience of the mining industry where a further 220,000 jobs have been lost since 1979. This decline has been related to general patterns of change associated with the implementation of new technologies and the rise of low cost production facilities in the newly industrializing countries of the Pacific. One account from the textile and garment industry tells a familiar story:

> On Friday, workers at the Coates Viyella factory at Rainhill Merseyside picked their notices up off the floor of a Portacabin outside the plant. Their envelopes had been left in little piles by a management anxious to close the door at 1 p.m. sharp. For Pat Donoghue and Lisa Kelly, it was the final humiliation. 'People had to grovel on the floor to pick up their notices. They didn't have the decency to hand them to us', said one of the workers.
>
> The factory at Rainhill produces shirts for Marks and Spencer, but there has been no work since April 10, when the staff heard from the managing director that the plant was to close. All work would be transferred to Coates Viyella factories in Mauritius and Indonesia where local workers will produce the same shirts for less than half the wages paid at Rainhill.
>
> (*The Times*, 6 May 1996)

Table 2.1   Changing Patterns of Employment in the UK 1979–95 ('000s)

	Manufacturing	*Services*	*Totals**
1979	7,013	13,680	22,970
1985	5,307	13,860	21,073
1995	3,789	15,912	21,103

* Includes 'other activities'
Source: *Employment Gazette*, various years

In this way employment in the textile and leather industries which stood at 723,000 in 1979 was reduced to 366,200 by 1995. The process of plant closure and the relocation of employment has affected many branches of manufacturing industry. In sectors as diverse as clothing, vehicle and chemical manufacture, job losses have been linked with geographic relocation of production sites. It was seen dramatically in the operations of such giant manufacturing corporations as ICI which, in the early eighties changed the balance of its production from one which was dominated by its British plants to a truly diverse international operation. Its employment base altered in a similar way creating severe job losses in its main British locations on Teesside and Merseyside (see Beynon, Hudson and Sadler, 1994). As a *quid pro quo*, the UK has offered suitable production sites for the branch plants of US and German corporations as well as those from Japan, South Korea and Taiwan. These companies have formed the basis of the UK electronics and computing industries. The extent to which this emphasis upon 'inward investment' has come to form the keystone of employment policy in most of the cities and regions of the country, is an interesting phenomenon in itself. However, no matter how successful these operations have been, they have come nowhere near to replacing the manufacturing jobs that have been lost, and which continue to drain away.

Generally, the manufacturing plants which have arrived and those others that have remained open have been managed in ways which have seen their labour forces dramatically reduced. This process was referred to as *downsizing* (occasionally *right-sizing*) in the USA. It was seen to be a solution to the intensity of international competition in removing the sclerosis of industries dominated by 'jobs for life' practices and state support through subsidies and guaranteed contracts. More generally, machines (robots and computers) have been replacing jobs at a pace which has led to some observers predicting *The End of Work* (see Rifkin, 1996).

On both sides of the Atlantic these changes have been associated with considerable employee trauma. Most commonly it has been achieved through the introduction of various forms of redundancy schemes, combined with procedures and techniques aimed at increasing the productivity of those who remain. Employment levels have also been reduced through 'out-sourcing' techniques which sub-contract work to other, more specialized organizations. This 'out-sourcing' often takes the form of a sub-contract which operates *within* the parent plant. It has become common for employees on a particular production site (a car plant or a steel mill) to be in the employ of a number of *different* companies. In the car industry, for example, it was once common for assembly line workers after they had reached a certain age to move to less arduous work away from the assembly lines. The job of 'janitor' was one such and involved responsibilities relating to the cleanliness of the plant. When I visited the Nissan factory in the North East of England, I noticed that cleaning jobs were being performed by people in different coloured overalls; men in fact who worked for another company. When I asked about this I was informed that: 'we are a car company not a cleaning company'. Many manufacturing firms have done the same, reducing their labour force to its productive core, hiring additional help when needed and subcontracting many ancillary operations (Wood, 1989).

As a result of these changes, it is increasingly unusual to meet a factory worker or manager nowadays. The people we share carriages with on trains (many of them with cellular telephones) work in banks, in insurance companies or in the retail trade. They belong in offices, hotels and shops rather than on factory floors and down coal mines. Often though, the past is just a scratch beneath the surface. Most taxi drivers I've talked to have had a previous existence working in factories; so too the men who collect the trolleys from the car parks at Tesco and Sainsbury. Mostly these people express resignation over the ways in which their lives and the world around them has changed. Occasionally you encounter anger; especially, in my experience, in the steel towns. On one occasion in South Wales I was told with some feeling that

> it's your lot, the boys from the University who have brought this about. All your new ideas and messing with things you don't understand. You've sold us out to the bloody Japs. We could make steel as good as them. There's no doubt about that; no doubt at all. And where are we now – on the scrap heap.

In these towns, men (without formal skills and training) made their lives around the furnaces and the hot rolling steel. These were the men who talked to me of having 'broken hearts' as the result of 'downsizing'.

As manufacturing employment declined, new employment opportunities emerged in other expanding branches of the economy. The most dynamic of these in the eighties was the service sector most obviously visible on our High Streets as insurance companies and building societies opened new offices. The rise of these financial services associated with the borrowing, investing and lending of money was a dramatic phenomenon. So powerful was it that by 1995, over half of the regions in Britain (including the famed industrial economy of Scotland) earned more from financial services that they did from manufacture (HMSO, 1996). To this can be added the revolutionary changes that have taken place in the tourist and retailing sectors. In 1995 a million and a quarter people were employed in the hotel and catering industries; more than the combined labour forces of almost all the industries we associate with traditional manufacture. Retailing is another buoyant sector where the development of the super-store, located away from city centres, has done so much to rearrange the shopping and leisure habits of large proportions of the population.

These changes are considerable ones and have combined in ways which have produced a significant shift in the pattern of work and employment. They have also had a deep and profound effect upon the sensibilities of our society, in ways which

Table 2.2   Changing Patterns of Gender Employment 1979–95 ('000s)

	Manufacturing		*Services*		*Totals*
	Male	*Female*	*Male*	*Female*	
1979	4,964	2,050	6,674	7,006	20,692
1985	3,738	1,570	6,373	7,488	19,166
1995	2,659	1,131	6,861	9,052	19,702

Source: *Employment Gazette*, various years

social scientists are beginning to reflect upon. It is clear from Table 2.2 that the shift away from manufacturing has also been a shift in favour of the employment of women. Many of the expanding service industries (notably the ones that I have just mentioned) employ more women than men, and this heightens the sense of transformation and change. However, many of these service jobs have characteristics which are not dissimilar to those in manufacturing. In large hotels, waitresses are responsible for laying tables for breakfast, lunch and dinner. They often do it to a set routine: one laying the soup spoons, another the desert spoon and fork and so on. At MacDonalds we are told that

> 'a quarter-pounder is cooked in exactly 107 seconds. Our fries are never more that 7 minutes old when served'. In any one of their restaurants they 'aim to serve any order within 60 seconds. At lunch time in a busy restaurant we serve 2,000 meals an hour'. (Beynon, 1992, p. 180).

In his account of these developments Ritzer talks of the new 'MacDonaldized society':

> MacDonaldism shares many characteristics with Fordism, notably homogeneous products, rigid technologies, standardized work routines, deskilling, homogenization of labor (and customer), the mass worker and homogenization of consumption....in these and other ways, Fordism is alive and well in the modern world... (Ritzer, 1993, p. 155)

Continuities clearly exist in the lives which people lead in this new service driven economy. Nevertheless, a recognition of this should not obscure difference (between an assembly line and a dining room) and the quite fundamental changes that are taking place both in people's perceptions and in the ways in which economic organizations pattern themselves. Most clear is the ways in which service organizations are driven by a particular conception of the customer and that many service sector jobs involve workers in direct (social) relationships with people (du Gay, 1995). As a consequence 'the customer' has taken an ascendant position in our understanding of work, and this has worked back into manufacturing. At the Nissan company, the assembly line workers are told to 'build the car as if your work mate was going to buy it'.

Furthermore, these changes have produced new kinds of occupations and activities which have had a significant effect upon the structure of society and the ways in which we understand our position within it. It has become a more 'visual' society (see Jencks, 1996). We are surrounded by more and more complex forms of visual communication on television and in advertisements on street hoardings. More and more students spend time in universities and colleges as education, training and communicative skills become crucial attributes in the labour market. All this is supportive of a view of a society which is being *culturally transformed* and of the view of a *post-industrial society* which is both democratic and liberating; inside and outside of work.

The new service workers are a mixed bunch however. They include the very rich (like Elton John) and the very poor (like the many thousands of office cleaners). In the USA, Reich calculated that just 20 per cent of the jobs in the new economy were ones which were intrinsically satisfying and economically rewarding. He refers to these as the work of the *symbolic analysts*, (the journalists, designers, architects, lecturers) whose work has creativity at its core as they communicate complex ideas to a broader audience (clients, customers, user groups). They represent his 'fortunate fifth' (Reich, 1991) and they match the 30 per cent identified by Will Hutton in the 30:30:40 society (Hutton, 1995). Their working lives can be contrasted with those of another 25 per cent who regularly perform routine tasks and the 30 per cent who are responsible for the daily delivery of a variety of mundane services. Clearly views of this new world vary with your position within it; ironically, of course, part of the function of the *symbolic analysts* is to perform such a task as 'spin doctors' or public relations experts. We live uneasily in *their* interpretive world. The fact that it is also a world of inequality is made clear in Table 2.3.

Since 1979, the real wages of manual workers have lagged behind those of non-manual employees. Female part-time manual workers have fared worst of all with their wages only increasing by 1.7 per cent in real terms. Amongst non-manuals however, and especially middle and senior professionals, wages have increased significantly and with them changes in pattern of demarcation. Here women's wages have increased at a

The Changing Shape of Work

Table 2.3   Changes in Weekly Earnings 1979–95* (in 1995 prices)

	Full-Time				Part-Time	
	Manual		Non-Manual		Manual	Non-Manual
	Male (£)	Female (£)	Male (£)	Female (£)	Female (£)	Female (£)
1979	278.0	165.01	337.7	197.29	75.3	89.6
1995	291.3	188.10	443.3	288.10	76.6	114.2
Real Increase (per cent)	4.8%	14.0%	31.2%	46.0%	1.7%	27.3%

* Excluding overtime payments
Source: *New Earnings Survey*

higher rate than men's. This was confirmed in a report by Susan Harkness for the Institute of Fiscal Studies:

> women who worked part-time did not do as well as those in full-time employment...the gap between the highest and the lowest paid has risen for women as it has for men: which makes the real winners high paid women who have seen their wages almost double in real terms since 1973. Those who have done worse – but who have still narrowed the gap with men – are part-time low skilled women. (Harkness, 1996)

The overall effect of these changes upon working life is unclear. They serve to direct our attention upon the nature of industrial and commercial management and its role in organizing economic activity under these new conditions (see for example Scase and Goffee, 1989; Streeck, 1987; Webb, 1992). The new theories of 'post-Fordism' and 'flexibility' emphasised the importance of labour and the need for management to involve people in decision-making as organizations cope with an increasingly complex and unpredictable world. The failings of British management in this regard were brought out forcefully by Nichols (1986); conclusions which were reinforced in two recent case studies. In a factory in North Wales, 'the workers argue that management do not know how to do the jobs but insist on telling the workers that they do'. A common reaction here was expressed in this way:

> when decisions come, most men in my department keep quiet...in the workers' experience, nobody ever listens...so we don't say much now. (Jones, 1993)

Similar reactions were found in an automotive component plant in South Wales. Here a major organizational change was introduced in which management estimated that 88 per cent of all the jobs had taken on increasing numbers of tasks; for this to succeed the company needed to call increasingly upon the trust of the workforce. A common response here was:

> For eighteen years [this] has been a standard company. If they could kick you in the teeth they would and did. Now they expect trust merely because they ask for it. (Trotman, 1993)

In spite of comments like these 'downsized' companies and their managements are placing more and more emphasis upon the need to involve their workforces, to develop 'team-working' and to improve the education and training opportunities available to people who are increasingly seen as one of the corporation's most valuable resources. The shelves of the management sections in book stores are packed with texts on Total Quality Management which feature heavily in contemporary courses in business administration. These are the 'buzz words' of the decade. In the British publishing industry publishers like Harper-Collins have introduced its 'Visions and Values' initiative involving team building and the various arrangements involved in Human Resource Management. Staff are involved in measuring their own performance through GRPI (goals, roles, processes and inter-personal relations). However many were unconvinced of its applicability to a working context which thrives on creativity and imagination. One reported that 'it seemed to have no practical application for us. It made me very angry and it made me very ill'. (*The Observer*, 21 April 1996)

There is a lot of ambiguity and tension in these developments. In the context of a competitive economy which has displaced the producer from its centre, companies have to deal with the need to sell and to please their consumers. The market has taken an ascendancy which relegates the workings of offices and factory floors to subordinate status. Here, Anthony has pointed out, with much perception, managements now claim the right not only to manage but to 'manage the meaning of events'. It is they who form the conduit between producer and consumer. But they are often inadequate to the task. In his researches, Anthony (1994) detected a 'schizophrenia' in British management; on the one hand, emphasising 'team working' and togetherness while on the other being swamped by the onset of further 'downsizing' as the market takes its toll. In his sympathetic investigations into the operation of 'team working', Wilmott discerned a considerable level of 'confusion and emptiness' amongst the workers he talked with (Wilmott, 1993).

This, of course, raises some very interesting questions about the changing position of women within the authority structure of the new economy. Historically this has been the domain of men, and Board Rooms tend to maintain their masculine ethos. However there are arguments which maintain that, in the new contexts, women managers will increasingly come to the fore (Maddox, 1996). Cary Cooper and Marilyn Davidson, the authors of *Shattering The Glass Ceiling*, see the 1990s as a major turning point. In Davidson's view:

> Management literature in the seventies and eighties was all about how to adapt, cope, power-dress and fit into male culture...After downsizing, you want to utilise what's left and that's when barriers of race or sex don't make economic sense. (*The Guardian*, 10 June 1996)

It seems that many of the managers of the future (the time co-ordinators, the flexible workers, the team workers) will be women and in the considered view of Professor Cooper: 'the quicker we get women up there and dump men the better'.

THE RISE OF THE 'HYPHENATED WORKER'

If we attempt to relate these changes back to the ways in which work and employment relations have altered a number of complex processes become evident. Most clear is the fact that the stable superannuated labour force which characterised the 1950s has been severely eroded. The labour force of the 1990s is made up of a number of different kinds of employees: part-time-workers, temporary-workers, casual-, even self-employed-workers. As we enter the twenty first century these *hyphenated workers* are becoming a more and more significant part of the economy.

Table 2.4 documents some basic patterns of change within the labour force since 1979. It illustrates the way in which the number of *employees* has declined both absolutely, and as a percentage of the economically active labour force. In 1979, employees made up 88 per cent of the labour force, in 1996 the percentage was 75 per cent. The difference is explained through the increasing numbers of unemployed people and the rapid growth in those registered as self-employed. The numbers in both these categories have almost doubled, and in their different ways they have often been used as an indication of the increasing dynamism of the economy and its changing relationship with society. Unemployment and self employment have often been seen as two sides of the same coin which moved people out of inefficient, declining industries (often seen as 'featherbedded' with state subsidies) through temporary periods of unemployment and retraining into new, more demanding and enterprising contexts.

I talked with one man who had worked in a large company of architects. He had been provided with a company car and, by his account, his working environment was stress free and easy-going. The company had grown on the basis of

Table 2.4   Labour Force Changes 1979–95 ('000s)

	Employees	Self-employed	Training	Unemployed	Total
1979	22,432	1,778	–	1,428	25,638
1985	20,746	2,713	390	2,990	26,840
1995	21,675	3,269	273	2,376	27,726*

*Includes unpaid family workers
Source: *Labour Force Survey*, various years

public-sector contracts; designing housing schemes, municipal swimming pools, leisure centres and the like. In 1989 his firm, and many like them across the country, had a major financial crisis and he was made redundant:

> It was a large company, and looking back, it was very badly organized. They didn't need to be efficient really with the kinds of contracts they were negotiating; we charged £120 an hour on those big contracts with local authorities and the government departments. Everything was big: it had a big main-frame computer which contributed very little. Today, the industry has changed completely. In fact it's unrecognizable compared with what it was like ten years ago.

John experienced redundancy and employment as a trauma. However with the help of an Apple Mac he trained himself in Computer Aided Design. Within three years he was set up in his garage with two large colour screens running *Microstation* and tendering for small and large contracts in his local area. He described the enjoyment he gets from working with the computer programme:

> it's amazing to think that not so long ago I used to have to draw all of this on a board; it's really quite amazing what I can do with the Apple Mac; how I can change things in ten minutes which before would have taken me a day!

A clear 'success story' therefore; but one which gets more complicated as we take it further and John describes in more detail how he fits into the new industry:

> As I said it's unrecognizable from what it used to be. All the big firms got rid of staff in 1989, they retained core employees who are now used to set up new projects. Everyone else is registered with an Agency; that's where I get most of my work from. We register with the agency and then we get recruited as the firms need architects – on a temporary contract.

Although 'self employed' and working for himself, John employs no-one and obtains most of his income from large architectural companies. He often works in *their* offices (with his new skills) and travels much further in search of work than he ever did before. He has been very enterprising (retraining himself, investing in computers in his home) but he is not a classic *entrepreneur*.

This story is a common one. In one way or another it applies to most of the people who appear in the 'self employed' category, and this casts doubt on the usefulness of the category as an indicator of radical change toward entrepreneurship. A closer examination of the data on self employment reveals that it is concentrated in a relatively few industrial sectors. In transport and communication and the group of industries associated with banking and financial services, self-employment makes up 13 per cent of the total workforce; in distribution, hotels and catering it is 14 per cent and in construction a massive 45 per cent. In his detailed study of the self-employment phenomenon, Harvey (1995) has argued that the case of the construction industry is revealing and more representative than that of architecture. In this industry, self-employment increasingly relates to manual production workers and not professional or white collar employees. In 1992, fifty eight per cent of the manual workers in the construction industry were self employed. As Harvey puts it:

> It is legitimate to speak of *mass self employment*...moreover the expansion of self-employment has not taken place at the expense of the large contractors...(who) now undertake major contracts using predominantly self-employed workers. The self employed are indeed the core workforce. (Harvey, 1995, p. 3)

These people work as bricklayers or steel erectors or labourers on the large building sites of companies like Costain and Tarmac. They are paid by the company and to all intents and purposes they are employees; but the companies do not recognize this relationship. Like John they are self employed and register with Agencies.

The data in Table 2.5 make clear that, along-side the self-employed worker, part-time work stands as the main source of employment growth in the 1980s and 1990s. In 1995 there were three and a half million fewer full time jobs than there were fifteen years earlier. The dynamic in the jobs market has been in part-time employment, usually for women. This 'gender bias' in part-time work is being modified slightly as increasing proportions of men find employment on this basis.

The Changing Shape of Work

Table 2.5   Changing Labour Contracts 1979–95 ('000s)

| | Male | | Female | | Total |
	Full-time	Part-time	Full-time	Part-time	
1979	13,032	605	5,560	3,781	22,978
1985	10,922	808	5,407	3,937	21,074
1995	9,536	1,106	5,650	4,812	21,104

Source: *Employment Gazette,* various years

In the hotel industry, for example, part-time employment made up 26 per cent of all jobs in 1971 (21 per cent for women and 5 per cent for men). By 1991, the proportions had almost doubled with the part-time jobs of women (33 per cent) and men (11 per cent) providing almost half of the jobs in the industry. This practice has been encouraged by government initiatives (like *Job Match)* which emphasise the attractiveness of this type of employment, seeing it as indicative of an increasingly flexible labour market. To these part-time and self-employed workers can be added the numbers of employees who (although not 'self-employed') work on a succession of temporary contracts.

The kinds of changes indicated here can be seen to offer great opportunities for employers. Some authors have emphasized the advantages for workers also, stressing the ways in which deregulated labour markets facilitate people moving into and out of particular jobs, careers and markets. The practice of holding more than one job has extended beyond company directors and members of parliament. Its advocates have developed the idea of a job *portfolio,* although for most people these are not as lucrative as those which hold stocks and shares. Nevertheless, Hakim, and others, have pointed to the benefits which self-employment and non standard work contracts offer for women reentering the labour market. These authors argue for greater flexibility and for employment arrangements which permit a range of possible living and working options. Patricia Hewitt (1993) has been adroit in pointing out unnecessary inflexibilities in work contracts and the potential advantages that could flow from altering our use and understanding of time. In fact many women have developed their employment careers through a complex process of time juggling. A waitress at a Yorkshire hotel explains how

> Craig my eldest son was five when I started work here. It was just evenings then. I started off as casual at night when the children were little and my husband looked after them. I just did banquets... Then I gradually started doing weekend breakfast and the odd lunchtime. Then I did the week breakfasts and it fitted in quite well as my husband was working local and he could see them off in the morning for me. Then they grew up and they got to an age when they could be left on their own. (Charles, 1994, p. 146; see also Crompton and Sanderson, 1990)

These arguments often resonate with the discussion of industrial transformation, the role of innovating firms and other radical changes within the workplace. Here too, however, the evidence is both patchy and contradictory. Attitudinal surveys have indicated that women are happy to combine paid employment with the demands of child-care and a family, (to get out of the house, to meet people, etc.). They also show the importance of the need for money (providing independence and necessary household income). But, for women (like men) the experience of paid employment can be a source of tension as well as satisfaction. Furthermore, the emphasis upon choice often obscures the fact that, in many circumstances, market and power relations favour employers, and that these changes taken together may well trap some women in low paid employment rather than liberate them. Ted Johns, consultant with Minitruth Management takes this view arguing that

> only 57 per cent of the workforce is now employed on a full time permanent basis.
> The other 43 per cent work part-time or on fixed term contracts or have a 'portfolio' career. This kind of employment contract gives organizations much greater power over the employee. It increases the pressure to conform on those who want to retain employment. (*The Observer*, 21 April 1996)

Certainly this view would be supported by some advertisements in places like Consett:

we are seeking people who are prepared to work on a casual basis, with extremely flexible hours. We can accommodate from 3 to 10 hour stints throughout the 24 when work is available. Applicants must have very nimble fingers to cope with the work involved, and be prepared to work at 24 hours notice. (quoted in Wray, 1993)

Furthermore, 'non-standard work contracts' may be imposed, rather than freely negotiated. This has been the case in the retail sector where many employees have found their full-time contracts revoked in favour of part-time ones. A recent MORI poll of senior personnel managers found that:

More than half the managers believed that the desire to cut over-heads by avoiding the legal terms and conditions due to full-time workers might influence decisions to introduce flexible working patterns. (*Financial Times*, 31 November 1993)

The situation is made more complex in industries like the hotel industry where the use of split shifts and casual labour is such that the difference between 'full-time', 'part-time' and 'casual' employment has become very blurred. One manager from the industry explains the difficulties of defining a 'casual':

We have very few workers who are the sort of casuals where you ring up and say 'can you work tomorrow'. They're more permanent casuals in a way – but it's because of the number of hours they work a week; that's why they're casuals as opposed to part-time.

Another reflects on the nature of 'full-time' employment:

We have two different sorts of full-timers. Some are on the 'inclusive' which means that they do 39 hours a week. If they do under then they're still paid for 39 hours but they owe us the hours. The others are on a 'maximum 39' and they only get paid for the hours that they do and that can be anything between 16 and 39 hours. (Charles, 1994, p. 107)

This pattern was observed nationally, as Department of Employment researchers estimated that as many as half of the people employed on 'full-time' contracts were, in fact, involved in working arrangements that were less stable than this term implied. This indicates the pace to which casualized or 'non-standard contacts' have become a generalized aspect of working life, applying to men as well as women.

These are the *hyphenated workers* in the *hyphenated economy*. The old industrial economy of Britain was highly regulated; it employed large numbers of highly unionised workers employed on full-time contracts. As we have seen, most of these were men, and they were paid what was recognized as 'a family wage' a form of payment which sustained the idea of the man as the bread-winner. This 'family wage', like coal and steel production, is a thing of the past. Most generally the standard of living for families in the UK is sustained by more than one income. Women's wages (once slandered as 'pin money') have become an essential part of household income. Oddly, at a time when 'work is becoming scarce', more and more people are working longer hours. In my journeys around the country I have talked with many people who have made what Schor (1992) has termed 'the Faustian contract': trading time for money – spending too much time earning and not enough living. In Britain we work longer hours than anywhere in Europe. Twenty per cent of us work on Sundays and 15 per cent of us are routinely paid to work over 46 hours a week. Low wages contribute to this of course, and before accepting the overarching benefit of these changes it is worth paying attention to the words of warning spoken by the Director General of the Institute of Personnel Management. In his view, 'flexibility' had led to abuse by many employers with workers being hired and fired on terms determined by employment legislation rather than the needs of the individual, or the dictates of the production process. Such policies were leading to

> the creation of a permanently casualized industrial peasantry, with little protection and no stake in the future.

In his view, this situation 'can't be in the interests of organizations or society' (*Financial Times*, 31 November 1993). This opinion is reinforced by research into home-working which indicates that the experience of unskilled, less privileged workers is more exploitative than rewarding (Rowbotham and Mitter, 1994; Phizacklea, 1990).

Taken together these findings raise important questions about the employment rights of workers, and also raise questions about efficiency. These new arrangements (or more correctly the return to old arrangements of a previous century) may well conflict with the requirement for employees to be more committed to their work and to the company that employs them. Fukuyama (1995) has resurrected the idea of 'trust' as a crucial part of any employment relationship. This was the background to a decision by Yorkshire Tyne Tees Television to offer full staff status to contract staff. In the previous three years employment levels in the company had fallen from 2,400 to 650 staff, with a further 250 employees on short term contracts. In his assessment of the situation, Mr Ward Thomas, Chairman of the company, recognised the self deception involved in defining many of these workers as 'short term'. While their contracts were of a fixed term (involving no liability to the employer) they were being systematically renewed. He added that 'it is right that they should feel secure about their employment'. This was welcomed by the trade union, whose representative, Tony Lennon, argued 'casual staff have less loyalty to their employers and there is little incentive to provide training' (*Financial Times*, 21 November 1995).

PRIVATIZATION AND THE SQUEEZE OF THE PUBLIC SECTOR

In the post-war period, the labour markets in many of Britain's industrial regions were dominated by state sector employment. People worked for a nationalized industry or for a public utility; they worked for local or central government; they worked in schools and hospitals, in the fire service or police force. In the decade 1982–1992 employment in this sector declined by over a million (Table 2.6). This was almost entirely due to the process of privatization which moved nationalized industries like aerospace and steel into the private sector to be joined there by the major public utilities. Once sold off, these corporations experienced radical restructuring. Changes were most obvious in the privatized utilities with water, gas, and electricity each shedding over 25 per cent of their labour forces while generating increasingly high wages and dividends for their senior executives; the so-called 'fat cats' (see Froud et al., 1996). For their part, employees in these corporations have found their working days increasingly subjected to monitoring and regulation. Conversations with fitters and engineers working for British Gas produces a set of common responses:

> it's change after change after change. But I wouldn't say that these changes were done with our benefit in mind. For example they've just introduced this new machine which if we attach to the boiler flue measures the emission and lets us know whether it's necessary to strip down the boiler. Before, on a service we would strip down every boiler; now we don't need to. But it's not done to make our job easier. Now we have to do more jobs in a day and there are less of us.

The one major corporation remaining in the state sector is the Post Office, plans for its privatization being defeated in the House of Commons. While this reprieve has meant that many small local post-offices have remained open it has not slowed down the pace of organizational change within the postal service itself. It was this – the introduction of new rotas and team working – which produced a ballot in favour of strike action and a series of one-day stoppages in 1996. The greatest fear of these workers was that team working (why do you need a team to deliver mail!) would reduce the work task to the morning delivery and thereby facilitate the imposition of part-time contracts.

Table 2.6 State Sector Employment 1982–92 ('000s)

	Public Corporations and Nationalized Industries	Public Services	Total
1982	1,756	5,265	7,021
1992	588	5,210	5,798
Decline	1,168	55	1,223

Source: *Economic Trends,* 1995

The experience of the postal workers is shared by other state workers employed in the public services. While their number has remained around 5.2 million throughout the eighties, these people have seen their jobs and working arrangements changed dramatically. The introduction of budgetary constraints, new measurements of 'output' and the generalized introduction of 'Agencies' with management structures responsible for the monitoring and organization of work have involved little less than a revolution in many of these organizations. For example, in his assessment of the ways in which civil service employment has altered, Fairbrother has drawn attention to the ways in which the Benefits Agency has transformed the organization of the Department of Social Security which is now

> organized on the basis of three territories rather than seven regions, and 500 offices have been grouped into 159 district management units – DMUs.

In these new arrangements 'staff deal with claimants via an integrated computer system' and 'there has been the intensification of managerial work as well as the physical removal of managerial responsibility from the majority of local offices' (Fairbrother, 1995, p. 141).

Similar changes have strongly influenced the operation of schools, universities, hospitals, local authorities, the BBC and the emergency services (fire, ambulances, the police). In each of these areas there have been similar responses of protest, and complaints about increased work-loads. As a result, in the 1980s, industrial disputes in the UK are becoming increasingly concentrated in the public sector, with public sector unions increasingly dominating the politics of the Trades Union Congress. Regularly these workers and their representatives draw attention to issues of work intensity and stress associated with the organizational changes.

At one point it seemed as if these professional groups would reinvigorate the work ethic. Teachers talked of being 'at the chalk face'; and 'workaholism' became a legitimate illness as people turned up earlier and earlier for work, and often boasted of it. However, there are signs that this phase is over. Throughout the public service sector employees have been complaining about the lengthening and restructuring of the working day.

A recent national survey by the Association University Teachers indicated that 'academic staff are working an average week of 55 hours, with one group, women professors, working an incredible 65 hours per week' (AUT, 1994). In response, one senior academic told me that he'd

> been working in the University for over thirty years, and I've always turned up for my lectures and classes. This term, for the first time, I rang in to cancel my classes saying that I was unwell. I had so much work to do that I just had to have two days alone at home – 'on the sick' – to catch up.

In response to this situation the AUT launched its 'Lessen the Load' campaign which aimed to draw attention to the fact that:

> Since 1983–4 student numbers have increased by nearly two thirds while staff numbers have risen by a mere 11.4 per cent...it is the staff who have borne the brunt of this dramatic change and whose work loads have increased massively (AUT, 1996, p. 6)

Others have commented on the increasing demands upon working time and the ways in which these are increasingly resolved in relation to external criteria established by the funding council in relation to teaching and research. Many have questioned the impact of these changes upon previously established professional ethics (see for example, Harley and Lee, 1995; Minkin, 1996). The British Sociological Association conducted its own survey and found that

> no-one reported any positive effects of the research assessment exercise. Most thought it detrimental to quality, of both teaching and research...although one respondent noted that deterioration in output was not to be put directly at the door of the RAE, everyone else accepted that it was responsible for a series of consequences that were described as 'appalling', 'obscene', 'greatly detrimental' and so forth. (Warde, 1996, p. 2)

This disenchantment with imposed work norms was demonstrated graphically by one delegate at the Nation Union of

Teachers' Annual Conference in 1993 who arrived to speak at the rostrum bringing with her on a porter's trolley the documentation relating to the National Curriculum.

Within the National Health Service, the development of private Trusts and the introduction of management systems built around the internal market have produced considerable friction. The parallels here with some of the more rigid management systems introduced into private manufacturing are quite strong ones. One medical secretary described arrangements in one of the departments in her hospital, in ways which reminded me of the early Ford system (see Beynon, 1984). There, she said, 'laughing is forbidden; even smiling gets you into trouble'. To ask hospital workers whether the TV series *Cardiac Arrest* resembles life in their hospital is to produce an immediate response:

> everything that has happened in it has happened in our hospital. Except on one occasion when the administrator helped some-one who was on a trolley. Ours wouldn't have. He would have filled in one of his chittys and walked away.

Regularly, nurses say that they 'love the work but hate the job'. Accounts of increased work loads and perceived irrationalities are repeated throughout the state sector. In one of the Social Services Departments I visited I was told that:

> The pressure of work has got such lately that people are regularly taking days off work 'on the sick' as the only way of coping with it. As soon as a new virus appears, everyone develops the symptoms: one after the other. I've started to make a joke of it. I call into the offices and ask 'has anyone got something that I can catch: I need a few days at home'.

All this is suggestive of important changes taking place within the state sector which relate to changes in state policy and the imposition of external, budgetary constraints upon activities which were previously delivered on the basis of 'service' and 'need'. They form an arena in which conflicts over purpose, and the evaluation of work are fought out. That the conflict over values seems to be so acute in the state sector illustrates the extent to which these state workers and public service professions drew upon ideas of public service as a means of establishing their collective identities and developing their complex interests within society. It was these codes which were being contested and broken down by the managerialism of the eighties and nineties.

In turn, many professional people resent the increased demands placed upon them in a world where their 'service' isn't valued. As one teacher put it to me:

> I went into this job because I was interested in it; interested in teaching kids. But that isn't valued anymore. Not by the government or even by the parents. It's 'money' that counts nowadays. There are a lot of things – extra-curricular things – which I just won't do anymore.

INSECURITY AND STRESS

In Britain the most dramatic changes over the past decade and a half have been associated with the rate of unemployment and with increased insecurity (and 'fear') expressed by employees and the self-employed worker alike. As we have seen (in Table 2.4) unemployment increased in the early 1980s and has remained high since then. However, the unemployment data alone underestimate the numbers of people who, for one reason or another, are not in employment. The number of those 'out of work' is best measured through the idea of 'economic inactivity'. These data are contained in Table 2.7 and it indicates the extent of the gap that exists between this measure and the unemployment data. It demonstrates a long term decline in the percentage of men who are 'in work' and a corresponding increase in the percentage of women, especially married women. It demonstrates too how the labour force, in addition to being more balanced between men and women, is increasingly unrepresentative of people under eighteen and over fifty four. In the view of Schmitt and Wadsworth (whose more refined data suggest that inactivity rates are in fact higher than is suggested here):

> The evidence suggests that a shift in demand away from low skilled work, rather than any voluntary reduction in labour supply, was responsible for the rise in inactivity. (Schmitt and Wadsworth, 1994, p. 115)

Table 2.7   Economic Activity Rates 1975–93 (percentages)

Economic Activity of Men: percentage economically active by age

	1975	1981	1985	1991	1993
16–17	55	47	65	68	63
18–24	89	89	91	89	83
25–34	98	97	97	97	94
35–44	98	98	98	95	93
45–54	98	95	93	92	92
55–59	94	90	82	79	76
60–64	84	73	53	52	51
65 and over	16	11	8	8	7
16–64	93	90	89	88	86
Total	81	77	76	75	72

Economic Activity of Non-Married Women: percentage economically active by age

	1975	1981	1985	1991	1993
16–17	52	40	66	74	58
18–24	82	83	81	79	75
25–34	76	76	74	70	69
35–44	75	75	78	78	70
45–54	77	74	73	76	70
55–59	62	61	51	55	53
60–64	34	23	16	23	19
65 and over	6	4	2	2	2
16–59	72	70	74	74	69
Total	42	44	45	46	43

They add that the depressed state of wages and employer preferences which favour part-time work have also had an effect. This is borne out in research commissioned by the Rowntree Trust which argued that economic growth would not, in the nineties, have a significant effect on unemployment rates. Like Schmitt and Wadsworth, the editor of the study's findings, Pamela Meadows of the Policy Studies Institute, argued that

> unemployment at less that 2 million is simply the tip of the iceberg. We are entering the twenty first century

Table 2.7   *Continued*

Economic Activity of Married Women: Percentage economically active by age

	1975	1981	1985	1991	1993
18–24	54	57	62	71	74
25–34	52	51	57	71	72
35–44	66	69	69	77	79
45–54	67	69	67	75	74
55–59	49	54	50	55	56
60–64	26	21	20	25	22
65 and over	6	5	4	5	4
16–59	59	61	62	72	73
Total	51	51	51	59	59
All Women					
16–59	62	64	66	73	72

Source: *General Household Survey*, various years

> with 7 million people of working age who have no jobs (Meadows, 1996, p. 6)

This report indicated that employers increasingly favour women and part-time contracts. It also indicated that companies increasingly lay off older staff, hiring cheaper younger replacements, resulting in non-participation rates of 50 per cent in these older age groups. Further support for this line of argument comes from research commissioned by the Carnegie UK Trust which raised concern over the way in which

> the decline in the numbers of full-time secure pensioned jobs in favour of sub-contracting, part-time working and short term contracts has serious consequences for both young and older people, especially when coupled with discrimination against both young and old on grounds of age.

They added:

> in the 1980s, during the period of recovery following the early 1980s recession, employment levels first regained their

pre-recession level and then went on rising so that by the end of the decade they were 2 million above their pre-recession peak. In the 1990s even the restoration of the pre-recession level cannot be taken for granted. (Trinder and Worsley, 1996)

While the recession of the early eighties affected manu-facturing and the old industrial regions, the last recession hit directly at the new post-industrial, service economy and its heartland in the South East. An investigation by *World in Action* (10 November 1992) into the local economy of Slough (the boom town of the 1980s) documented 'the fear that affects every office and shop-floor in Britain'. In a sample of 1,000 they found that nine per cent had recently been made redun-dant; 43 per cent were worried about being made redundant and 60 per cent expected there to be an early redundancy within the family. The leader of the local Council remarked:

> everyone is depressed on the borough council...this country seems to be geared up for one thing – unemploy-ment. You can't plan your future.

A year later, a MORI/IRS survey commissioned by the *Financial Times* found that:

> the number of workers who fear they might lose their jobs in the next twelve months rose to more than 50 per cent in December – in spite of last week's sharp fall in unemploy-ment (*Financial Times*, 20 December 1993)

This survey revealed some interesting variations in the pattern of change. In referring to a 'surge' in the increased fear of redundancy, particular groups were highlighted:

> Part-time women workers are taking most of the jobs being created but this group has seen the biggest rise in job fears.... The anxiety ratio also rose among white-collar staff and lower managerial staff...possibly reflecting the likeli-hood of more public-sector job cuts.

In a reanalysis of Labour Force Survey data, Philip Bassett and Patricia Tehan estimated that in the three years 1990–1993 as many as 28 per cent of the labour force (that is 7 million people) experienced periods of unemployment (*The Times*, 11 January 1994). The *British Social Attitudes Survey* for 1994, registered a significant increase in the proportion of employees who saw job protection as their most important concern. Fourteen percent of the sample had been made redundant in the past five years, 52 per cent had worked in workplaces where there had been redundancies and 80 per cent knew someone who had experienced redundancy. These data are supported by a survey conducted at the University of Warwick by Whitston and Waddington. Focusing on issues relating to trade unionism, they recorded only six per cent of respondents claiming that their job was secure. Shop stewards and workplace representatives stressed managerial attitudes and the abuse of authority as giving greatest concern to their members. These feelings were felt most strongly in the public services.

While the earlier period of uncertainty had affected manual workers in the manufacturing and extraction industries, by the 1990s insecurity was widespread. For example, on 3 March 1994, *The Times* noted that

> more than 1,000 young business travel agents will be looking for jobs in corporate management this year after graduating from new training schemes.

It added that

> a recent study has said that up to 700 students on new tourism degree courses could fail to find jobs within the travel industry because of the recession.

Eighteen months later, the *Financial Times* was commenting on the fact that

> there has been a sharp increase in the number of travel agencies which have collapsed. In the three months to the end of September, the number of failures rose by 46 per cent compared with the same number last year.

In its view:

> the industry is bracing itself for another tough year in the face of erratic consumer behaviour in a market which most

describe as 'not buoyant'. (*The Financial Times*, 28 October 1995)

Perhaps the most interesting survey has been the one conducted recently by Mintel into 'Marketing to 45–64s' (Mintel, 1995a). This group has hitherto been the source of considerable purchasing power with no mortgage to pay, and children who have finished their education and are employed or married. The survey reports an astonishing change in the circumstances of this age group which it depicts as 'the sandwich generation'; caught between the changed demands and circumstances of their parents' and their children's generation. Caught too in the changed circumstances of their own employment. The study highlights 'a new mood of disenchantment with the world of work' with a significant decline in the proportion indicating that they would continue working if they didn't need the money. In its view

> it is certainly true that the widespread changes in working practices across the decade (including greater reliance upon new technology and a more 'results oriented' approach in many occupations) are likely to have been unsettling for established members of the workforce.

This report, helpfully drew attention to the ways in which fears and anxieties about security compound the stress which is related to the intensification of work itself. In the year to March 1993, Britain's largest 1,000 companies shed 1.5 million workers (*The Director*, March 1993), cutting costs and restructuring their operations. In the view of Alistair Anderson, managing director of Personal Performance Consultants UK, 'downsizing in companies has meant that often people have been left ill-equipped and ill-prepared for the job expected of them. This itself creates great stress.' He added that, in his belief 'the demands on the workforce are greater than they have ever been' (*The Financial Times*, 8 December 1993).

Here as everywhere there are ironies. So acute is the stress experienced by the 'survivors' of corporate shake-outs that many of them wish that they had been 'let go'. In a recent survey of 40 UK organizations in the public and private sectors, all of whom had undertaken at least one redundancy exercise, Drake Bean Morin (1995), the management consultancy found that

> survivors frequently feel confused and insecure about the future, and envy their former colleagues' lump sum payments and the opportunities opened up by career counselling... It is common for productivity to nose dive.

More recently, a survey of 1,300 managers carried out by the Institute of Management pinpointed 'recession survival strategy' as the source of significant levels of stress.

> Four out of five of the managers in the survey said that their work loads had increased in the past two years and the same numbers were worried about their future financial position. More than half the managers said that they were concerned about future career opportunities.
>
> As companies emerged from recession, however, the new management job structures were not offering improved job security, reduced stress levels or the easing of work loads. (IM, 1995)

In this respect these responses fit well alongside the findings of Cary Cooper's researches into the work habits of industrial managers. These confirm that many managers are rejecting the demands of the office in favour of time spent in more rewarding relationships beyond the workplace.

In the 1970s, the problems of British employment relations were strongly identified with the days lost through strike action. In the 1990s it seems that work-related stress (accounting for the loss of as many as 90 million working days a year) has replaced it. This helps to highlight the ways in which the most significant changes taking place in employment relations involve an interplay between the labour process and the content of the job on the one hand and institutional and external factors on the other. Of these, the depressed nature of labour markets; the reorganization of labour contracts and related changes in the composition of the labour force; and the changing nature of public sector employment are of considerable significance. In this context the decision by the Department of Health to shred printed copies of the commissioned publication, *Mental Health and Stress in the Workplace: A*

Guide for Employers, is of some interest. As Cary Cooper, one of
the authors, put it:

> Obviously it struck a nerve somewhere.... [but] it is clear
> that long hours do not mean good health. (*The Times,*
> 6 October 1995)

In assessing the current situation in labour markets across
the UK the Pennington column of *The Times* put the matter
rather succinctly. Responding to the Bank of England's
puzzlement over the failure of earnings to push up in the
period of recovery, it argued thus:

> Ask anybody working in the real world why earnings have not
> risen during this recovery as in past ones and they will come
> up with a much more sensible answer, which is blind terror.
> The industrial reforms of the 1980s have rendered the
> labour market permanently less secure for large swathes of
> the work force. Many more people work part-time and on
> temporary contracts and the use of casual labour is
> widespread.
> The jobs market is stacked dramatically in favour of the
> employer rather than the worker. Look no further than the
> fear of unemployment for the reason for low earnings
> growth. (*The Times,* 9 November 1995)

This was supported by an investigative report by *The Observer*
in which Neasa MacErlean interviewed a variety of different
employment consultants in order to establish 'How to make
sure that you don't get sacked'. Some of her findings were
these:

> Jo Bond of Coutts Career Consultants said: 'Keep fit and
> healthy. The older you are the more important it is to
> project a fit and healthy outlook; it's highly important for
> people over forty'.

> Elaine Aarons, employment solicitor of Eversheds, advises:
> 'Keep a distance from **the** politics of the organization. It
> doesn't do someone any good to be going to official or
> unofficial union meetings. These people often don't do well
> when a redundancy situation is going on. Unfortunately, it is
> as if we are going back into the Dark Ages where employees

have to take everything on the chin'. (*The Observer*, 26 May 1996)

Given this, it is perhaps not surprising to note that trade union membership in the UK has declined by 5 million since 1979. Unemployment and the closure of unionised enterprises provide the main explanation of this decline. This together with the difficulties involved in unionising many of the new workplaces and the growing tendency for employers to *deunionise* companies and establishments. A survey conducted by Industrial Relations Services of 98 companies in 1993, revealed that 25 had derecognized unions in the previous twelve months. The third Workplace Industrial Relations Survey data suggest that such derecognition and the removal of collective bargaining rights lead to a substantial decline in union membership. On its evidence density rates fall from 54 per cent to 15 per cent after derecognition.

In his interpretation of these data, Millward has argued that:

> Britain is approaching the position where few employees have any mechanism through which they can contribute to the operation of their workplace in a broader context than that of their own job. (Millward, 1994)

It would be possible to interpret this decline in unionisation and the response to deunionisation as evidence of the rise of individualism and the decline of a collective ethic. There are signs that the new leadership in the Labour Party take this view, stressing that trade unions should cease to behave as (putative and imperfect) organizations of class, and rather emphasise their role as service organizations capable of providing individual services for their members. Several trade unions have taken this path and there is some evidence that their members appreciate these new advantages of union membership.

However a recent major survey conducted at the University of Warwick seriously questions this interpretation, and the salience of individual benefits in the minds of union members. The authors of this survey concluded that their data

> emphasise the continuing relevance to workers in all occupations of the traditional reasons for trade union organization and membership – their need for an independent

collective means of defending and promoting their interests. (Whitston and Waddington, 1994)

Their respondents repeatedly mention the need for support at
work in the event of a problem. Shop stewards and workplace
representatives stressed managerial attitudes and the abuse of
authority as giving the greatest cause for concern to their
members. Across the sample only six per cent of the workforce
felt secure in their jobs. These feelings were felt most strongly
in the public services.

CONCLUSIONS

Things are changing in our society: sometimes imperceptibly,
sometimes dramatically and before our very eyes. Much of
this change is associated with work and employment. The
processes whereby new labour forces were reproduced (many
of them unchanged for two or three generations) have been
radically transformed. As a consequence dockers in Liverpool
strike for months attempting to prevent the imposition of a
contract which, in their view, would reintroduce the casualization of the nineteenth century. Thousands of people queue in
Manchester for the chance to work for Euro-Disney in Paris. A
man kills his friend in Bristol in a conflict over a part-time job
desired by both. Trainee managers for retail companies, like
'Toys R Us', are informed that the company demands 'total
commitment' and a working week of at least 100 hours.

Undoubtedly, many people's lives have improved immensely
in the last twenty years: both in terms of their real wages and
in the opportunities which have opened as a consequence of
rapid social and economic upheaval. However in its new form,
organized around a dynamic new technology, the economic
system produces high levels of insecurity and involuntary
economic inactivity. In the UK this has combined with the tacit
ending of 'the family wage'. As a result more and more of us
need a job in order to keep up our standard of living just at
the time when jobs are becoming scarcer. Nowadays more and
more people are being pushed to the edges of the labour
market; often to fight their way back in again but with little
guarantee of security.

This 'deregulation' of the British system of employment relations has brought it more in line with the US. However it has failed to deliver new jobs at anything like the US rate. At the same time there are grounds for feeling that it has done damage to the normative attachment of employees to their occupations and to their particular employer. Historically this relationship has been strongly underpinned by the state. For this reason the withdrawal of the state from the labour market has produced a situation of moral turbulence. In reflecting upon the situation in the USA, Edward Luttwack has argued that conventional politics of left and right can no longer deal with 'the central problem of our days: the complete and unprecedented personal economic insecurity of working people; from industrial workers and white collar clerks to medium high managers'. He adds, ominously, that 'it is not necessary to know how to spell *gemeinschaft* and *gesellschaft* to recognise the Fascist disposition in today's turbo-charged capitalism' (Luttwack, 1995). In the US, this route is seen to be represented in the new populism of Perrow and Buchanan. In the UK, the trajectory of such a politics is unclear; but there are worrying developments.

In this context it somewhat galling to read that Stephen Roach, the chief economist at Morgan Stanley in New York and the key advocate of 'downsizing', has had a change of heart. In his words: 'I am now having second thought as to whether we have reached the promised land'. Increased productivity and profits have been achieved but at what cost?

> in the face of intense competition, managers may simply have pared the largest chunk out of bloated costs – worker compensation… If this is so, the so-called productivity resurgence has been built on slash-and-burn restructuring strategies that have put extraordinary pressures on the workforce. This approach is not a permanent solution. Tactics of open ended downsizing and real wage compression are ultimately recipes for industrial extinction. (*The Financial Times*, 14 May 1996)

Many redundant steel workers would say 'amen' (or something stronger) to that.

3 What is Work for? The Right to Work and the Right to be Idle

INTRODUCTION

While working on this paper I remembered that in the late 1970s an elderly neighbour gave me a pamphlet with the title, *The Right to be Idle* (La Fargue, 1937) which she explained had sustained her throughout her working life in the textile mills of West Yorkshire. The arguments in it are relevant to much of my chapter, providing a salutary reminder that work and idleness are both part of life. 'What is Work for?' is not a question that is often asked, possibly because the answer seems so obvious. It is to make life possible, to produce things to eat, to wear, to provide shelter, to sustain not only ourselves, but those too young, too old or too ill or disabled to provide for themselves. Human beings have devised divisions of labour with the aim of fulfilling these needs. In some societies these divisions are relatively simple, between men and women and between age groups, for instance, while in others they are extremely complex, encompassing age and gender, but also between classes and ethnic groups with fine gradations within them. Theories of divisions of labour seek to explain not just what work is done by whom, but the kind and degree of social integration this produces. Durkheim built a typology of societies on this basis and it is still regarded as one of the keys to understanding the economy, power structures and social change (Durkheim, 1960; Sayer and Walker, 1992).

It is also the case that work establishes a right to respect, to a feeling of self-worth and some argue to an identity. How work is valued and how it is rewarded gives us many clues to the person's standing and life style. The question 'What do you do?' is often asked when people meet for the first time and is well understood in our culture to refer to work – to an occupation. From the answer we learn what level of income they are likely to earn, what kind of house they live in, what type of school their children attend and so on. It is still clearer if the person is a man rather than a woman. When the answer is 'I'm just a housewife', rarer now than in the past, this speaks volumes not about income levels, but about the differential evaluation given to unpaid work performed for husbands/partners and children and that which is part of the financially rewarded occupational or career structure. These two dimensions of work – the material and the evaluative – are intertwined in personal and social relations, yet they are not fixed or inevitable, but shaped to some degree by the choices that are made, most significantly by those with power.

In a world in which some kinds of work are disappearing and where some have too little work and others are burdened with too much, the problems we face require clarification through analysis and the options before us need discussion and informed choice. I will concentrate in my chapter on some of those aspects which are frequently pushed to the back of our minds either by everyday concerns, or because we can see no solution. The sound bite responses given by politicians, amount to little more than slogans either of the 'a return to full employment' or 'the free market' variety which neglect the evidence of the social and economic transformation which is taking place.

THE PRESENT CONTEXT

According to some authorities we are experiencing a global restructuring of economic activity. This involves on the one hand a re-emergence of the free market for capital, initially among Western type economies, but since the downfall of states in Central and Eastern Europe, the break-up of the Soviet Union and the changes in China, it has become world wide. Capital is ever more concentrated in fewer hands and able to move across borders in search of profit, outwith the political or economic control of the institutions of any individual society, either governments or private organizations. On the other hand changes in the international division of labour have occurred as the production of manufactured goods moves away from the older industrialized economies to the sources of cheap labour found in what are referred to as peripheral locations, for example, to Latin America, parts of the Pacific Rim or the Caribbean (Froebel et al., 1981; Grunwald and Flamm, 1985; Nash and Fernandez-Kelly, 1983). At the same time new forms of technology allow services of many kinds to be located almost anywhere, away from the older industrial and commercial centres and the motorway corridors, in what were previously construed as remote areas. In Britain, for instance, these include the Yorkshire Dales, the Highlands and Islands of Scotland and the Welsh mountains (Morgan, 1986). In much popular literature there is a marked tendency to portray such changes in a technological determinist framework accompanied by a misplaced romanticism and with little reference to the social relations in which such work is embedded.

From a national perspective these changes are frequently seen in terms of the radical political rhetoric characteristic of Mrs Thatcher's years in office and as consequences of the social and economic policies her governments pursued. Such rhetoric and policies are still advocated by among others, those whom Edwina Curry recently described in a television interview as 'young, fit men in the Cabinet', in contrast to the views being voiced by her constituents with children, mortgages, elderly or sick relatives and neighbours. The contribution of the Thatcher years to breaking the post war consensus on full employment and the welfare state which held for almost forty years after the Second World War across the political parties, and between them and the electorate, is a matter over which there is much debate (Cross and Payne, 1991). Our present economic and social situation is certainly not unique to Britain. The forces for change are much broader and their contours more complex. However, they are experienced in specific local contexts and these play their part in the responses people make, as individuals and members of collectivities (Garrahan and Stewart, 1992; Sadler, 1992).

WORK: EMPLOYMENT, UNEMPLOYMENT AND
SELF-EMPLOYMENT

Work

Work covers all kinds of activities which in the end shade off
into something which is not work, but play or leisure, rest or
relaxation and in some contexts, idleness. The distinction
between work and non-work and between different forms of
work is not the activity engaged in, but by the relationships
among those organizing and/or undertaking it and the
circumstances under which it is undertaken (Pahl, 1988;
Thompson, 1983). Work or labour is as old as humankind
itself, while employment came to prominence as a dominant
form of social organization only relatively recently, a mere two
and a half centuries ago in this part of the world and much
later in other parts of Europe and further afield.

Work in all its forms is about more than putting bread on
the table, or shoes on children's feet or paying the rent or the
mortgage. It is infused with moral and political values, with
ideas about social worth and has figured prominently in many
religions, not least in Christianity, especially the Protestant
work ethic which it is now commonplace to associate with the
development of capitalism in England and the Northern states
of North America. A system which had global effects, cultural,
political and social as well as economic, in addition to altering
the face of Britain – or the United Kingdom as it came to be.

Many of these still form a backdrop to our everyday lives.
The transatlantic slave trade, experienced by the forebears of
many British citizens, the transferring and transporting of
millions of others across the British Empire, to work as labourers or to farm and to own and to people, so-called empty lands
or lands made virtually empty of the indigenous inhabitants
are but two examples. They are not distant in time or space,
nor simply reminders of the past. The physical and social
landscape of Britain is replete with them. Some gathered in
collections in museums or private houses, some in the location
of major cities and their magnificent buildings, the city halls,
the shipping offices, the warehouses and commodity exchanges of Manchester, Liverpool, Bristol and Bradford to say

nothing of London or Glasgow. Many others are to be found in the multiplicity of backgrounds of the population of contemporary Britain. Where we live, what we do and how we are identified and evaluated owes not a little to this history, for most, if not all of us. Whether or not we identify ourselves in relation to any of this history is entirely another matter.

Employment

Employment, often called having a job, is a relationship between buyers and sellers of labour and labour time. This relationship between capital and labour is typically one in which the employee carries out certain activities, in a certain place at particular times to produce a good, or part of one, or to provide a service and be rewarded financially by the employer for doing so. The degree of discretion and control the employee has varies. It may be full-time or part-time, permanent or temporary. In the 1980s, for a variety of reasons, 'new ways of working' were increasingly advocated. Flexible work organization is one of these and represents a way of reducing labour and related costs for the employer. Most flexible jobs produce for the employee insecurity, a lack of protection and lack of permanency (Allen, 1989a; Allen and Wolkowitz, 1987; Christensen, 1989; Pollert, 1988; Rainnie, 1992; Rubery, 1988). Such forms of work organization are not new, but a return to those used throughout the industrial period.

To return to my neighbour, her family's experiences were shared by countless others in the first 60 years of the 20th century. She was a textile worker from leaving school at 14 until she retired and was employed for 30 years at Salts Mill, in the Victorian model village of Saltaire built by Sir Titus Salt in the mid nineteenth century (Reynolds, 1983).[1] In contrast to the mills he owned in Bradford, where he made his wealth, and the housing conditions of the mill workers there, it was indeed a model village, a symbol of paternalistic philanthropy, combined with a keen business sense. The control exercised over those employees who lived in Saltaire extended beyond the mill gates to their personal lives. This is evident from the layout of the houses with those occupied by the overseers being strategically placed at the corners of the rows from where all comings and goings could be seen.[2] The surveillance and the rules were anathema to many mill workers who avoided living in the village whenever possible. As late as the 1970s those who lived there were regarded with pity by local people.[3]

Born in 1900 and being the youngest of a family of five, my neighbour had been allowed to finish her schooling without becoming a part-timer. Not so her eldest sister, who began as a part-timer before the First World War and spoke of drinking water from rusty ladles as they worked at the looms in immense heat and dust. When dying in the late 1960s, she begged 'don't make me go back to the mill'. In the depression of the inter-war years their father obtained work in the mills on condition that the labour and skills of his wife and unmarried daughters were available to his employer when they were needed; a practice that existed until at least the 1950s in the wool textile industry. The outbreak of the Second World War, however, brought them for the first time regular work and regular, if low, wages. Though the details differ, whether one lived in the country or in town, what kinds of industry existed in the locality or the region, whether one was male or female, and so on, for working class people work dominated their lives. The conditions on and under which they worked were largely outside their control, only a minority being organized in trade unions which sought to improve and maintain working and living conditions.

The high point of the establishment of a floor of basic economic and social rights in Britain came in the late 1960s and mid 1970s, with legislation on contracts of employment, redundancy pay, health and safety at work, the outlawing of racial and sex discrimination. Even these did not cover many sections of the working population, those who worked for pay at home, most part-timers and those employed casually or defined by those for whom they worked as self-employed (Allen and Wolkowitz, 1987; Burchell and Rubery, 1992).

The majority of jobs created at the end of the 1980s were in the service sector across the European Community and these were overwhelmingly taken by women. Many jobs in this sector are part-time or temporary with no career prospects and are frequently low paid and casualised. In the European Union, women make up two-fifths of the labour force, but 80 per cent of part-time employees are women. Temporary contracts are equally distributed between men and women. The term 'the working poor' is now becoming commonplace along with the 'feminization of the labour force' (Jenson et al., 1988; Brown and Scase, 1991). Both are linked to the recession and restructuring. The decline in skilled manufacturing has left those who were or would have become industrial workers competing for low level jobs in the service sector and for more and more of them the terms and conditions under which they are employed have become poor and insecure – a feature formerly associated with women's employment.

At the other end of the job hierarchy there has been some growth in managerial, professional and administrative positions and employment requiring new skills has followed the application of information and communications technology. There is therefore a marked increase in the polarization of the labour market between the working poor and those earning high rewards. The term recession carries with it connotations of a temporary phase from which the economy will recover rather than longer term structural change in the economy itself. The recession and the restructuring trends have had widespread effects on the social and political fabric of Britain.

Marshall argued that as well as civil and political rights, social and industrial rights were necessary to the exercise of full citizenship and for effective integration into society. He took for granted the arguments for full employment put forward by Beveridge and was concerned with the problem of how social justice and market price could be reconciled in a mixed economy (Beveridge, 1944; Marshall, 1950). The relevance of this question to the problems of the 1990s could not be greater. The lack of affordable housing, the widening inequalities in health care and education and the crisis around the care of the frail elderly are to a great extent associated with the lack employment. For many unemployment is the most significant of all the problems facing us.

Unemployment

My neighbour was well aware of the scourge of unemployment and its consequences and to her, along with millions of others, 'the right to work' was a basic right. Beveridge's view that 'the greatest evil of unemployment is not physical but moral, not the want which it may bring but the hatred and fear it breeds' (Beveridge, 1944, p. 15) would have had her qualified support. From her experience physical want, in the shape of hunger, cold, lack of shelter and avoidable sickness and premature death were not lesser evils but the material base of the fear and hatred to which he refers.

For most of the modern period, the vast majority of the gainfully occupied in Britain have sold their skills and labour to an employer in return for a wage or salary as their only source of a livelihood. To lose one's job usually brings an immediate loss of income, and is '...accompanied by a loss of status, identity and rights through the multiplicity of rules and regulations to which the unemployed and their families are subjected. Additionally those without jobs are frequently denigrated and their abilities and motivation openly questioned. The wage relationship, previously a main source of integration into wider structures of society, is for more and more individuals and families severed.' (Allen and Waton, 1986, p. 1; see also Pixley, 1993). The distribution of unemployment varies according to region, age, gender, educational level and race. During the 1980s the rise in unemployment was heavily concentrated among council and housing association tenants (Cooper, 1995). For 'never employed' young people making the transition to adulthood, independence from parents or other carers and setting up their own family/household, becomes increasingly difficult. Those too young to draw income support may be forced into homelessness and begging for a living. This is particularly the case for those growing up in the care of the Social Services, or on one of the 2,000 estates (housing 5 million people) where average incomes are below the European poverty line and unemployment is well above the national average.

In contrast to our European neighbours, unemployment rates in Britain are consistently reported as higher for men than for women. This was due in part in the 1980s to the loss of jobs in heavy industry and manufacturing which were largely the preserve of men. By 1990 only 43 per cent of male and 18 of women employees, less than 30 per cent of the workforce, were in industry compared with Germany where a stronger industrial base has been maintained which provides over 50 per cent of male and 25 per cent of female employment.

Other factors are involved which make comparisons between men and women difficult. These relate both to the methods used to count the unemployed which consistently underrecord women's unemployment, and as research has increasingly shown, to the gendered divisions of labour in the household and the labour market.[4]

Despite the fact that there is much hidden unemployment what we can see is that even recorded unemployment indicates in a particularly sharp way what work is for.

Creating Jobs: Self-Employment and Small Business

Much was made in the 1980s of the growth of the small business and self-employed sectors in terms of economic recovery from the recession and as evidence of the emergence and durability of the 'enterprise culture' (*Employment Gazette*, May 1989, p. 218). There are statistical and conceptual problems with the data used to substantiate the first claim and much debate around the meaning of the second which politically was set in opposition to the 'dependency culture' (Burrows, 1991). The confusion and ambiguities which surround self-employment and small business arise from the complexities and variety of the relationships to which they refer and from the reality that individuals can participate in more than one of these relationships (Leighton and Felstead, 1992). Someone who is self-employed may also employ others and be categorised as a business owner or a small firm.[5] As the system of collecting the data relies largely on self-classification, and conflicting advice is given by different government departments on how to complete the forms, there is both underestimation and overestimation in the official statistics on self-employment (Allen and Truman, 1992, 1993; Burchell and Rubery, 1992; Casey and Creigh, 1988; Felstead, 1992). Some of those classified as self-employed may be so only in a formal legal sense, undertaking work for others who then sell the goods or services produced. The majority of homeworkers have always fallen into this category, as have many workers in the building and construction industry (Allen and Wolkowitz, 1987; Phizacklea and Wolkowitz, 1995). The advantages to employers in using this method of work organization lie in the on-cost savings they make and the ease with which they can freely take on and dispose of labour, advantages which have been exploited throughout industrialization. The number of self-employed in the UK grew between 1978 and 1989 from 7.5 per cent to 12.2 per cent of the employed workforce (from 1.84 to 3.18 million) (Meager, 1992). These data reflect an increase in the use of this method of work organization by employers in the recessionary 1980s which was facilitated in some cases by developments in information and communication technology which allows homebased work to be undertaken at or from home, rather than in an office or factory.

The self-employed sector includes a wide range of activities and though it remains high in agriculture across Europe it is in services of all kinds that it grew fastest in the 1980s. These range from those supplying professional services, for instance lawyers or architects, or literary, dramatic and artistic/craft workers, freelance journalists, screen writers and film makers to those providing goods or services, such as jobbing builders, small shopkeepers, prostitutes, childminders, painters and decorators, gardeners and many more. Where athletes, boxers, footballers, cricketers, mountain climbers and explorers fit is a good question, but not one I shall pursue. Like all the others referred to above their conditions of work and levels of reward vary widely, as does their social status and the esteem in which they are held.

The use of 'family labour' by the self-employed or small business owner is not commonly and systematically recorded in Western European statistics (Allen, 1992; Kovalainen, 1993). Besides distorting the numbers involved it marginalises the work undertaken, typically by women, but also by men, and by children. Some of the most successful micro-enterprises are of this type, not least because the work of family members is rewarded below the market price or is unpaid, particularly in the case of wives, for whom subsistence is the reward. Exploitation is an enduring feature of most forms of work organization, but in self-employment and micro-enterprise exploitation – of self and of others – is especially marked.

If we accept at face value the numerical increase in self-employment and small business, it remains the case that the majority of the population of working age rely on employment for an income, not only in the UK but across the European Community (European Commission, 1993).

The 'enterprise culture' as a solution to unemployment, so popular in the 1980s among some politicians, those looking to be their own boss, or to make a fortune, began to wane in the 1990s. As a change in approaches to work organization, as a necessary part of restructuring it remains strong. It is to some issues relating to this that I turn in my conclusion.

CONCLUSIONS

Work is central to our material existence, to our place in the world and in fact to every aspect of human life. It encompasses all those activities which produce our subsistence and the caring and servicing on which every one depends. It produces works of art as well as shoes, religious texts as well as scientific instruments, poetry and false teeth. It takes many forms and uses many methods and covers much more than employment or self employment. Social life depends in large measure on invisible, unpaid work which is *discounted* in economic statistics and financial projections. It involves soothing crying babies and attending to the dying as well as making cars or pots or computers. Work is for the production of wealth and for the production of social life. Consideration of the terms and conditions on which it is undertaken is therefore crucial.

Present political concerns about our relations to the European Union and which of its rules and regulations we are prepared to accept, are not just about national sovereignty, with policing our borders, or defending our culture. These arguments are often couched in nationalistic terms, in the language of our way of life, in claims to defending freedoms enjoyed by Englishmen over many generations, which are now being threatened. What is abundantly clear is that many of the substantive objections relate to the terms and conditions of work organization. Opting out of the Social Chapter is only part of maintaining poorer conditions for workers in Britain. The British government's reluctance to accept rulings on employment law, such as paternity leave, outlawing child labour and discrimination in pay and conditions between nationals of member states, and between men and women, are just a few examples. It is claimed these will undermine Britain's competitive position and slow, if not reverse, its economic recovery. These arguments are not new, nor is the language in which they are delivered. Every improvement in working conditions or in rates of pay or towards more equal treatment between men and women, between migrant and indigenous workers, between those deemed as different racial or religious groups or between the able-bodied and the sensory, physically or mentally disabled has met, to a greater or lesser degree, with opposition on economic grounds. The gains made in the 1960s and 1970s in employment rights have been eroded by piecemeal legislation (Hepple, 1986) passed by the British Parliament and underpinned by an ideology of enterprise. In many respects the legal rights of workers existing in much of Europe are well in advance of those in the UK.

New technologies free us from much hard manual labour, from the drudgery of routine, repetitive work, from the threats of starvation, avoidable illness and disease and produce information more rapidly than was possible even a decade ago. As yet we do not have technologies to perform so many tasks which are necessary for social reproduction and survival. The information which technologies enable us to produce is not the same as the production of knowledge. Knowledge involves much more than information. It requires a plan, a scheme, a theory to order it and make sense of it. At its most creative it is based on the thought of previous generations, anchored in knowledge of the social world and is an open activity, not the prerogative of any one collectivity or category.

The potential impact of technological changes, associated first with automation and later with computing, led to debates around post-industrial society in which it was argued that knowledge and information would be at a premium, with manufacturing production decreasing in importance relative to education in structuring societies (Bell, 1973; Stonier, 1983). These arguments were not accepted by many social scientists who developed a major critique around the relations of technology and social organization. Technology is never neutral and by itself does not determine the direction of social change. First, its application or non-application can not be understood apart from the choices and decisions made by those with economic and political power (Lyon, 1986). Second, those with this power are, in turn, constrained by existing structures (Mackenzie and Wajcman, 1985). The ownership and control of property now includes the ownership and control of information on a vast scale. Access to it is not freely available any more than its construction is a neutral, disinterested undertaking. A free market of information means a competitive struggle between sellers operating in a global framework, but a range of interests including those of private corporations, governmental agencies and military alliances are also involved. Touraine argued that the post-industrial society would be one of conflict in which 'class situations, conflicts and movements' would be of fundamental importance (1974, p. 28). The differential control and access to information between classes is already very evident, but to this must be added the other dimensions of systematic inequality such as those between women and men and among different ethnic/racial groups. Information technologies can widen the gaps already existing between those with access and those without. But equally, if not more importantly, they bring a potential for controlling the production and dissemination of knowledge which will deprive yet further already disadvantaged groups.

There are options about how technologies are to be shaped. These depend on political and economic decisions and strategies which offer alternatives. One alternative is to continue with policies based on an impoverished notion of economic growth which is not only environmentally damaging and heavily dependent on arms sales, but widens the gaps between rich and poor nations and within them between classes. The other is to use the knowledge that is available to devise sustainable development, to begin to take steps to design a system of reward to include all forms of work and provide collective ways of dealing with the social and material infrastructure essential to everyone. These choices are value laden – from which we cannot escape. What kind of society we envisage depends crucially on how we reshape the ways we think about and organize work.

An inclusive society means that all have a right and an obligation to share in work activities, to share in its products, material and non-material, and a right to be idle. This would not be a 'free for all' form of society, envisaged in romantic, glamorized versions of some of the post-industrial, information society literature (Gorz, 1985; Lyotard, 1984; Toffler, 1981). On the contrary, the potential for abolishing material scarcities through relevant technologies, liberating those presently confined to impoverished lives is possible only by renegotiating social, political and economic relations. Technology, though essential to the scale and means of the holocaust, does not explain why it occurred nor who was involved (Bauman, 1989). Such explanations can only be arrived at by analysing policy decisions by those with power, the codes of morality on which they are based and the options open to and the choices made everyday by ordinary people.

My neighbour's belief in the right to be idle, as a human right, flew in the face of the dominant morality and was denied to her and those like her by the social and economic system under which they lived. The pamphlet provided her with the language in which to express her belief. It reflected an alternative set of values, based on empathy for and solidarity with others which gave rise to resistance and to collective endeavour to change living and working conditions produced by the 19th century 'enterprise culture'. In the last decade of the 20th century despite major advances in the application of technology to producing and consuming goods and services, neither the right to work nor the right to be idle has been achieved. The discussion on 'new ways of working' requires both to be taken seriously.

NOTES

1. Titus Salt has been described as

    a highly successful entrepreneur who developed a new branch of the worsted textile industry and as the creator of the model village of Saltaire. When he died his fame was international and in England he was regarded as the epitome of all that was best in the enlightened Victorian capitalist (Reynolds, 1983, p. 1).

2. An African economist friend remarked that the layout resembled that of compounds in South Africa.

3.   It is now a tourist attraction with boutiques and gift shops and the former workers' cottages sell at inflated prices. The mill is used for offices of high technology firms and the Area Health Authority, a restaurant, an art gallery, upmarket shops and newly developed luxury apartments overlooking the canal and the river. What is being preserved and celebrated is hardly the history of the textile workers or the vision and purpose of Sir Titus Salt.

4.   A more detailed discussion of these points is to be found in Allen, 1989b.

5.   Small businesses can be defined in a number of ways. One of the most commonly used is the number of employees and any firm with below 200 employees is classified as small. The recognition that having 199 employees is a very different matter from having only very few led to those employing between 0-9 being designated in some research and official categorization as 'micro-enterprises' (Leighton and Felstead, 1992, p. 18).

4 Flexibility and Security: Contradictions in the Contemporary Labour Market

INTRODUCTION

We live in a society where the vast majority of us depend directly or indirectly on the labour market for our livelihood. The income which supports us comes from our ability to sell our labour power, to secure paid employment or to have done so in the past, or the ability to do so of those on whom we are dependent. The proper operation of the labour market, the institutions which allocate people to jobs and jobs to people, is therefore crucially important for our well-being. Yet throughout the past 15 to 20 years the labour market in Britain has been characterized by too little effective demand for labour to provide employment for all those who would like or need to have a job. There have also been difficulties arising from mismatches between the jobs which are vacant and the qualifications, skills and experience of available workers. These difficulties, however, cannot account for the levels of unemployment experienced since the 1970s.[1]

It is important to make this point at the outset because it is not what I want to discuss in detail. It is, however, the crucial context for the issues which are the main focus of this chapter. We must not forget that continuing high levels of unemployment have been the dominant feature of the labour market since the 1970s. One part of the answer to the question, 'what sort of labour market do we need?', must be that it is a labour market which provides the possibility of employment for all those who want or need paid work; and also, but perhaps not quite as important, that it is a labour market which can provide suitable employees for all those employers who have jobs to fill.[2]

For several decades after the end of the Second World War it was widely accepted that the 'Keynesian revolution' had provided a solution to the problems of unemployment which had been so prominent in the inter-war period, and indeed before that. By the 1970s, however, the degree of management of the economy by the state which Keynesian policies demanded was felt by many to be a cause of problems – inflation, poor productivity, lack of competitiveness, industrial disputes – rather than the answer to them. The Conservative Government elected in 1979 was determined to adopt policies guided by quite different economic doctrines, policies which had to some extent already been foreshadowed by the actions of the Labour Government after 1976. Only in this way, it was argued, could Britain survive in the increasingly competitive world economy which had developed following the oil price rises of the 1970s.

Perhaps the most important element in the Government's policies for employment has been the search for a labour market which is freer, less regulated, more competitive and more flexible. This has been combined with an emphasis on the need to strengthen education and training so as to provide a more highly and appropriately qualified workforce. The 1985 White Paper, for example, argued that 'The biggest single cause of our high unemployment is the failure of our jobs market, the weak link in our economy'. It went on to emphasize the need for improvements in four areas:

'quality, so that businesses can find the increasingly demanding skills they need';
'costs and incentives, so that people are neither prevented from pricing themselves into jobs, nor deterred from taking them up';
'flexibility, so that employers and employees adapt quickly to new circumstances'; and
'freedom, so that employers are not so burdened by regulation that they are reluctant to offer more jobs' (Department of Employment, 1985, pp. 13–14).

Since then there have of course been numerous changes in the details of Government policy as 'schemes' aimed at improving training or assisting the unemployed to find jobs have been modified or replaced. The overall intentions of Government policy for the labour market have, however, remained essentially unchanged. They have been embodied in the legislation of the 1980s and the early 1990s which greatly reduced trade union powers and employment protection and created a more nearly deregulated labour market. They have informed the measures to reduce the size of the public sector, with its relatively more highly protected workforces, by means of privatization and compulsory competitive tendering. They were reiterated, nearly a decade after the White Paper, when the Department of Employment described its 'overarching aim' as 'To support economic growth by promoting a competitive, efficient and *flexible* labour market' (Employment Department, 1994a, quoted in Beatson 1995, p. 1. Italics in the original). These broad aims for the labour market have even influenced recent statements of policy by the European Union, in response to persistent high levels of unemployment throughout Europe (for example CEC, 1993).

That unemployment in Britain in 1996 remains stuck at well over two million, even using the official and much adjusted figures, might suggest that either these aims for the labour market have not been achieved, or that a less regulated, more competitive and flexible labour market will not prove to be a solution to unemployment, or indeed both. My aim in this chapter is to explore in a little more detail what is meant by the central plank in this policy, the increase in labour market 'flexibility'; to review the evidence regarding the extent to which there has been increased flexibility in the labour market and in employment; and then to suggest not only that one of the main and unavoidable concomitants of labour market flexibility, increased job insecurity, is unwelcome to most employees, but that these policies have a number of consequences for economy and society which exacerbate rather than help solve the very problems of unemployment, poor productivity, and so on, for which they have been seen as the answer. The corollary of this argument, of course, is that we 'need' a different sort of labour market from that which is currently being pursued.

A FLEXIBLE LABOUR MARKET?

The term 'flexibility' has come to have a variety of not altogether consistent and unambiguous meanings. The 1985

White Paper, for example, uses 'flexibility' to refer to adapting quickly to new circumstances, by adjusting patterns of work, hours and job demarcations (Department of Employment, 1985, p. 14). The other changes it advocates – improvements in labour costs and incentives, and the ending of expensive, time-consuming and complicated employment regulation – are both seen as aspects of labour market flexibility by other commentators. Indeed, these three assumed 'needs' are closely parallel to the definitions of 'functional', 'pay' and 'numerical' flexibility which are the attributes of the putative 'flexible firm' described by Atkinson and Meager (NEDO, 1986, pp. 3–4). Similarly, in a recent comprehensive review and assessment of *Labour Market Flexibility*, published by the Department of Employment, Beatson (1995, p. 1) identifies 'flexibility on the extensive margin' by which he means 'the ability of firms to change the number of people they employ'; 'flexibility on the intensive margin', 'the ability of firms to vary the amount of labour they use without resorting to the external labour market', for example by varying working time, or the range of tasks that employees perform; and 'wage or reward flexibility', 'the ability of pay and payment systems to respond to labour market conditions and to reward and encourage improved performance'. Whatever the terms used these distinctions between flexibility in numbers, in tasks and in rewards can usefully be adopted here to take the argument forward.

In his report Beatson (1995) has assessed the main developments. He drew on an extensive literature, including the three Workplace Industrial Relations Surveys of 1980, 1984 and 1990, and the Social Change and Economic Life Initiative research programme of the mid-1980s, as well as more recent studies. In relation to numerical flexibility he argued that – although there is little evidence for an increase in temporary work – part-time employment, especially of women, self-employment and sub-contracting have all increased considerably since the 1970s. Indeed, employers 'face relatively few constraints on their ability to exploit external flexibility' (to vary the size of their workforce), but 'there is insufficient data to reach firm conclusions on whether turnover of people or jobs has increased or decreased over time' (pp. 36–7). However, compared to other countries in the European Union the UK has relatively high rates of mobility into and out of employment and unemployment, and between industries and regions, though the rates are higher in the USA and Australia, and the evidence on trends over time is uncertain (p. 68). The evidence also suggests that employers have taken advantage of the scope for increased flexibility and diversity in the structuring of working time, which is greater in the United Kingdom than elsewhere in the European Union (p. 49).

In contrast, the degree of functional flexibility may be low in Britain by international standards, although there is evidence that manufacturing firms have taken steps during the 1980s to remove some of the barriers, especially rigid job demarcation (pp. 51–3). Wage determination has become increasingly decentralized and a substantial majority of employers make use of performance related pay (p. 84), and there is some (limited) evidence that short-term wage flexibility has increased since the early 1980s (p. 110). Thus, after summarising this and other evidence, Beatson argued that 'it can reasonably be concluded that the labour market has become more flexible over the last fifteen years or so'; and that even in areas where adequate information is not available 'there is no evidence that the labour market has become less flexible' (p. 134). The Department of Employment's own report on *Labour Market and Skill Trends 1995/96* comes to a very similar conclusion (Employment Department, 1994b, pp. 20–1).

THE 'FLEXIBLE FIRM'

It can be argued that there is a basic contradiction in much of the discussion of flexibility: workers who are employed on short term contracts and likely to be dismissed at short notice will have little incentive, or opportunity, to acquire the skills and to develop the commitment needed by a functionally flexible workforce. Equally, workers who have the skills and the willingness to undertake a range of tasks, to be functionally flexible, will expect, and may well be able to demand, job security, thereby making it more difficult for the employer to achieve flexibility in numbers.

The idea of the 'flexible firm' represents an attempt to deal with this dilemma. It is the notion which has perhaps aroused the most heated debate in all the lengthy and convoluted discussions of various aspects of flexibility, and I do not intend to try to resolve the questions which have been raised (see, for example, the discussion in Pollert, 1988a and b, and 1991, and Proctor et al., 1994). However, the 'model' of the flexible firm implies that employers would respond to the changed labour market conditions and industrial relations climate of the 1980s by, on the one hand, retaining a **core** of skilled and versatile employees, able and willing to carry out the central tasks of the organization in a 'functionally flexible' manner; and, on the other, by supplementing this with a 'numerically flexible' **periphery** of less secure, part-time, temporary, short-term contract and casual employees, who could be taken on or dismissed as demand dictated, together with subcontractors, agency temps and self-employed who were 'distanced' from direct employment. Dividing an organization's workforce into a 'core' and a 'periphery' in this way, and offering the core very different terms and conditions of employment from the rest, provides, in theory, a way of resolving this basic contradiction of a flexible labour market.

We can note in passing that there is little evidence that employers have been explicitly pursuing flexibility in the form of the flexible firm, or indeed that they have explicit strategies for utilising labour which recognize these problems (see, for example, Hunter et al., 1993). Rather decisions and actions tend to be opportunistic and ad hoc. The most that can be claimed is that some such 'strategy' may be considered to emerge from the pattern of a stream of decisions about the ways in which workers are to be recruited, employed and dismissed (Proctor et al., 1994).

Whether or not it has been altogether intended, however, one clear concomitant of these labour market policies, if and in so far as they are implemented, is increased uncertainty and insecurity for many, perhaps a majority, of those in or seeking employment. The removal of protective regulation, allowing employers to take on and dismiss employees more easily, thus achieving flexibility in numbers; the requirement that workers be prepared to undertake a wider range of tasks and to vary their hours and times of work to achieve functional flexibility; the linking of pay to performance as an incentive to accept these changes; all these developments may make for a more flexible and competitive labour market, though this can be questioned, but they also make for one in which employees have less security and less ability to control their own working lives and to plan for the future. 'Flexibility' for employers, and in the labour market as a whole, implies 'insecurity' for their employees.

INSECURITY

It seems difficult to capture the extent of job insecurity in conventional statistical indices. It can be reflected in the proportion of jobs which are labelled 'temporary' or 'fixed term contract', and in increased rates of dismissal and redundancy, but these measures almost certainly understate its extent. Indeed, one of the apparent paradoxes of discussions of flexibility is the evidence from many sources that the numbers and proportion of explicitly 'temporary' jobs have not greatly changed for fifteen years or more. The Workplace Industrial Relations Surveys (WIRS), for example, record little change in the incidence of temporary work during the 1980s, and Labour Force Survey data, which use respondents' own assessment of whether a job is temporary or permanent, showed little change in the number of temporary workers between 1984 and 1991. There has, however, been an increase in workers on fixed term contracts since 1992 (Millward et al., 1992, pp. 337–9; Beatson, 1995, pp. 7–11).

Similarly levels of recorded redundancy have not increased straightforwardly over time but rather fluctuated in relation to overall levels of unemployment. The WIRS, for example, reported fewer workplaces shedding workers in 1990 than in 1984 or 1980, largely, they argued, because of the expansion of the economy in 1989–90. Even so a third of all establishments surveyed reported workforce reductions in 1990, though this was a reduction from two-fifths in 1984 and 45 per cent in 1980; and in nearly a third of these cases compulsory redundancy was involved (Millward et al., 1992, pp. 320–2).

More important, perhaps, is the more diffuse influence of the overall levels of unemployment, and the knowledge that if one loses one's job there is quite a high probability that it will be some time before another one is obtained, if indeed, especially in the case of older or less skilled workers, this happens at all. The chances of redundancy and unemployment are much higher, and the chances of quickly obtaining another job much lower, – and felt to be so – than they were in the 1950s and 1960s.

Reactions to labour market flexibility are crucially affected by the extent to which employment is seen as secure, and likely to remain so. Subjective evaluations that jobs are less secure than they were may or may not be justified – though I would agree with most commentators that they are – but, in the familiar truism, if people 'define situations as real, they are real in their consequences'!

In this context it is important to note the suggestion by the Social Change and Economic Life studies that employees' feelings of security in their jobs are influenced not so much by the sort of employment contract they have as by 'whether or not their employer had cut the work-force' (Gallie and White, 1994, esp. p. 293). The threat of workforce reductions has been a common experience. In each year between 1984 and 1991, for example, the *British Social Attitudes* surveys found that between 20 and 30 per cent of all employees expected there to be workforce reductions at their place of work, though rather fewer expected to leave their own employment for any reason, and only five per cent or fewer of them expected to be made redundant (Social and Community Planning Research, 1992, G.3 – 5–9; R. Jowell et al., 1991, p. 211; R. Jowell et al., 1992, p. 30).

Thus, expectations of job cuts and feelings of job insecurity are much more pervasive and affect far more people than those experiencing unemployment and/or redundancy directly. This is reflected in and reinforced by the mass media and other non-academic writing on the subject (see, for example, Handy, 1994). Their pervasive message on employment issues is that no one can expect 'a job for life', and that having a full-time permanent job is likely to be confined to a smaller and smaller proportion of those in the labour market, if indeed it is an option for anyone. Towards the end of 1994, for example, Will Hutton described the changes as follows:

> If more than half the working population had full-time, tenured jobs 20 years ago, now the proportion has fallen to

barely a third. Even if you include those self-employed who are secure and the part-timers who actively want to work part-time, barely more than half the working population are working in conditions that earlier generations would recognize as secure employment. The rest have been plunged into a maelstrom of uncertainty, and conditions that 19th-century factory workers would have recognized. (*The Guardian*, 28.10.1994, 2, p. 2)

JOB SECURITY

However much increased labour market flexibility may be in the employers' and the government's interests – and I shall question that in a moment – it is very unwelcome to the majority of employees. One of the more consistent findings of social science research is that those looking for work, or evaluating alternative job opportunities, give high priority to job security, especially when levels of unemployment are high. In a review of research on attitudes to employment carried out in 1983 my colleagues and I found that a range of varied evidence from studies carried out over the previous 25 years showed job security to be one of the most frequently desired attributes of a job; and that the trend towards the end of the period was towards placing even greater emphasis on job security (Brown et al., 1983, pp. 14–45). More recent data from the surveys of *British Social Attitudes* in the second half of the 1980s show that between two-thirds and three-quarters of respondents would advise a young person looking for their first job to consider 'a secure job for the future' as one of the two most important factors; and that forty per cent or more of those in employment regarded 'job security' as one of the three most important factors to consider if they were looking for another job (Social and Community Planning Research, 1992, G.1 – 1; G.3 – 20–22). Similarly Gallie and White report from their 'Employment in Britain' survey, carried out in 1992, that 'a secure job' was seen as 'essential' or 'very important' by 83 per cent of their respondents (and was given slightly greater emphasis by men than women), and that 59 per cent of men and 49 per cent of women now attached greater importance to having a secure job than they had done five years earlier (Gallie and White, 1993, pp. 13–15).

There is a lot of evidence, therefore, that those in or seeking paid work want the labour market to provide them with secure employment. Yet, as we have seen, for the past fifteen to twenty years it has failed to do so. What are the consequences of this discrepancy between expectations and reality?

It is difficult to demonstrate conclusive links between job insecurity and any actions in the workplace or the labour market. One possible consequence, which may be desired by the government ministers and employers who advocate greater flexibility, and insecurity, in the labour market, is that employees work harder and more 'conscientiously' in order to hang on to the job they currently occupy. There is certainly evidence to suggest an increased intensity of work in the past decade or more. Some of this is 'popular' rather than re-search-based, contained, for example, in newspaper accounts of the intensification of work not only among manual and routine white collar workers but also among professionals, managers and others: accounts of head teachers, and their staff, retiring early, and of doctors and nurses suffering illness and breakdown through overwork. Indeed it can be argued that those in more skilled and/or responsible jobs, who have realistic chances of moving into a more secure status, are pre-cisely the employees who are likely to respond to job insecurity by performing to the limits of their energies and abilities in order to create a good impression with their employer.

It is, however, more difficult to establish the intensification of work in general in any reliable way, in part because of the difficulties of measuring levels of effort directly (see Nichols, 1986, esp. pp. 42–5). Possible indicators like official statistics about hours of work, and the prevalence of overtime and of payment by results, show very little change and not all of it in the same direction, though the 1990 Workplace Industrial Relations Survey did report that the use of incentive pay was more common (Millward et al., 1992, pp. 258–264). Industrial relations specialists differ as to whether Thatcherism has 'worked' in the 1980s in producing increased worker effort (compare, for example, Metcalf, 1989, and Nolan and Marginson, 1990, with Guest, 1990). On the other hand, case study evidence does tend to support the argument that there has been an intensification of work during the past decade and a half, for example in manufacturing industry (Elger, 1990), in the ports (Turnbull, 1991), in coal mining (Winterton, 1993), in contract cleaning (Rees and Fielder, 1992) and in the public sector (Pulkingham, 1993). Neither the studies based on aggregate data, nor case studies, can demonstrate conclusively that any intensification of work they do show to have occurred is a consequence of job insecurity; there may have been other factors at work.

Other evidence suggests that those who feel their employment to be insecure will take whatever measures they feel to be available to them to retain the work they have. This can be seen very clearly and explicitly in the various campaigns and other action in opposition to plant closures and job cuts. Only in a relatively small minority of cases have such protests prevented the job losses, particularly in the last two decades when levels of unemployment have been so high. It might be argued, however, that the threat of such opposition has influenced the ways in which employers have behaved and, maybe, prevented or delayed justifiable 'rationalization' and restructuring.

More important is the possibility, for which there is a lot of evidence in the literature of industrial sociology, that employees who are or feel that they are insecure will take measures to try to protect work they have. So-called restriction of output – to make existing work last as long as possible – and the defence of jobs through demarcation and opposition to dilution, as was common in shipbuilding for example, can all be plausibly attributed to the employees in question fearing that they would otherwise lose their share of available work. As has already been suggested, a situation which makes it easy for employers to achieve numerical flexibility in the labour market, to vary the numbers they employ, may well militate against functional flexibility, their ability to deploy workers to best advantage in the workplace. This is also particularly likely to be the case when levels of unemployment are high, and when payments to those made redundant or unemployed have been cut in real terms or made more uncertain. These less welcome consequences of job insecurity for the employment relationship will be explored further below.

There are other less direct but equally or even more damaging consequences. Producers are also consumers, a fact which often appears to be ignored when wage cuts or job cuts are demanded. The evidence of the last few years suggests that those who feel that their employment is insecure will, understandably, be reluctant to spend, particularly on less essential purchases and those, like cars or major consumer durables, which involve loans or hire purchase and repayments for months or years ahead. Thus consumer expenditure remains 'flat'. In a period when the economy is supposedly growing in strength, there was, for example, barely any increase in private purchases of new cars in August 1995 as compared with 1994; and 'retail sales in volume terms were up only 1.4 per cent year on year in July' whilst later figures showed that the annual increase in total consumer spending remained just over 2.5 per cent. (*The Guardian*, 5.9.95, p. 17; 7.9.95).

It is the housing market which provides perhaps the starkest example of this consequence of insecurity in the labour market, though exacerbated by the fall in house prices since the boom at the end of the 1980s. The (understandable) reluctance to enter into the major commitment which buying a house represents, when future levels of income are so uncertain, not only has deleterious effects on the employment prospects of estate agents, solicitors, furniture removers and others directly involved in the process, but also means that demand for furniture and fittings, home improvements and so on remains lower than it would otherwise be – with obvious consequences for levels of employment in the relevant industries.

It can also be argued that a further consequence of labour market insecurity is to store up problems for the future. There are increasing demands, and a growing need, for individuals to make their own provisions for old age, and the health costs which are likely to go with it, rather than relying on the threatened and diminishing collective provisions of the 'welfare state'. This means undertaking long-term commitments to private pension and health care plans. Yet few of those with insecure employment will feel able to enter into such expenditure, or – even if they do – be able to sustain it for long enough to gain full or adequate benefits.

Thus this basic contradiction behind the demand for a more flexible labour market can be expressed as follows. Flexibility in the labour market necessarily creates insecurity of employment. Those employees who have insecure jobs, and the even larger number who feel that they have, will tend to limit their expenditure on goods and services. This depressed demand means that there are fewer jobs in the affected industries, and thus levels of unemployment remain high, reinforcing feelings of insecurity. Such limitations on purchasing power will also occur in the future because people have been unable, or unwilling, to make adequate provision for their old age.

THE LABOUR MARKET

There are two further and perhaps more fundamental aspects of this situation which I would like briefly to explore. The first is to question the conception of the labour market which informs the advocacy of labour market flexibility.

Markets are rarely if ever neutral allocative mechanisms which efficiently secure the best possible outcome for all participants. The buyers and sellers in any market typically possess differential resources, and the more powerful can to a greater or lesser extent dictate the terms of the exchange to those with fewer resources. This is especially true in the labour market. Employers are fewer in number, and have greater resources, than employees. Unless employees are able to combine, in trade unions or professional associations, to protect and further their interests, they are likely to have little or no influence over the terms and conditions of employment offered by employers. This is particularly the case, of course, for those without scarce skills or qualifications, and they are in the majority.

Current labour market policies appear not to recognize these characteristics of the labour market. This may be the result of poor understanding, or it may reflect the deliberate but mostly unarticulated intention to ensure that the power of employers will be maximized and their interests dominant. There is an inherent imbalance in the market for labour in favour of employers rather than employees. There are basically three ways in which this can be remedied, in whole or in part, the three methods identified earlier this century by Sidney and Beatrice Webb: the method of mutual insurance;

the method of collective bargaining; and the method of legal enactment (S. and B. Webb 1913). Mutual insurance (the friendly society functions of trade unions) has largely atrophied as a result of the development after 1945 of the more general and adequate collective provisions of the 'welfare state', though there may be signs of a revival. In the name of labour market freedom and flexibility there has been legislation which makes it more difficult for trade unions to engage in effective collective bargaining. Legislation which protected employees and employment has been repealed or amended. In addition the pursuit of economic policies which give no priority to full employment, but rather have the effect of creating and perpetuating relatively high levels of unemployment, further reduce the ability of employees to influence the outcome of labour market transactions. It seems to me that policies which fail to recognize these characteristics of the labour market are bound to be one-sided and inadequate.

THE EMPLOYMENT RELATIONSHIP

Secondly, we need to consider the employment relationship. Labour, or more precisely labour power, is not a commodity like any other. Nor is the exchange of a wage or salary for work comparable to other purchases and sales in the markets for goods and services. What is purchased is the employee's capacity to work. The exchange of pay for work cannot take place instantaneously but has to be realized over time and this involves an on-going relationship between the employee and his or her employer, or their agents – managers and supervisors. This relationship is important because it is typically impossible to specify in advance precisely what work is to be done. How hard an employee is expected to work, what responsibilities they will have to take, even what skills they will be expected to exercise, are worked out in the course of employment rather than clearly specified at the start.

These continuing negotiations are inherent in the employment relationship. Employers, managers and supervisors have to clarify in practice what levels of effort, skill and discretion are expected of the employee in return for their wage or salary, and any other rewards; employees have to try to establish what they think reasonable in terms of how hard they work, what skills they may need to acquire and use, and how much responsibility they take in return for the rewards they are being offered. The situation is made even more complex by two further aspects of the employment relationship.

First, to some, but a considerable, extent employer and employee have conflicting interests in the outcome of these 'negotiations'; pay is a cost for the employer, but income for the employee; the employee's contribution of mental and physical effort equally represents a cost to them, but is essential for the production of goods and provision of services which the employer needs. Thus the 'negotiation' of the employment relationship is likely to be made more difficult by these differing interests.

Secondly, even within the on-going negotiation of the employment relationship it is difficult if not impossible to specify completely what is required from employees, still less to control it in every detail. Rather employers depend on their workers' co-operation in carrying out instructions intelligently, in exercising discretion in ways which further the aims of the organization, in using tacit skills to get the job done effectively and to co-ordinate their work with that of others. Forced labour and slave labour are generally agreed to be very inefficient systems of production. The labour of workers who have 'voluntarily' entered into a contract of employment is likely to be more effective and productive, and possibly even cheaper. For that to be the case, however, employers need to have employees' commitment, to try to get them 'on their side', at least to some extent. (For further discussion see, for example, Brown 1988; Cressey and MacInnes 1980; Manwaring and Wood 1985.)

If this analysis is correct, and I believe it is, then it has important implications for the labour market. Only in a situation where employees have some expectation of job security is their contribution likely to include the fullest possible commitment of effort and skill, the greatest willingness to work responsibly and flexibly. Insecurity will tend to make for restriction and rigidity, and for an economy which is correspondingly less productive and less competitive than it would otherwise be.

WHAT SORT OF LABOUR MARKET?

It appears to be generally agreed that we are not likely to
return to the sort of labour market conditions we experienced
in the first two or three decades after the Second World War.
This may or may not be seen as regrettable, but this is not the
place or time to challenge such a judgement. Yet, if my
account of it is even partially correct, the situation we are in is
far from satisfactory. Is there any way of resolving the problems which arise from the likelihood that employment will
remain insecure, at least for a substantial proportion of the
country's workforce? It is only possible to suggest a few
pointers.

The search for labour market flexibility at all costs should be
abandoned. It may not be possible to provide everyone with a
secure job, still less 'a job for life', but the aim should be to
provide as much security as circumstances allow rather than
maximising numerical flexibility and insecurity. This may mean
both reinstating some of the employment protection measures
which have been eroded since 1979, and creating the circumstances in which collective organizations of employees can
properly defend their members' interests. There will be psychological and social benefits for individuals and general
benefits for the economy arising out of increased confidence
about prospects for employment and incomes; and the benefits
in employee performance may well outweigh any cost.

Secondly, governments should intervene to protect individuals – their citizens – from the downside of a more flexible,
and insecure, labour market. Compensation for the loss of a
job, as was attempted, albeit with limited success, in the
Redundancy Payments Act in the 1960s, and more rather than
less generous unemployment benefit would reduce the impact
of job insecurity. If insecurity of employment is going to be
the general experience for those in or wanting paid work,
then the possibility, for example, of a basic income for all
deserves close scrutiny. If these or other similar measures
mean that those in employment have to pay more in National
Insurance contributions, and those with higher incomes more
tax, that would seem a proper redistribution from the more to
the less fortunate – and self-interested provision against
possible future insecurity.

Thirdly – and this is perhaps already on the agenda – if we are all to be expected to change jobs, and occupations, and to retrain and undertake life-long learning, then proper provision must be made by governments and/or employers to cover or at least share the costs involved, rather than leaving them to be carried solely by those making such transitions.

Finally, is it too much to hope that the 'need' for full employment will once again be given priority in framing economic policy? It is no longer possible, if it ever was, to claim that in the long run the 'market' will somehow adjust itself without intervention. There is too much evidence that high levels of unemployment do not lead to labour pricing itself into jobs; those in employment for the most part do not suffer wage cuts; and there are insufficient incentives to induce those with income from capital, or from employment, to engage in the investment necessary to create new jobs. Government intervention is necessary particularly in encouraging, facilitating and undertaking investment, in the public as well as the private sectors, which will not only create jobs directly, but also help create the conditions for full, or fuller, employment in the future.

In the world at the end of the 20th century, in contrast to 50 years ago, attempts to create a fully employed economy will necessitate concerted international action. Keynesianism, let alone socialism, in one country is no longer a realistic aim. The Commission of the European Communities has set out an agenda which includes creating 15 million jobs by the end of the century (CEC, 1993). It is questionable whether this target, and the means suggested to achieve it, are adequate, but at least it represents a cross national step in the right direction. Many more such steps are needed.

NOTES

1.   The view that unemployment is in large measure due to lack of aggregate demand is not one which would be accepted by the present Government. For example, the 1985 White Paper on 'Employment' argued:

Unemployment rises when we move too slowly to meet new customer needs, overseas competition and technological change, and when pay and prices – the link between supply and demand – adjust too slowly. *There is no basic lack of demand* (my italics); the reason why we cannot use our full labour force is that we have not adapted well enough, particularly in our jobs market, to be able to exploit it. (Department of Employment, 1985, p. 3)

It is not possible to pursue this argument in detail here. However, the Government's view does appear to show a faith in the ability of markets to adjust autonomously which flies against the evidence of much 20th century history, and to underestimate the impact on the demand for labour of restrictive monetary policies, which give priority to containing inflation, and of continuing attempts to restrict public expenditure, including expenditure on capital projects, in order to keep levels of taxation low.

2.   As Beveridge memorably put it, when arguing for a labour market in which there should always be more vacant jobs than unemployed men (sic):

A person who has difficulty in buying the labour he wants suffers inconvenience or reduction of profits. A person who cannot sell his labour is in effect told that he is of no use. The first difficulty causes annoyance or loss. The other is a personal catastrophe. (Beveridge, 1944, p. 19)

5 Gender and Change in Employment: Feminization and Its Effects[1]

INTRODUCTION: EMPLOYMENT CHANGE AND FEMINIZATION

During the 1980s and 1990s there have been major shifts in the structure of the labour market, in employment practices and policies, and in the sectoral make-up of the British economy. Such changes have been variously interpreted in terms of a switch to a 'post-industrial' or 'post-Fordist' economy or to a 'post-modern' phase in social development. Such changes are often considered to involve major challenges to existing gender relations, both at home and within the workplace.

First, the gender composition of the labour force has been affected by various developments. The long-term decline in employment in manufacturing, particularly in heavy industry, has brought increased male redundancy and unemployment, especially among younger men (in the Northern region 16 per cent of the male workforce was unemployed in 1993 (Coombes et al., 1994)). A decline in male employment has also been influenced by the trend to early retirement among men in their fifties and early sixties: between 1971 and 1991 there was a 32 per cent decrease in the economic activity rate of men aged sixty to sixty four (Bradley, 1996). Meanwhile, any new job creation has been concentrated in the service sector often in areas assigned as 'women's work' (for example, retail, catering, clerical work in the finance sector, leisure and other personal services).

Many new jobs in these areas are part-time, temporary or seasonal. This results from employers' desire for flexibility in their production methods. Not all researchers accept that flexibility in employment relations is demonstrably on the increase (Pollert, 1991; Millward et al., 1992). However, others believe that the drive for flexibility has contributed to a climate of increasing economic insecurity for the workforce, with the rise of part-time work, short-term contracts, new types of self-employment and so forth, forms of employment which Brown and Scase have characterized as 'poor work' (1991). The Labour Force Survey of 1993 suggested that some 38 per cent of the workforce can be categorized as 'flexible workers'. In line with this, Will Hutton (1995) describes Britain as a 30–30–40 society (30 per cent marginal to the labour force, 30 per cent in newly insecure employment situations and 40 per cent in stable and economically reward-ing employment). Hutton's view is confirmed by recent re-search findings that only 36 per cent of the British working population now occupy full-time tenured jobs compared with 56 per cent in 1975 (Murdoch, 1995). The other aspect of the climate of insecurity relates, of course, to high levels of unem-ployment, the threat of redundancy, and the continued efforts of firms to become more efficient and 'lean' by shedding labour (see Chapter 4).

These trends have contributed to what has frequently been described as a 'feminization' of the labour force (Jenson et al., 1988) with women's share of employment creeping up slowly towards men's. Feminization has been seen by some post-industrial theorists as a characteristic of the emergent post-industrial economies. For example, Gosta Esping-Andersen and colleagues (1993), speak of a 'female bias' in the six coun-tries they studied; employers considered female labour more suitable for the new service jobs, so that opportunities for women were opening up as they closed for men. Similarly Fred Robinson, in discussing 'post-industrial Tyneside' (1988), noted the decline in full-time male jobs and rise in part-time opportunities for women.

Such changes have knock-on effects for gender relations in the family. One outcome is that women may take over the role of main household breadwinner. However, as Lydia Morris' re-search into unemployment has shown (1990; 1995), benefit rules can deter women from taking employment if the only jobs available are insufficiently rewarding. Other research confirms that wives of unemployed men are more likely to be unemployed than those of men in employment creating a pattern of 'work-poor' households (Pahl, 1984). But as this paper will show, more fortunate couples may adopt a strategy of dual earning as a protection against employment insecurity.

These developments have been linked by some commentators to stress and breakdown in the family. As the above listed options suggest, the traditional model of male breadwinner and female domestic carer is becoming increasingly less viable in the face of new employment realities. Some believe this causes family conflict and role strain (Murray, 1990; Young and Halsey, 1995). Others have linked the changes at work and in the home to a 'crisis of masculinity', as long-standing male social and economic dominance is undermined by feminization and by female competition at work (Morgan, 1990). This may help promote a 'backlash' among male employees in the workplace (Cockburn, 1991), while young men, finding themselves socially redundant, resign themselves to a life on the dole or erupt in manifestations of resentment such as violence, crime or street disturbances (Campbell, 1993).

The impact of feminization, however, has been interpreted in a number of ways. In line with the 'crisis of masculinity' thesis, recent attention has been given to the idea that it may no longer be a man's but a 'girl's world' (Furedi, 1995). Evidence for this is disputable, but it is suggested that women will soon outnumber men in the workforce; girls have overtaken boys in school examinations performance and women now slightly predominate as undergraduate students; it has been claimed that female graduates are finding it easier to get jobs than their male compeers. Crompton and Sanderson's research (1990) highlighted the use of the 'qualifications lever' by younger women as a challenge to male domination and gender segregation at work. Male fears of female takeover lie behind recent agitation against affirmative action programmes in the United States, a campaign that may well be replicated in Britain, despite the relative weakness of British Equal Opportunities programmes.

Others argue that the feminization of the labour market has had limited effect in improving women's position and overcoming male dominance in the workplace. Surveys and studies, such as the recent government report *Social Focus on Women* (CSO, 1995), have demonstrated that segregation persists and women are concentrated in low paid jobs. The ILO (International Labour Office) reported that in 1993 women's hourly earnings were 71 per cent of those of men, only a rise of two per cent since 1985.[2] There is little evidence of an end to women's double burden of tiring paid work combined with responsibility for the bulk of unpaid labour in the home. Women may be the losers in the move to flexible labour markets as the 'new opportunities for women' presented by labour market change so often take the form of low-paid, casualized jobs. Indeed, Murdoch and Furedi argue that feminization is bad for both sexes, since rather than the upgrading of women's labour market position, all work is being dragged down to share the conditions of traditional 'women's work' (Murdoch, 1995, p. 16). Furedi, following the literature which suggests that women bring different values into the workplace (see for example Adler et al., 1993), discerns negative political results in the decline of the 'bold pretensions' of traditional masculine behaviour which has informed employee resistance in the past, as it is replaced by 'the low expectations of a caring femininity' fostering 'the values associated with postmodern "femininity" – like acquiescence, flexibility and passivity' (Furedi, 1995, p. 13).

Nor has the idea that feminization has occurred gone unchallenged. Catherine Hakim (1991; 1993) has argued that the apparent rise in female employment over the century has merely been in the form of part-time jobs (although she concedes some real rise in female full-time employment since the late 1980s); as she points out, men still carried out 67 per cent of the total volume of work in Britain in 1988. Hakim distinguishes between 'work-committed' women, who share men's values and career patterns, and 'family-centred women', who prefer part-time work (or not to work at all) and who hold traditional views on sex roles. The persistence of family-centred orientations among women means that change in employment has been less extensive and its effects on gender relations less far-reaching than implied in the literature discussed above. Moreover, as Allen points out (in Chapter 3) a great deal of women's employment in the past went unrecorded, again suggesting that the extent of feminization may be exaggerated.

In this paper, however, I accept the notion of feminization in the limited sense that the proportion of women recorded as being economically active is increasing relative to men, in view of the unchallenged fact of falling male employment. I seek to explore the contentions concerning feminization and its effects on gender relations, by means of data from a set of case studies of employment carried out in the North East region in 1991–3. 198 employees in five organizations were interviewed about their jobs and work histories as part of a study of gender differences in trade unions, funded by the ESRC. The organizations were chosen to represent typical areas of current female employment (retail; banking; the NHS; the civil service; and line work in a chemical factory). Approximately 20 women and 20 men working in matched occupations were interviewed in each workplace. All except 20 employees in retail were currently on full-time contracts. Since each sample of women and men was working in similar jobs, the study allowed for comparison of women's and men's experiences, attitudes and behaviours in comparable employment situations.

A FEMINIZED WORKFORCE?

Feminization as defined here (increased numbers of women in the labour force relative to men) is a macro phenomenon. Certainly, the North East labour force has been feminized through the loss of male jobs and rise of part-time employment for women. In 1928 women were 20 per cent of the Tyneside workforce, in 1988 45 per cent; women are now 49 per cent of employees in the Northern region (Robinson, 1988; *Regional Trends*, 1996). Four fifths of Newcastle's workforce is employed in services. However, since feminization relates to the balance of jobs *across the nation or region*, it will not necessarily be reflected within particular workplaces. Three of the organizations in my study were in areas which have long been characterized by high levels of female labour: the NHS, banking and retail. At the hospital 81 per cent of employees were women, at the bank 66 per cent and at the supermarket 63 per cent. In the other two organizations I was informed that some degree of what we might call 'internal feminization' was taking place. Currently female employment in the civil service agency was 70 per cent, but I was told that the proportion of women had increased over the past ten years largely because more women had gained entry to the top executive grades, previously dominated by men. In the factory, where 60 per cent of non-managerial employees were women, there had been some minimal feminization; women had some access to two jobs which previously had been male monopolies (process operation and warehousing).

All these organizations, then, could be categorized in a purely numerical sense as female-dominated; but it was noticeable that marked structures of vertical segregation remained in all of them, with men predominating in the top grades, especially at managerial level. For example, of the 74 managerial staff in the factory, only five were women; in the Civil Service agency there were no female managers and only two per cent of women had reached the top executive grade as opposed to ten per cent of men; in the hospital only five per cent of female nurses had reached top grades F and G, compared to 43 per cent of men. In all the organizations, there were clear signs that personnel managers had attempted to implement equal opportunities policies on gender, opening up possibilities for women to gain promotion into middle grades; and training programmes targeted at women had encouraged some women to develop managerial aspirations, an effect which can be seen as another kind of 'internal feminization'. But whatever the long-term effects of such initiatives may be, as yet structures of gendered power had altered little in these organizations.

The message then is clear. Feminization as currently operating has not brought an end to male domination at work. Rather it implies increasing numerical dominance of women in low-ranked jobs. However, that does not mean that gender relations are unchanged by feminization. While structures of male power within the organizations remained fairly intact, the operation of feminization at a regional level appeared to have had clear effects in terms of attitudes to work and the employment strategies adopted by individuals and households.

WOMEN'S GROWING COMMITMENT TO WORK

Hakim's contention that overall women are less committed to their careers than men gains support from Coward's research

(1992) among married women. But my study revealed strong attachment to the labour force among this sample of women workers: they took their jobs seriously, wished to develop careers and often indicated that they felt women's skills and talents were undervalued. A small number of women did display the more traditional attitudes identified by Hakim, stating they would have preferred to work fewer hours or none at all. But the seriousness towards employment demonstrated by most of the interviewees accords with recent qualitative research conducted by Spencer and Taylor (1994) in five parts of Britain, including Newcastle and Gateshead. While they found some women who chose to stay at home and put domestic responsibilities first, their interviews indicated a growing commitment to employment among many women. Research by Demos found that 51 per cent of young women in classes A, B and C considered work a source of meaning in their lives compared with 45 per cent of the young men (quoted in Walter, 1996). My research confirmed these findings.

When the interviewees were questioned about their motives for having a job, financial reasons for going out to work predominated among both sexes, but women were more likely to mention intrinsic factors as well. Significantly, many women described their jobs as an escape from being 'stuck at home' and being treated as 'just a wife and mother'. For these women employment did indeed appear as a source of meaning in their lives and a route to self-development:

> It's changed my life it has, going out to work. I couldn't bear to stay in the house and not work. (factory operative, aged 52)

> I consider it my sanity. I like to feel that I have my own little bit of independence. (part-time shopworker, 35)

> It helps us be a person in our own right, not just mam, not just the wife. I'd hate to be home all day. (factory operative, 38)

Table 5.1 gives an indication of female and male attitudes to employment. Several questions about respondents' views of their jobs and their reasons for going out to work were taken together and the answers categorized as positive, neutral or negative.

Table 5.1   Employees' Attitudes to Employment

	Women	Men
Positive	62%	53%
Neutral	23%	38%
Negative	15%	9%

The table shows that a majority of both sexes viewed employment positively. However, women tended to express more strongly positive or negative views, while men's attitudes were more likely to be classifiable as neutral. Many men seemed resigned, weary, and cynical about their jobs. This might reflect Furedi's view that men have higher expectations and protest more when they are not met. But it was noticeable that men tended to impute meaning to their jobs within the traditional framework of the male's duty to be a breadwinner. 'To earn a living', 'to pay my mortgage' and 'to support my family' were typical reasons given for going out to work:

> I've always been the breadwinner... I've enjoyed the various jobs, but the end of the line is, I come to work to exist. (factory operative, 60)

> If they'd send me cheques to stay at home I would. (laboratory scientist, 39)

By contrast, the most enthusiastic comments about employment came from women, for whom employment is contextualized in terms of options, namely the choice (real or illusory) of staying at home and caring for children. Many women enter the labour market from the context of full-time domestic work and this shapes their responses to their job experience:

> There was no way on God's earth I would be stuck in the home. It's mind-numbingly boring being at home...Women are the independent ones. (factory operative, 38)

> I like working. I like being with people. I don't want me life revolving around me husband and kids etcetera... It gives

you more of an outgoing personality when you're at work. (factory operative, aged 34)

For women from working-class backgrounds, in particular, the difficulties of running a home where economic resources are limited may make the housewife role a less attractive option.

GENDER AND CHANGE IN WORK HISTORIES

If women are becoming more employment orientated as a result of the feminization of the labour force, we would expect a marked decline among the younger age groups in time taken out of employment for raising a family. This was the case, as Table 5.2 shows.

The oldest age-group had spent an average of ten years seven months out of the labour market, as compared to one year among the youngest women. The fact that some of the younger women have not yet completed their families must be taken into account. Nonetheless, the trend is clearly downwards. Significantly, some of younger women had only taken up the minimum period of maternity leave.

If this trend keeps up, we should see a shift away from the characteristic postwar bi-modal pattern in women's work histories (Rees, 1992). However, women in the sample *had* experienced more interruptions to their employment than men. 61 per cent had spent time out of the labour market compared to 39 per cent of men. Women were more likely to report themselves as having worked for two or more other

Table 5.2 Time Taken Out of the Labour Market to Bring up Children

Age	No. of women	Average time out of employment
Under 30	7	1 year
31–40	12	2 years 9 months
41–50	21	5 years 3 months
50 +	5	10 years 7 months

employers (49 per cent of women as opposed to 35 per cent of men). Women reported holding an average of 3.22 jobs each, while men had held 2.82; however, if the ten part-time female shop assistants are excluded (who reported an average of 7.1 jobs), the female figure is almost identical to men at 2.80. To sum up, while a minority of the sample displayed the 'typical' female pattern of a highly fragmented work history, with long breaks for family formation and movement between a number of low-skilled jobs, the work histories of the full-time female employees were not so markedly different from those of men.

Analysing national data, Tomlinson (1994) has also suggested that the employment histories of women and men are showing signs of convergence. Given the context of growing insecurity in labour markets, it is not surprising that two-fifths of men in my sample had experienced breaks in their work histories, often because of redundancy. Increased male unemployment and quicker return to work after childbirth lie behind such a convergence.

PREVALENCE OF DUAL-EARNER COUPLES

Clearly such changes will have implications for household arrangements. In my sample 87 per cent of the married or cohabiting employees were part of a dual earner couple. This reflects the national trend to dual-earning as 'the most common form of family life' (Harrop and Moss, 1995, p. 433). Of the 27 men with children under school age, only eight reported that their wives were not in paid work. Moreover, women in the sample were nearly as likely to be sole earners as the men. 28 men were sole earners (19 of these being single) as compared to 26 women, including 12 who were single. This reflects the national rise in one-person households, which have doubled in number between 1961 and 1994, and single-parent families, which have increased from three to eleven per cent over the same period (*Social Trends*, 1996). Some of these women were separated or divorced and were working to support their children; others had a sick or unemployed husband. A few married women reported that they were the main family breadwinners and that husbands were sharing the responsibility for child-care.

Dual-earning strategies can be linked to the perception that both partners need to work if a decent standard of living is to be attained and maintained. As one young shop assistant stated:

> To have a good standard of living, with your own car and holidays and that sort of thing, I think the woman has to work all her life.

Two-thirds of the women considered their earnings were essential for their household, and another 28 per cent described them as important though not essential. Despite some negative comments by men in the sample, it is clear that few of these women are working for 'pin money': only six per cent considered their earnings unimportant to the household and these were mainly young women living with their parents.

The rise of dual earning couples is a complex phenomenon. It would be imprudent to impute it to a single cause. But I suggest that it can be linked to the climate of insecurity at work, which emerged as the major problem respondents identified about their jobs. A quarter of the sample expressed anxieties about the future, about possible redundancies and cutbacks in staffing. That the figure is not higher reflects the fact that the five organizations were seen as providing some of the best jobs in their localities, and in the past employment within them had been prized for its security. Respondents were uneasily aware of the fate of the unemployed people living around them in the region.

ASPIRATIONS FOR PROMOTION

As I have argued, dual earning reflects the desire for a better standard of living than can be secured by a single wage, and acts as insurance against job loss in a labour market perceived as insecure. Moreover, in a climate of rising family breakdown, today's young women are aware of the danger of assuming that they can depend on a husband to maintain them and their children for the whole of their lives. Such an analysis, then, might indicate that many women are being pushed into taking up employment because of the economic climate, when they would have preferred to stay at home and care for children.

However other evidence from the survey suggests that the greater priority given by women to employment is not purely the result of push factors. We have already seen that many women held very positive attitudes towards their paid work. Another important indicator of commitment to employment is attitudes to promotion. Hakim and Coward imply that men are more ambitious in their careers than women. The data from my study challenge this view. Table 5.3 shows the proportion of respondents in each age group who expressed a desire for promotion at work.

Among younger age groups similar proportions of women and men wished for promotion. Men did tend to express longer term ambitions, while women set their sights on moving up one stage at a time. Yet, some of the youngest women wanted to get into management and made it clear that work ambitions were central to their sense of self-development, what Grey has called 'the entrepreneurial project of the self' (1994, p. 482):

> I want to feel as if I've done something with my life. I won't be happy with an assistant's job. I want to get on. (shop assistant, 19)

> Self worth. I was always determined to do something with my life. (civil servant, 19)

Table 5.3 shows the greatest disparity between women and men aged 30–39. This is the age when women are most likely to be preoccupied with domestic concerns, with the anxieties

Table 5.3   Percentages of Women and Men Wishing for Promotion at Work, by Age (Full-time Workers only)

Age group	Women	Men	All
under 25	86	89	88
25–29	78	79	78
30–39	33	78	56
40 plus	39	17	28
All ages	56	64	60

– and the pleasures – of home life and caring for children. Some women explicitly cited these as a blockage to thoughts of promotion:

> It usually involves a move; and I wouldn't like to be away from the children.

> Not with having a family. I like to do my work and to do it well, but with the responsibility of having a family... I have got a system for managing. But it's hard.

However, women in the oldest group, whose children are older and families completed, appeared more ambitious than men. In part this reflects the fact the older men have already been promoted or have reached a position where they know that they cannot realistically expect promotion. But these men in particular seemed disillusioned and negative about their jobs, in contrast to the vigour of their female counterparts. Many women appeared frustrated at the lack of opportunities for promotion for older people, which they linked to their lack of qualifications. Choices they had made earlier were a source of regret:

> I wish I did something else years ago, went to college and studied and maybe got a better job. I would have liked to have been a nurse. (factory operative, 43)

> They ask for so many qualifications, sometimes I think experience doesn't count. When I left school you didn't sit the GCSEs. I wish I had. (factory operative, 47)

It seemed to me that these older women were responding to a public climate which places more emphasis on women's talents and potentials and that they were more ready to challenge traditional practices which had confined them to low-status, subordinated women's work. But unfortunately such heightened aspirations run up against the problems of gender segregation and male power at work.

BACKLASH AND CONFLICTS OF GENDER

The discussion so far has suggested that in the context of feminization, women's commitment to employment and aspirations to promotion may be heightened. Positive results for women's self-esteem are indicated. But, since I have suggested that, in these organizations at least, male power has not eroded, can it really be stated that feminization is creating new opportunities for women? Or, following Furedi, are both sexes being faced with declining opportunity and instability?

Some men, certainly, are feeling threatened by female competition. In all the organizations except the supermarket employees expressed considerable frustration about limited career opportunities. Some gave this reason for their lack of aspirations for promotion. The public sector employees tended to blame government policy for this situation. But in the bank, the hospital and the factory some men expressed hostility to equal opportunities principles, stating that women were being preferred to men who were more deserving, or complaining that women were being given jobs they were unequipped to perform.

But women did not see things in quite the same way! Over half of them (55 per cent) stated that men were favoured in their workplaces, while a majority of men felt equality had been achieved. Women felt that men still got more opportunities and that women had to work harder to get their achievements recognized. Many felt that managers displayed sexist prejudice, especially towards married women:

> It's the women who do the hard work. Women do quite a variety of jobs before they can go up a grade. (bank clerk)

> When it comes down to the nitty-gritty you still have to be twice as good, being a woman. (factory operative)

> Men get more opportunities than women, definitely... The bank feel that women are going to leave and have children so they promote men. (bank clerk)

In fact gender differentiation was still marked in these organizations. I have already spoken of the persistence of vertical segregation. The level of horizontal segregation varied: it was virtually absent in the bank, but present to some degree in the other four organizations with the traditional pattern of sex-typing strongest in the hospital and the factory. Significantly, in the three organization with least horizontal segregation (the bank, civil service and supermarket) an important source of gender differentiation was part-time working.

But, as I have indicated, the position was not static. Some women, taking advantage of the equal opportunities climate were pushing towards top posts. A few were venturing into areas traditionally considered 'men's jobs', some against resistance, some not. These workplaces were characterized by upheaval in gender roles, which reflects both the commitment of some managers to equal opportunities and women's growing resistance to being channelled into subordinated positions. Unfortunately this is happening at a time of restricted opportunities caused by the cost-cutting strategies of organizations as a result of government stringencies or heightened international competition.

CONCLUSIONS

As I hope to have shown, the effects of feminization are complex. Moreover this study can only illuminate these effects with regard to one particular segment of the community (full-time employees in reasonably secure employment) in one particular region. However, the findings are not out of line with other recent research. I have suggested that there are some positive effects for women in terms of somewhat extended promotion opportunities and, particularly, of heightened aspirations and growing self-confidence to challenge gender norms. Choices made by younger women show a determination to combine career and family. This is reflected in household choices and strategies, with dual earning consolidating itself as the norm; there is likely also to be a rise in the number of non-partnered single earners. If women are, as I have argued, becoming more assertive and confident, Furedi's gloomy prognosis about female passivity may be misplaced.

The downside to this is increased workloads and heightened stress as women juggle domestic and employment commitments. A recent Mintel survey found that the relative gap between male and female leisure was at its greatest in the North East; women had 10.5 fewer hours of free time than men (Mintel, 1995). Possibly couples will renegotiate the domestic division of labour as dual earning becomes the expected practice. My survey yields no systematic data on domestic labour, but the impression I gained was that women still expected to do most of it, a finding in line with other recent research (Brannen and Moss, 1991; Devine, 1992).

To such changes, men are responding in various ways. While some welcome and actively encourage women's greater participation, others find it hard to adapt and are bitter about the heightened competition at work. It is too much to expect that a dominant group will give up power and privileges without some kind of struggle. As I have shown, so far men have not actually lost their dominant position at work. But it is being challenged and my prediction must be that in the next ten years contestation around gender roles will be intense.

In this paper, I have drawn out the consequences of the feminization of the workforce for gender roles. But the final point to make is that feminization cannot be understood in gender terms alone. The changes in economic organization which promote feminization result from changes in capitalist accumulation in its post-industrial, consumerist phase and must be seen in this light. Feminization occurs in the context of pressures for increased competitiveness within and between organizations and of heightened capital power, bringing stress, extra competition for opportunities and insecurity to the majority of employees, be they female or male.

NOTES

1. A shorter version of some of the material in this paper appeared in 'Social Change in Tyne and Wear', University of Sunderland School of Social and International Studies, Working Paper No 1, edited by M. Erickson and S. Williams, 1995. The research on which it is based was funded by the ESRC, research grant R000 23 4124.
2. Reported in *The Guardian*, 28 August 1995.

6 Informal Working, Survival Strategies and the Idea of an 'Underclass'

INTRODUCTION

Teesside – famous world-wide in the 1950s for its success in steel and chemical production – has in the 1980s and 1990s become notorious for its persistently high levels of unemployment and the socio-cultural problems which accompany mass joblessness. The locality is now probably better known as the 'Car Crime Capital of Europe' than for its proud industrial heritage. The securities of full employment just thirty years ago have given way to the uncertainties of massive economic collapse and the social changes have been so deep and far-reaching that commentators such as Charles Murray now single out the place as home of what he calls the 'New Rabble' underclass (1994).

This chapter argues, however, that the majority of accounts – both popular and academic – of the decline of Teesside and places like it fail properly to comprehend the diverse and active ways in which people respond to unemployment. Bill Jordan and Marcus Redley, in reviewing studies of polarization and debates about the 'underclass', make a similar point and call for research to 'investigate the survival strategies [of the poor] and their cultures of resistance' (1994, p. 156). What this chapter attempts to do is examine some of the dynamic, cultural responses of the excluded working-class as they seek to re-create working lives through more informal economic activity. A review of evidence on informal working hypothesized that more may be found 'in areas of "catastrophic" economic collapse' (Roberts et al., 1985, p. 522). Teesside provides a useful test case.

WORK AND UNEMPLOYMENT ON TEESSIDE

The focus of this discussion is Teesside, the industrial heart of the County of Cleveland, in the North-east of England. Here – between 1975 and 1986 – one-quarter of all jobs were lost as industrial giants like ICI and British Steel retrenched in the face of fierce global competition. During the same period nearly half of all those with manufacturing and construction jobs were made redundant (Cleveland County Council, 1986), leaving many thousands permanently excluded from the labour market of 'proper jobs' (McLaughlin, 1994).

In the mid-1990s, the picture is still bleak despite recovery from recession at a national level. In January 1995, according to *official* statistics, unemployment in the county stood at over 15 per cent with 40 per cent of these being long-term unemployed (Cleveland County Council, 1995). More than one man in five is unemployed and certain neighbourhoods, particularly the outer estates of East Middlesbrough, fare even worse. Despite recent rises in (part-time) employment, prognoses are not good:

> ...there is every indication that unemployment in Cleveland will remain a significant problem as the county enters the twenty-first century (Cleveland County Council, 1993, point 4.10).

Even Teesside Training and Enterprise Council (which can normally be relied upon to accentuate the positive aspects of the local economy) recently acknowledged that even many of the new jobs which might be created in the coming years will be:

> part-time, low-paid, low status, temporary contract positions and will be unattractive to many people (1995a, p. 45).

RESEARCHING CHANGING CULTURES OF WORK

The following discussion is based on research which examined the changing cultures of work associated with the decline in standard employment.[1] Following Hakim (1987, 1989a), the research investigated the growing significance of alternative, non-standard work by exploring the informal patterns of work being developed by working-class men and women who were neither properly employed nor yet completely unemployed.

The design of the study was as follows. Fifty-two interviews were held with professionals involved in local employment and welfare issues (for example, TEC staff, volunteer bureaux workers, small business advisers). The core sample consisted, however, of 214 people with whom ethnographic interviews were held in the early to mid 1990s.[2] They were selected via enterprise agencies, volunteer bureaux, co-operative development agencies and through a snow-balling method whereby early informants suggested further interviewees. Interviews explored holistically the working lives of informants (who ranged in age from sixteen to over seventy and were able to provide a fascinating insight into changes in work not only in their own individual biographies but across generations). The sample was predominantly working-class and sixteen were from ethnic minorities, mainly from the British Pakistani community on Teesside. None were in formal employment but all were involved in some form of non-standard work through, in the main: (a) self-employment in very small businesses; (b) voluntary work; (c) 'fiddly jobs' (working undeclared whilst in receipt of unemployment benefits); or (d) community enterprise and co-operatives (which are not discussed here). The results of these studies are reported in full elsewhere and only brief summaries can be given here.[3]

INFORMAL WORKING IN TEESSIDE

(i) Young People, Adults and the Enterprise Culture in the 1990s

The revival of small business and self-employment in the UK was '...one of the most significant economic and political events' of the 1980s (Stanworth and Gray, 1991, p. 228). The numbers of people self-employed multiplied from 1.76 million in 1979 to 3.27 million or around 13 per cent of the work-force by 1994, despite a temporary downturn with the early 1990s recession (*Employment Gazette*, 1995; Campbell and Daly, 1992).

Much of the growth in self-employment has been in very small, service sector 'microfirms'; 70 per cent work alone with no employees (Stanworth and Gray, 1991). Furthermore, there is evidence that many of these self-employed were new recruits to the enterprise culture with little previous experience of business and often drawn from social groups (for example women and young people) previously under-represented in the small business population (Hakim, 1989b; Storey and Strange, 1992). It is exactly these sorts of people in these sorts of enterprise who are often missed out of surveys of the small business world but who were the focus of this study.

Whilst numerous explanations have been given for these dramatic national rises (see Stanworth and Gray, 1991; Campbell and Daly, 1992) it became clear that two factors were important in explaining why Teesside people were making the move into self-employment. Firstly, the decline in manufacturing employment and rise in unemployment have resulted in 'forced entrepreneurship' (Storey and Strange, 1992) with self-employment being perceived as the only remaining option for those excluded from the labour force.

Secondly, government efforts to create an enterprise culture (Bright et al., 1988) reached their zenith in the 1980s (Burrows and Curran, 1991). Over 200 policy measures have been introduced to support small business development (at a cost of over £1 billion) since 1979. The Enterprise Allowance Scheme, in particular, had by 1991 assisted over half a million unemployed people to become self-employed with varying degrees of success (Department of Employment, 1991; National Audit Office, 1988).

During the 1980s Teesside became a focus for attempts to generate an enterprise culture. Previously an employee culture, the area had levels of self-employment well below the national average. With massive rises in unemployment during the decade a veritable industry of agencies, schemes and initiatives sprang up to spread the gospel of enterprise and encourage the unemployed to start new businesses (MacDonald and Coffield, 1991).

Participation of Teesside people in the Enterprise Allowance Scheme (and its renamed successors) in the mid-1990s does show a decline from the 'halcyon decade' of the enterprise culture. Yet Teesside still has some of the highest levels of unemployment and the lowest levels of self-employment (under 10 per cent of all employment) in the country (*Employment Gazette*, 1994). Consequently the local TEC continues to promote self-employment and new small firms as the key to reviving the economy, claims that '70 per cent of businesses are surviving after 18 months' and predicts that such businesses will create around two-thirds of all future jobs (Teesside TEC, 1995b, p. 31).

The successes and failures of people who have drawn upon such support and who are regarded as contributing to a new, local enterprise culture were examined. The evidence would suggest that, on a quantitative level, the longer-term survival rates of the new, self-employed would seem to fall far below those estimated officially and that, more importantly, the quality of their experiences do not support the idea that we are witnessing the (re)birth of a local enterprise culture.

One element of the research attempted to track the progress of the young 'entrepreneurs' who were first contacted in the late 1980s (MacDonald and Coffield, 1991). In 1989 a reasonable cross-section of the young self-employed in Teesside were interviewed (n.86). Some were then still in the planning stages (n.12), some had closed down businesses (n.15) but most were trading at the time of interview (n.59). What had happened to their businesses by 1995? Table 6.1 describes their fortunes.

Table 6.1   The Status of Young Adults in 1995 who were Involved in Enterprise in 1989

Status	Number
'Runners'	4
'Plodders'	10
'Fallers'	50
Never started	8
Unknown	14
	86

The most striking figure is the number of people left in business (either 'running' successful firms or 'plodding' along in the hope of becoming more successful). Only 14 people from the 71 who had been self-employed or on the way to start up in the late 1980s were trading in the mid-1990s. Of these, only a handful (n.4) could be categorized – by themselves or by the author – as being successful 'runners'. 50 people who were or had become self-employed were, by the mid-1990s, known to be no longer so. The whereabouts of 14 remains unknown (although there is a suspicion that they might also have 'fallen': their business 'phone lines were disconnected and their premises vacant).

These basic statistics confirm the picture that was painted of these new, small firms in earlier work. It was predicted that many of them – even those that seemed to be doing well after the first year or two – would be unable to continue in the long-term (MacDonald and Coffield, 1991). Qualitative interviews were used to explore their experiences of starting up, running and closing down new, small businesses and the stories told by young people were compared with the accounts gathered from adults who had become self-employed.

There were some differences (in the adult group) in the reasons behind start up which reflected longer and more varied work histories. In broad terms, the informants in their thirties, in particular, stressed their negative experiences of employment, those in their forties talked about the push of unemployment resulting from mid-career redundancy and those in their fifties and sixties saw self-employment as a last chance to salvage working lives from the beckoning chasm of permanent labour market inactivity.

In the main, though, the experiences of younger and older informants after start up were found to be strikingly similar (despite an expectation that age would bring various advantages in self-employment). One of the main conclusions is that age is not a significant factor in attempting to understand the experience of self-employment in these marginal microfirms. The younger informants four or five years on experienced similar problems to their first years in business and adults talked of the same things.

A small minority of young people and adults – those called the 'runners' – established successful, employment-generating, commercial firms. A larger group – the 'fallers' – suffered devastating business failure, often returning to the dole queues burdened with the psychological traumas of failure and considerable personal debts. A small number owed several thousand pounds to creditors and one thirty-year old man had had to sell the family house as part of bankruptcy proceedings. The majority of both younger and older self-employed only 'plodded along', working long hours (averaging over 60 per week) for low pay (often around £1 per hour), hoping through dogged persistence and self-exploitation to become one of the 'runners'. The primary experience of running new, small businesses in Teesside in the late 1980s and 1990s was of struggle and survival.

National surveys suggest that the 'smallest and youngest firms are the least likely to survive and grow' (Chittenden and Caley, 1992, p. 9) and, as predicted, the 1990s saw many of these enterprises collapsing. Only a few still traded and most of these could not be described as successful. The typology of 'young entrepreneurs' (as 'runners', 'plodders' and 'fallers') developed in 1989 still applied in the mid-1990s, although the numbers of people in the latter group had been greatly swelled as the 'plodders' closed down businesses. Even the most successful young business, a manufacturing firm with 35 staff run by a 27-year old man, had gone bust, leaving the owner £200,000 in debt.

The source of their collective difficulties lay not in issues of age but in more general factors. Both young and old were encouraged along much the same path in much the same way and took much the same steps to get their businesses going. The difficulties they encountered sprang from the fact that such enterprises were – in the main – never likely to succeed, despite all the effort and enthusiasm invested in them.

Even with sufficient finances to set businesses off on a decent footing, the hold they would have in the market place would still be precarious. Given the types of businesses established it is improbable that many could ever succeed. Both the younger and the older interviewees typically started businesses in the service sector where little capital investment was required (for example as clothes retailers, beauticians, car valets, sandwich deliverers, sign-writers, 'horror-grams', counsellors for the unemployed, writers, car mechanics, private

detectives, bicycle repairers, dancers and so on). They traded
with skills informally learnt and experience gained from personal hobbies and pastimes. But competition was too fierce.
The market place was already saturated with similar businesses
run by similar people with similar motivations in similar ways.
The local economy simply could not support another budding
free-lance photographer, another cheap mobile hairdresser,
another keen graphic designer.

The usual course of action was to pare labour costs to the
bone (that is the income derived) – the take home pay of the
mature informants never rose much above that of the younger
ones – in the hope of killing off some of the competition. In
time, they were themselves often killed off by an even newer
business setting up and competing in the same way (National
Audit Office, 1988). This was the brutal cycle of hopeful business start up and disheartening business failure that characterized the 'enterprise culture' of places like Teesside in the
1980s and into the 1990s.

A 1990 survey in Teesside found a massive increase in the
rates of new firm formation, particularly amongst older,
unemployed people, compared with the 1970s (Storey and
Strange, 1992). The authors remark that:

> if this alone constituted the basis for 'the enterprise
> culture', then it would be valid to infer that a significant
> change had taken place from one decade to the next
> (p. 94).

However, they also note that the quantity of these firms had
apparently increased at the expense of quality with over one
quarter of those studied being in hairdressing or vehicle-
related activities, with a poor chance of survival or growth.
Storey and Strange refer to such self-employed people as
'forced entrepreneurs' and other writers have referred to
'recession-push' (Stanworth and Gray, 1991) to explain the
effect of recessionary unemployment upon the growth of self-
employment. This interpretation of the 'appeal' of self-
employment is a more convincing one than that which refers
to the inculcation of entrepreneurial values amongst the previously unemployed (or employed).

In Teesside, however, the move into self-employment is
caused not so much by recession (although this compounds

the problem) as by long-term economic restructuring and high rates of unemployment which seem set to become permanent. In this context of declining opportunities for decent, secure, full-time employment – in the absence of 'proper jobs' – it is likely that the unemployed and precariously employed will continue to see self-employment as a way of resisting long-term labour market exclusion.

This view of the 'enterprise culture' from below – from the perspective of working-class men and women caught up in self-employment in the 1990s – illustrates that the businesses they temporarily ran, contrary to the claims of the local TEC, were not part of some new, thriving, entrepreneurial culture deserving of Ministerial plaudits and encouragement by state policy.[4] Rather, their time in enterprise can be better understood as survival self-employment: one element of an incipient culture in which those excluded from the shrinking core of secure employment seek less formal ways of making a living.

(ii) Voluntary Working

As with self-employment, it is difficult to estimate the extent of volunteering in Teesside. Much is done which is unrecorded and unregulated. One local agency, however, attributes a value of £24 million per annum to voluntary work in Hartlepool alone (deeming volunteers to be worth £4 per hour). There are around 6,000 organizations that relied upon volunteers in the county and a recent national survey also found that levels of voluntary activity amongst the general population were high and had risen significantly over the past decade (Joseph Rowntree Foundation, 1991). Despite all this volunteering has received relatively little academic attention in the United Kingdom (Harris, 1990).

The volunteers in the sample ranged in age from sixteen years old to over seventy, with the majority being over the age of forty and a slight majority being women. They were predominantly working-class which is not representative of samples from national surveys (for example, Joseph Rowntree Foundation, 1991). It is argued, however, that in economically depressed localities volunteering is being taken up increasingly by working-class people not in employment. Within the study attention was given to unpaid, regular and sustained voluntary effort by individuals for national, county-based or neighbourhood voluntary organizations. Volunteers also constituted a critical section of the work-force of the growing 'Third Sector' of community businesses, Credit Unions and co-operatives in this locality and elsewhere (MacDonald and Coffield, 1993).

As in national surveys (Joseph Rowntree Foundation, 1991) the volunteers were predominantly engaged in the welfare of the disadvantaged, either as carers (for example for the elderly) or as fund-raisers (for example for foreign aid appeals). The sort of work they did included: collecting second-hand clothes; driving minibuses; caring for the elderly and people with disabilities; providing counselling to victims of crime; and working in charity shops. A minority worked for only a few hours per week but most worked virtually full-time for no pay.

Although all were motivated by a moral concern for the disadvantaged in their communities – describing their voluntary work as 'labours of love' – there were variances in the appeal of volunteering which can be explained by the sample's different age, gender and class-based experiences, particularly of work in the labour market and in the domestic economy.

Firstly, some – particularly middle-aged and older women – rebuilt lives left empty through redundancy or bereavement by volunteering as carers. For women, volunteering tended to confirm their socially ascribed roles as carers and served to extend the associated responsibilities into later periods of their life (when husbands had died, children left home and employment in service jobs ceased). The opportunity to maintain such self-identity, and the sense of purpose that went with it, was welcomed even if these roles were acknowledged to be traditional and narrow. Volunteering replaced many of the positive social psychological 'categories of experience' (Jahoda, 1982) normally provided through employment and stripped away in unemployment.

Secondly, volunteering was pursued as a semi-permanent response to increasingly lengthy periods of exclusion from employment. This was particularly true of the middle-aged men interviewed who had been made redundant from jobs in manual employment. Voluntary work, for them, was a response to the realization that unemployment was likely to be their normal condition if alternatives outside of the formal labour market could not be found. For men like these, volunteering provided new opportunities and challenges; the chance to surrender time-honoured, masculine self-images as worker and breadwinner in the light of the novel experiences for providing social care that volunteering provided. In an increasingly flexible labour market, characterized by fewer jobs in the traditionally male manufacturing sector and increasing part-time, service-oriented work, volunteering could have an effect in broadening men's work aspirations and expectations.

Conversely a third motivation perceived volunteering not as a strategy for coping with unemployment but rather as a strategy for finding 'proper jobs'. This was the typical view of the teenage and young adult volunteers interviewed. The work experience, skills, contacts and references gained through voluntary work were thought to be useful additions to a curriculum vitae largely devoid of regular jobs, although some did acknowledge that long-term volunteering might diminish their chances of employment ('if we work for nothing why should anybody ever pay us').

Finally, some of the young informants found their way on to new schemes to encourage 'active citizenship'; for the majority these schemes were not chosen positively, nor were they regarded highly. They perceived themselves as 'forced volunteers' and volunteering was a strategic response to the negative experience they had of the alternatives open to them in their early careers (poor quality training schemes, unemployment, dead-end jobs).

Overall whilst interviewees talked positively of the benefits that this informal work brought them it was clear that their 'labours of love' were becoming increasingly subjected to patterns of organization and control which threatened both the personal satisfactions it brought and the welfare it provided to the local community.

A first set of criticisms centred upon the type and amount of work that volunteers were asked to do. Some informants spared a few hours per week but most worked almost full-time. Often their work was very hard – both physically and emotionally – and informants reported being treated 'like skivvies' and being 'drained' by the sheer effort. Some of the younger women who volunteered to work with the elderly, infirm and severely disabled, gave harrowing accounts of work expected of them; they felt their treatment came close to 'exploitation'.

One volunteer bureau manager reported being 'bombarded by requests' from social services for volunteers following the enactment of 'Community Care' legislation in 1993. Cutbacks to Cleveland County Council's budget have resulted in many services being 'transferred to the voluntary sector' (Brindle, 1993). The shortfall in funds facing many local councils, coupled with the impact of community care policies, will mean increasing reliance upon unpaid volunteers, particularly women, to shoulder the burden of caring for the sick, disabled and disadvantaged.

As second set of related concerns centred on the political agendas which were transforming the nature and quality of voluntary work. The voluntary sector is becoming increasingly colonized by the new welfare ideology of the Conservative government. Within their broad attack upon the 'nanny state' and 'cultures of dependency', and their proclamation of the values of enterprise, 'active citizenship' and de-regulation, the radical and broader goals historically pursued by the voluntary movement (Hedley and Davis Smith, 1992; Sheard, 1992; Gladstone, 1979) are ignored in a focus upon how the comfortably off might share their time and wealth with the less fortunate (see the Speakers Commission on Citizenship, 1990).

The Government (and the Opposition) have become keen on a more formal organization of voluntary opportunities, especially for the young and long-term unemployed because training and enterprise policies have proved only partially successful in denting persistently high unemployment rates. So far open compulsion in the 'workfare' mode has been resisted in favour of schemes like *Community Opportunities*, operated by TECs across the country as a way of encouraging graduates from Employment Training (ET) into the 'positive outcome' of voluntary work (Cleveland Council for Voluntary Service, 1990). *Community Opportunities* was reported as suffering from the same stigma as ET: it was seen as semi-compulsory and very much second best to a 'proper job' (i.e. with pay). Forced volunteering would serve to further downgrade the status of the sector and undermine attempts to create more professional styles of operation. Nevertheless, an increasing proportion of funding for posts in volunteer bureaux was coming from TECs and such organizations were spending more and more of their time trying to encourage reluctant ET trainees to become volunteers. Such resourcing of voluntary agencies suggests that we are again witnessing a government scheme more concerned with reducing unemployment figures (and increasing the 'positive outcomes' of ET) than the quality of the volunteers and of the voluntary work that they are encouraging.

To summarise, a massive amount of voluntary labour was uncovered. Whilst much of this was often poorly organized, under-resourced and administered by workers whose own jobs were insecure, it did provide alternative ways of working to thousands excluded from the formal labour market and served huge numbers of disadvantaged people whose needs are no longer being met by the welfare state. And whilst, on the one hand, volunteering is experienced positively (in various ways and for various reasons) by people who would otherwise be without work, on the other, there is great potential for the political and economic exploitation of their 'labours of love', as the state cuts back on welfare spending and transfers responsibility for social welfare on to unpaid individuals and voluntary groups (thus making jobs redundant in this field). Elsewhere a number of policy developments are suggested which might assist in overcoming this contradiction (MacDonald, 1996a). These relate to: the way the state at national and local level intervenes in the voluntary sector; the dangers of forced volunteering and conscripting the young and unemployed onto semi-compulsory government make-work schemes; the individual situation of volunteers in relation to unemployment benefits and their need for greater material (as well as social) support; the benefits for both the potential providers and recipients of voluntary care of expanding opportunities for volunteering.

(iii) 'Fiddly' Jobs

A third aspect of the informal work carried out by informants is done through what are known locally as 'fiddly' jobs. Sometimes referred to as 'doing the double', 'taking a backhander', working 'on the side' or 'off the cards', fiddly jobs refer to work that is carried out for pay by individuals who are also claiming various social security and unemployment benefits to which they would not be wholly entitled if they declared this work to the benefit authorities.

Again, academics have shown surprisingly little interest in this sort of work. At the start of this project the few extant studies suggested that, in the main, the unemployed are far less likely than the employed (with their skills, experience, contacts and other resources) to engage in illicit work. Ray Pahl's (1984) study on Sheppey found that, contrary to early expectations, the island was not 'a seething centre of fiddles' (p. 145) and when Bradshaw and Holmes (1989) examined the living standards of families on benefit in Tyneside they found that 'only one seventh of the sample had received extra income above the then permitted levels' (p. 137). On the other hand, a more recent study by Jordan and associates in the South-west of England found that around two-thirds of their sample of poor households had benefited from undeclared working (1992).

This qualitative study cannot comment on the prevalence of fiddly work in Teesside. The sample was not randomly selected nor can it be claimed to be representative of the unemployed population as a whole. Nevertheless, it does allow for an investigation of the way people accessed (or were excluded from) such jobs, the sorts of work undertaken, the motivations for doing fiddly jobs and the normative perceptions of such work which held sway locally.

Of the 214 people in the core sample, around one-third (n. 70) had done fiddly jobs and many more gave their views of it. In addition, interviews were held with fraud investigation managers of the local Department of Social Security (DSS) and Department of Employment (DE), to gather their accounts of policing this area. A full discussion of all the findings is presented elsewhere (MacDonald, 1994). Only general conclusions are made here:

(a) Fiddly jobs were not preferred to 'proper jobs'. Combining fiddly work and unemployment benefits was not preferred to more standard employment but a survival strategy initiated in the face of mass, structural unemployment and a system of benefits which failed to meet people's material needs.

(b) Fiddly jobs tended to be short-lived (typically lasting for a day or two, possibly a few weeks but rarely for longer), irregular (demanding great flexibility), infrequent (sometimes cropping up once or twice a year for some informants) and poorly rewarded (fiddly jobs often involved hard graft over long hours for low pay).

(c) This sort of work seemed to be most common in particular sectors of the labour market (sub-contracted labour at the steel works, construction, car mechanics, taxi driving, cleaning, bar work). None of the normal conditions of employment (for example health and safety regulations, training, sickness benefits, etc.) were afforded to fiddly workers and when some suffered industrial injuries (at the steel works) no compensation was forthcoming.

(d) Changes in management practice, for instance the search for greater functional, numerical and pay flexibility (Fevre, 1986) has provided greater opportunity for 'fiddly work' as firms contract out services. Contractors, looking to win tenders, cut costs by offering low pay to people they know to be in receipt of benefit and therefore able to 'afford' to work cheaply. It has been reported that employers have used the recent recession to actively cut pay, increase hours and undermine workers' conditions of employment (Citizens Advice Bureaux, 1992), sometimes relying upon benefit payment to 'top up' wages (Bevins, 1993).

(e) Unfortunately it is not possible to use this evidence to determine whether fiddly work is becoming more or less prevalent. Pahl (1984) suggests that informal economic activity will be more apparent in times of fuller employment. On the other hand, recent changes in management strategy – most obviously the sub-contracting out of work – seems to provide fertile ground for fiddly work. Nor is it possible to say whether the experiences of Teesside will be typical of other high unemployment areas. However, the study by Jordan et al. (1992), conducted in the South-west of England, reached many similar conclusions.

(f) People were remarkably conservative in their views and accounts. Those who had done fiddly jobs – and those who had not – operated with a clear morality: most common types of fiddling (irregular, low paid, temporary) were economically necessary, given the level of benefits people were living on and fiddly work (normally done by men) was a vital way to provide for families.

More serious 'fraud' (consistent, lucrative fiddling) was uncommon but condemned as wrong when instances did occur. This public morality reflects both the long-running dichotomy in working-class culture between the deserving and the undeserving poor, and the official policy response to undeclared working taken by the DE and the DSS.

(g) There was some evidence that being involved in fiddly work ameliorated not only the material experience of un-employment, but also softened its social psychological impact and helped to tie individuals back into working culture. The close regulation and policing of this sort of activity by the state would seem to be inhibiting enterprise and self-reliance, the maintenance of work routines and work ethics, and deterring people from involvement in local cultural networks through which illicit and licit work was found to be distributed.

(h) Popular perceptions that the locality was 'awash with fiddly jobs' are probably exaggerated. Access to fiddly work tends to be restricted to certain social groups. White, working-class males in their twenties and thirties, in neigh-bourhoods of high and long-term unemployment, with tradable skills and/or reliable records of (manual) work experience, who possessed the necessary cultural capital and who moved in the localised, pub-centred social networks through which fiddly work was distributed, were the most likely to partake in this sort of informal work. Yet even many in this category in the sample had not been offered such jobs. The more common experience of un-employment (particularly the social isolation it entails) ex-cludes many from the networks through which they are distributed (Morris, 1987, 1992).

(i) Contrary to writers like Henry (1978), fiddly work was not found to constitute a separate or hidden economy (Harding and Jenkins, 1989). It was not a provocative subject, nor particularly difficult to research. Interviewees happily talked about it in the same breath as discussing, for instance, their experiences of starting up in self-employment or of voluntary work, but particularly of unemployment. Thus, it is only possible to fully comprehend fiddly work by understanding the cultural and economic context of the lives of people who 'fiddle'. For this sample of poor and long-term unemployed people fiddly work became a necessary way of maintaining individual self-respect and household incomes.

INFORMAL WORK, SURVIVAL STRATEGIES AND THE IDEA OF AN 'UNDERCLASS'

A growing proportion of the recent sociological and policy debate about the social consequences of persistently high levels of unemployment upon deindustrializing localities has hinged around the notion of an 'underclass'. From Murray (1990, 1994) on the political Right to Dahrendorf (1987) and Field (1989) on the liberal Left, commentators have claimed that we are witnessing the rise of an underclass of people who, over time, are becoming spatially concentrated in the poorest areas and increasingly dependent upon welfare benefits and unable through their own enterprise to provide for themselves and their families. Government Ministers too have claimed that they see the rise of a society in which sections of the unemployed insist on getting 'something for nothing', have lost the work ethic and prefer to sit idly scrounging benefits to which they are not really entitled (Lilley, 1992).

Of course, different reasons are offered for the emergence of this alleged welfare underclass, with the Right preferring to stress interrelated cultural factors, the supposedly voluntary nature of unemployment and the disintegration of the 'traditional' family unit (see Dennis and Erdos, 1992) and the Left emphasising structural changes in the labour market and the exclusionary impact of laissez-faire social and economic policies pursued by recent governments. There is similarly little agreement about how one might define this underclass and about which individuals and social groups might be claimed to be members of it. However, in most UK versions of the underclass thesis – including the more respectable variants (Runciman, 1990; Gallie, 1988; Giddens, 1973) – the long-term unemployed are seen as prime candidates for membership of the putative underclass.[5]

Whilst this study was not conceived as a contribution to the underclass debate the evidence that it has provided about the informal work carried out by those excluded from employment in the long-term therefore has some bearing upon the debate, particularly to the more right-wing thesis.

Certainly the locality is not short of the indicators (illegitimacy, crime and unemployment) Murray draws upon to warn of this emerging underclass (1990). The county has the second highest level of live births outside marriage in the UK (Cleveland County Council, 1992). Between 1971 and 1991 Cleveland recorded the highest per cent increase in crime (up by 186 per cent) of twenty three national police areas and it consistently appears near the top of league tables of police statistics for offences committed (ibid). Unemployment has been stubbornly resistant to a range of economic policy interventions making Teesside notorious for the joblessness of its workers rather than famous for the success of its industry, as was the case in earlier decades. Nine out of ten criminal offenders in Teesside are not in full-time work (Cleveland County Council, 1994) and that local rates of unemployment are causally related to local rates of (particularly acquisitive) crime is still a matter of dispute by government Ministers is rather surprising.

Given the depth and scope of the social and economic problems facing the area it is perhaps understandable that Murray should select Teesside as a typical underclass area and a home of what he calls the 'New Rabble' (Murray, 1994).

A full critique of Charles Murray's argument cannot be offered here and fuller and more nuanced accounts of this debate can be found elsewhere (for example, Smith, 1991; Bagguley and Mann, 1992; MacNicol, 1994; Morris, 1994; Byrne, 1995). In the remaining pages, however, some tentative conclusions will be drawn which will suggest that Murray's thesis about a dangerous, anti-social, anti-work underclass fails to appreciate the potential for working-class men and women to respond creatively to the changing organization of work in places like Teesside.

The evidence presented here has shown how individuals can develop a variety of cultural response (of 'survival strategies and cultures of resistance', to use Jordan and Redley's phrase) to living in times and places of high unemployment. Certainly, there are many unemployed people in Teesside who experience the depressing and deadening social, psychological and material traumas of long-term unemployment. A significant section of the unemployed, however, seem to be able to find more enterprising and resourceful ways to get by when jobs in the more formal sectors of the economy are in short supply. The pursuit of a 'criminal career' is just one of these (Craine and Coles, 1995).

Across the 214 people interviewed in the core sample of informants it was difficult to identify anybody who appeared to be content to be living on the dole. All reported that they wanted to work and that they would prefer a 'proper job' (ie. one which was relatively full-time, relatively permanent and relatively well-paid) to the sorts of informal work they were engaged in. Few, it must be added, thought it likely that they would get such a 'proper job' in the foreseeable future.

The evidence of their actions, as well as their claims, would seem to suggest that the work ethic remained strong amongst this group. They were strikingly entrepreneurial in their search for work and strongly committed to it when they found it, even if – as was often the case – it was poorly rewarded, insecure and, in the case of fiddly work, a risky and illicit enterprise. Indeed, fiddly work could be understood better as representing a culture of enterprise than one of dependency. The way people secured and kept these illicit jobs showed high degrees of personal motivation, initiative, local knowledge and risk-taking. Paradoxically, they fitted the model of the entrepreneur much more closely than the people who entered into the grimy, self-exploitative world of self-employment.

The self-employed group were working exceedingly long hours in order to make a living wage and for adults as well as young people personal income often never rose much above the equivalent of around £1 per hour. Neither were fiddly jobs particularly lucrative, despite the popular clamour about benefit fraud. One young woman (who was reasonably typical) had worked thirty hours one week as a care assistant in a residential home on the 'fiddle'. Together with her Income Support this netted her the grand sum of £75. Employers, it was reported, were consciously relying upon state unemployment benefits to subsidize the low wages that they were paying (see Dean, 1995).

It is also difficult to interpret the motivations to engage in these informal sorts of work as being in some way anti-social. Most obviously, all the volunteers had a clear and genuine altruistic desire to assist in the welfare of disadvantaged others. They described at length the social and psychological benefits they personally derived from volunteering, but rarely did it result in any financial remuneration. On the contrary, several discussed how they had lost, or been threatened with the loss of, benefits as they were deemed to be not 'actively seeking' or 'available for' work by the benefit authorities. One middle-aged man returned from delivering charitable aid to Rumania to find his Income Support stopped.

Fiddly workers, too, were not generally motivated by greed or the opportunity to get 'something for nothing'. Even DSS and DE fraud managers acknowledged that this was about need (not greed), that most 'benefit fraudsters' were receiving quite trivial amounts of income from fiddly jobs and that this was usually destined towards supporting minimal family budgets. Men seemed to be more likely to engage in this sort of work than women and they talked in quite conservative terms about how fiddly work was financially necessary if they were to continue to provide for their families. This runs directly counter to right-wing views about the welfare under-class and how feckless fathers are guilty of neglecting their traditional role as breadwinner (Dennis and Erdos, 1992).

The extent of informal economic activity also suggests that it would be difficult to categorize these informants as somehow responsible for their own unemployment or 'unem-ployable'. The labour of volunteers and fiddly workers was needed in some quarters and under some conditions. (This is less true of the self-employed group who aimed to trade in commercial ways but found the market unable to bear further cohorts of hopeful 'entrepreneurs' no matter how keen and cheap they were).

Fiddly workers had, apparently, become an important part of the sub-contracting culture of Teesside. Their capacity for physical graft, for working long shifts for low pay, for putting up with arduous, dangerous and unpleasant working conditions and their ability to respond at a moment's notice to a contract, were all qualities in demand in the less formal sectors of the labour market.

Similarly, the unemployed volunteers were not 'unemployable' – they had skills, experiences and contributions which were put to good use by official agencies increasingly reliant upon them. Although they are not required at the core of the labour market they are much in demand as a back-up army of free labour to fill the dirty and thankless jobs not allocated a wage.

To conclude: informants called their locality 'Schemeland', a place where seemingly everybody they knew now had working lives constructed – not as they might have been a generation ago around relatively secure and permanent careers in stable employment – but through a series of different forms of non-standard work (part-time, temporary, self-employed, quasi-criminal, voluntary, fiddly and on an array of government schemes) punctuated by periods of unemployment.

The accounts they gave of this place did not report a culture of welfare dependency, of a dangerous, parasitical underclass as Murray would have it. On the contrary, the research suggests that at least some of those left out of employment, even in the longer-term, are capable of finding informal ways of working. This was not an emerging underclass culture but an incipient culture of survival, of resilience, of getting by. And this study of the experiences of some of the unemployed in the North-east of England provides one qualitative illustration of how the re-organization of work in late twentieth century capitalist societies is forcing an increasingly large proportion of people to seek the means for their economic and social survival through various types of disorganized, insecure, risky, casualized and poor work.

NOTES

1. The research was funded by the Economic and Social Research Council (grant no. R000231976) from 1990 to 1993 and on-going study has been supported by the University of Teesside. I am indebted to both organizations. The research was conducted with Frank

Coffield and Sharon Pickavance helped with some interviews. This discussion is restricted to analysis of the fieldwork undertaken by the author, who must also take responsibility for the conclusions presented here. My main vote of thanks must go to the hundreds of people who spared time for me to talk to them.

2. Interviews were qualitative in nature, lasted for about an hour on average and took place in people's homes, business premises, in cafes and pubs and were tape-recorded. Given the qualitative design of the study this sample cannot be claimed to be representative of the local unemployed nor can estimates of the prevalence of these forms of work be given. Nevertheless, there was no shortage of possible interviewees and the size of the sample suggests that the forms of work described are being taken up by, at least, a significant minority.

3. See MacDonald (1994, 1996a and 1996b) for more detailed and extended discussions of 'fiddly work', voluntary working and self-employment and the enterprise culture, respectively.

4. In a more candid moment the local TEC acknowledged that: 'self-employment cannot always be equated with the spirit of enterprise, it may, in some circumstances be the ultimate in the casualization of the workforce' (Teesside TEC, 1995a, p. 47).

5. Even if recent surveys of the unemployed would seem to suggest that, at present, they cannot easily be so classified (Payne and Payne, 1994; Gallie, 1994).

7 Economic Change and Domestic Life[1]

This chapter reports upon research in Hartlepool, a town located on the North East coast of England, which stands as a case study of the impact of heavy manufacturing decline affecting Britain throughout the 1980s. Hartlepool had become established as a port for the export of coal by the mid-nineteenth century, and soon developed a thriving shipyard and associated metal industry. Decline began with the rundown of shipbuilding in the late 1950s, followed by the restructuring and gradual elimination of steel production, which by the early sixties had resulted in an unemployment rate of 15 per cent. The subsequent recession in the late seventies brought a 19 per cent reduction in job numbers and an overall restructuring of employment.

'Jobs for life' in heavy industry became prone to redundancy, and the hitherto constant flow of short term contract jobs was undermined as employment in construction, maintenance and haulage waned with the town's industrial decline. A number of processes lay behind the changing structure of employment: large and long established companies were seeking increased flexibility in working practice among core workers, and cutting back their use of contractors, whilst conversely certain areas of work, notably haulage and maintenance, were increasingly contracted out as a means of holding the core workforce to a minimum. Contract work was thus becoming more competitive and less secure, at a time when previously stable employment was under increasing threat from redundancy.

The data to follow compare three contrasting groups with reference to household circumstances, employment histories, and informal networks of association and support. Its central argument is that conventional approaches to social inequality, by the occupational ranking of either individuals or even by some composite household indicator, can provide only partial representations of social structure. Informal patterns of association and networks of exchange can add an important dimension of understanding which has direct bearing on material well being and future employment prospects. This happens by virtue of the influence social networks exert on both informal support and job search. Our understanding of the social ramifications of formal economic structures can thus be complemented by the study of the informal processes in which they are embedded.

The concept of the 'household strategy' has commonly been adopted as a tool for analysing the experience of economic change at the level of the household. It is argued here, however, that any approach to 'household strategies' must be set not only in the context of local labour market change, but must also take account of the mediating role of informal processes. Readers unfamiliar with the British welfare system should further note the role of state provisions, still extensive despite recent erosion. For example, the long term unemployed have access to means tested Income Suppport, as of right, for the duration of their unemployment, and the public housing sector, though much depleted, still accounts for about one third of accommodation. In addition, we find elaborate systems of informal support and exchange, and a significant role for social networks in job search. All of these factors affect the shaping of domestic life, though a full understanding of the internal dynamics of the household must also incorporate the informal work upon which domestic organization depends, and its relation to labour market activity. The first part of this paper will deal with the social location of the household, and the second with aspects of its internal organization.

RESEARCH DESIGN

The data considered in this paper were gathered by a formal survey in Hartlepool, which in November 1989 was experiencing male unemployment rates of 18 per cent. Interviewing was completed from October to December 1989. The unit of investigation was the married or cohabiting couple, though data were collected on all household members and on the extended family. Household selection was based on male employment status, and one requirement was that all male respondents should be active in the labour market. Accordingly an age range of 20 to 55 inclusive was specified. The survey objective was to achieve an initial random sample of 600 with reference to these critieria, and through house by house screening of an additional random sample to build to a total of 200 couples in each of the following categories:

Group A: couples where the man has been unemployed continuously for at least one year,

Group C: couples where the man has been recruited to employment within the last 12 months, though he may be currently either employed or unemployed.

Comparison could then be drawn with a third group (Group B) achieved within the first random sample; couples in which the man has been in continuous employment with the same firm for at least the last 12 months. This sampling procedure also yielded a fourth group (Group D) made up of couples meeting the age criteria but not included in the other three groups, ie the sick, disabled, early retired, etc. Because of the nature of the local economy the sample consists overwhelmingly (80 per cent) of manual working class respondents.

For inclusion in the sample both spouses were required to complete identical interview schedules of 1–11/2 hours in length, and given this demanding requirement the overall response rate of 61 per cent is good. When broken down by sample group we find group C, the recent job finders, to have the best response rate, at 72 per cent, whilst unsurprisingly the long term unemployed were somewhat less co-operative with a response rate of 56 per cent, as were the securely employed with a rate of 58 per cent. The residual group, group D, gave a response rate of 65 per cent. Qualitative interviewing in the same area (Morris, 1987) suggests that those among the unemployed who would be least likely to co-operate would be the most withdrawn and cut off, whilst the employed least likely to co-operate were those most securely placed who could see no relevance in the research for themselves. These two low response categories represent the two extremes of the sample population. As a result our findings will if anything underestimate contrasts between the employed and unemployed, having lost from the sample those at each extreme. The numerical outcome in terms of completed pairs of interviews was: Group A, 159; Group B, 325; Group C, 214; Group D, 94. The random distribution of these groups in the married population aged 20–55 was respectively 13, 61.3, 17.2 and 7.5 per cent for groups A, B, C, D (adjusted for different response rates).

The point of defining group C with reference to recent job acquisition was to maximize the chances of detecting the existence of a group of male workers who typically experienced frequent and involuntary job changes. If such a group exists a recent job start would probably have been preceded by frequent entrances to and exits from employment such as to constitute a 'chequered' job history (cf. Harris, 1987). A scrutiny of the employment histories of the men in this sample group confirms the existence of a section of the male population who experience a distinctive broken employment history interspersed with periods of unemployment. The data show a sharp contrast with the more securely employed (group B) of whom only about 20 per cent have four or more employment spells in their 11 year history (1979–89), in contrast with 70 per cent of group C.

CONCENTRATIONS OF UNEMPLOYMENT

One obvious initial question concerns the possibility that the different groupings making up the sample are spatially concentrated, and here some understanding of housing provision is helpful. British housing patterns contrast sharply with, for example, those of the US, where public sector housing is extremely limited. In Britain state provision of housing has been much more important, and despite the recent sale of houses in this sector, public rented accommodation still accounts for about one third of all accommodation. There is a tendency towards a concentration of the least secure section of the population, who are clustered together on large estates. One such estate in Hartlepool houses a large proportion of people nearing the end of their working life, rehoused from the slum clearance of the fifties. Other more recent public housing has catered for young couples whose prospects have been badly affected by local economic decline, while owner occupation is more typical of a slightly older group who came of age in the more favourable conditions of the fifties and sixties, and took advantage of their position to purchase property. Even controlling for age, however, we find that employment status correlates strongly with housing tenure.

It is thus unsurprising that the three principal sample groups show markedly different residence patterns. Among the long term unemployed we find that 72 per cent are in local authority accommodation, 19 per cent in owner occupied housing, and eight per cent in private rented housing. The corresponding figures for the securely employed group are ten, 87 and two per cent, and for the insecure group 26, 67 and six per cent. Because of the arrangement of the housing stock in the town these figures translate into a distinctive spatial pattern, with high concentrations of unemployment in particular areas within the town. One of Pahl's early conclusions in research on the Isle of Sheppey (1984, p. 309) was that neighbouring households with broadly similar qualifications in terms of skill and experience could find themselves in contrasting positions. The data from Hartlepool, however, reveals a spatial dimension to social polarization.

The survey material was collected from the 15 administrative wards which constitute the built up area of Hartlepool. Just five of these wards account for 60 per cent of the total long term unemployed in the sample, a different four wards account for 42 per cent of the securely employed, and five wards account for 48 per cent of the insecure group. Of these five wards three coincide with the ward concentrations of securely employed workers, and one with the long term unemployed. Any casual patterns of social contact are thus disproportionately likely to be with others in similar circumstances, and we are likely to find concentrations of unemployment within social networks.

The other readily apparent dimension of concentration has been noted in a number of other studies (eg. Pahl, 1984; Harris, 1987; GHS, 1987) and that is the tendency for the employment status of spouses to coincide. The structuring of the present sample, and specifically the separate identification of the long term unemployed permits a more sensitive analysis than has been present in other studies, however, and unsurprisingly shows rather more marked contrasts. Thus, of the long term unemployed men (group A) only 13 per cent have a partner in employment, in contrast with 71 per cent of the securely employed, group B. Between these two polar positions we find the recently recruited group (C) of whom 55 per cent have employed partners, and the residual 'out of the market' group (D), 38 per cent of whom have employed partners.

We noted at the start that one distinctive feature of the British welfare system is the provision of income maintenance for the unemployed. Although this has been substantially eroded in recent years there is still a stark contrast with the US where there is no automatic right to benefit by virtue of unemployment. In Britain, provided conditions about availability for work are met, there is a universal right to means tested benefit for those aged over 17. The association of unemployment for husband and wife has sometimes been linked to this provision, in that additional income triggers deductions from benefit. There is clearly some disincentive effect built into the operation of the welfare system, and the findings on this issue will be more fully discussed later in this chapter. However, a woman's experience is not directly determined by that of her spouse, but is also intricately linked to lifecourse development. Those women with the lowest occupational standing are more likely to embark on motherhood early, and subsequently to suffer additional and related labour market disadvantage. The first section of this paper, however, asks is this household concentration of unemployment compounded by patterns of informal association as suggested above?

THE COMPOSITION OF SOCIAL NETWORKS

The tendency for unemployment to be concentrated in particular nuclear families has been long established (see Payne, 1987). The possibility that this concentration is also to be found within extended families has not, however, been investigated. The present research collected data on the 'close kin' of both members of each couple in the sample, close kin being defined as parents, siblings and independent adult children resident in Hartlepool. Among the long term unemployed men in the sample we find evidence of considerable concentrations of unemployment among close male kin, at

35 per cent as compared with 16 per cent for the securely employed and 19 per cent for the insecurely employed. Similar contrasts, though not so marked, are found when we look at the levels of employment for close male kin resident in Hartlepool. The male kin of the long term unemployed group had an employment level of 45 per cent, in contrast to 57 per cent for the securely employed group and 62 per cent for the insecurely employed group.

The differences were repeated in data on 'three closest friends', though significantly a greater proportion of the long term unemployed were unable to name any close friends (24 per cent) than were the securely employed (16 per cent). Of those friends who were named by the former group 32 per cent were unemployed, in contrast to five per cent for friends of the securely employed, and ten per cent for friends of the insecurely employed. The percentages of employed friends were respectively 32, 75 and 69 per cent. Contrasts of a similar kind are found among the kinship and friendship networks of the women in the three sample groups, although the proportions of employed and unemployed are generally reduced by the more common designation 'housewife'. One further point of interest is that women's friendship patterns seem to vary with their husband's status as well as their own. For women with husbands in employment the percentages with most friends employed varied according to the wife's status as follows: wife employed, 74 per cent; wife unemployed, 48 per cent; wife economically inactive, 30 per cent. For women with unemployed husbands the percentages with most friends employed were lower, but still varied by the wife's status; respectively 46, 22, and 19 per cent.

In summary then the long term unemployed tend to live on public sector housing estates with high levels of unemployment, tend to have partners who are also unemployed, to show concentrations of unemployment in their extended family networks, and to name close friends who are also unemployed. These patterns are not to the total exclusion of the employed population but there is certainly a strong tendency towards mutual association. It remains to spell out the possible implications of these concentrations and two main areas will be considered: the potential for informal aid, and the significance for informal job search.

INFORMAL ACTIVITY

Early expectations that the decline in formal employment would be offset by informal activity (Pahl, 1980) have not been substantiated, and the informal sector of the British economy is much less extensive than in third world economies, and even the US. Whilst there are some instances of unreported income, and periods of undeclared employment, these are the exception rather than the rule. There are a number of reasons for this, which are discussed more fully below. Briefly, the general features of informal sector work, which are captured by the notion of 'underemployment' and which serve to keep employer costs low, have been achieved by the restructuring of formal employment. Furthermore, informal (that is undeclared) earnings carry the threat of disqualification from eligibility for benefit. There are those who take this risk, but rarely for more than the odd day or week's work.

A rather different aspect of informal activity was investigated by Pahl's work in Sheppey, which raised the question of informal exchanges between households. The possibility that informal sources of work were used more by the poor than the rich was not, however, confirmed. In general the use of informal labour was low, and unemployed men particularly did not use such sources of labour. Finch (1989, p. 93) in a review of literature on family obligations, has commented on weakening kin ties among the unemployed such that: being unemployed reduces the capacity of both men and women to participate in the on-going patterns of activities on which such ties are based. At the sharp end, being unemployed reduces people's capacity to provide support in return for support received.

Finch's review of research on the general issue of informal support poses the difficult question of how far support will be given between kin when the element of mutuality is absent (p. 75) and she argues that there is no evidence of an automatic assumption of responsibility for kin unable to maintain themselves. Findings from my own qualitative research in Hartlepool (Morris, 1987) suggested that concentrations of unemployment in kinship and friendship patterns could affect the potential for informal support, and this seemed a possible direction for further research (Morris, 1988). Such ideas were taken up in the Social Change and Economic Life Initiative

(Gallie, 1990) which investigated support networks by asking whether there was anyone whom respondents felt they could rely on for help in a variety of ways. A majority of employed friends was found to produce a stronger support network than a majority of unemployed friends, and as in the present research, the unemployed were less likely than the employed to have such a network.

THE NATURE OF EXCHANGES

Unlike the Gallie data the present research has endeavoured to collect information about actual flows of aid rather than potential support. This has been achieved by identifying three different broad categories of aid – aid in services, in kind and financial aid, and compiling figures on the instances and distribution of types of exchange. Receipt of aid in services did not vary to a significant degree between sample groups, hovering at around 70 per cent for all groupings. The services vary from babysitting to household and car maintenance, gardening, etc. Couples most commonly identified an employed source of this aid, though this source figured lowest for the long term unemployed. Conversely an unemployed source was much more likely at 37 per cent as compared with 16 per cent for the securely employed group, though with employed givers still strongly represented (49 per cent among the unemployed as compared with 76 per cent among the securely employed). An important point to note is the high incidence of services from a 'housewife' source among women (37 per cent), and here the differences between sample groups were not statistically significant. This suggests a pattern of mutual support among women which is independent of the circumstances of the man, and it is a finding repeated for other types of aid.

Unlike the case of aid in services, aid in kind shows a statistically significant difference between sample groups according to whether or not aid is received at all. Contrasts are repeatedly found to be greatest between the securely employed and the long term unemployed households, with the other two groups always located somewhere between the two extreme positions. Thus more of the long term unemployed are in receipt of aid in kind than any of the other groups, usually in the form of gifts of food or clothes. Differences between the sample groups persist when we look at employed and unemployed sources, with fewer of the long term unemployed naming an employed source than any other group, and more naming an unemployed source. As with other findings the main contrasts were between the long term unemployed and securely employed, with the other two groups falling somewhere between. Again, however, there was a distinctive pattern of exchange between women, with 'housewives' as the source, and showing a much less marked difference between the sample groupings.

Turning to the receipt of financial aid we find that the difference by sample groups as to whether or not aid is received is much higher than in the other two types of assistance. The unemployed show much the highest level of receipt (71 per cent) and the securely employed much the lowest (39 per cent), though we should note that there is a distinctive pattern of mutual loans passing between unemployed people to accommodate the timing of benefit payments. The other, less regular, type of financial aid, usually from employed kin, takes the form of larger 'loans' to meet an unexpected cost, such as a fuel bill. Thus, when we consider sources of aid we find the familiar difference between the securely employed and the long term unemployed with regard to employed sources, but references by the unemployed to an unemployed source are much higher than for aid in kind (31 per cent), and almost equal references to an employed source (38 per cent). For each type of aid there is a small but significant proportion of the long term unemployed group who receive aid only from other unemployed. For the men, looking respectively at services, aid in kind and financial aid, the percentages are: 20.7, 14.9 and 16.5 per cent. For women the corresponding figures are 18.4, ten and 19.1 per cent. When we combine husbands' and wives' responses, however, the percentages fall to 15.9, seven, and 12.4 per cent, that is, one spouse may have an employed source of aid where the other does not.

KINSHIP OR FRIENDSHIP?

It remains to ask the more general question of sources of aid with regard to kinship and friendship links. Overall which is the more important source and under what circumstances does this vary? Across all three types of aid the long term unemployed are less likely than the securely employed to register a friend as the source of aid. This is particularly the case for financial aid, and especially among men. The contrasts between sample groups may be because friends are more wary than relatives of maintaining close connections with the unemployed. This would support Finch's suggestion (1987) that the unemployed will tend to show a reduction in social contacts and the data do suggest a weakening of friendship ties for the unemployed. We should note that within sample groupings women show a higher dependence on kinship than friendship as compared with men, and for them there is less of a difference by types of aid. For financial aid among unemployed couples women were slightly more likely than men to name neighbours and friends as a source. This suggests the use of neighbours for small but immediate pressing need, linked to women's role as budget managers where income is low.

A few other points of variation should be noted. Pahl (1984), for example, suggests the importance of the domestic cycle for the analysis of informal exchanges. The present research showed the presence of children to independently affect the propensity to receive aid, though the differences between the sample groups remained even where there were no children present. Those men whose fathers are living also showed a greater likelihood of receiving aid than those whose fathers had died. It was also the case that having at least one member of the kin network in employment improved the prospects of receiving aid for the long term unemployed.

The data on repayment or return of aid is also quite interesting. Couples in the long term unemployed group are most likely to give nothing in return for services, whilst the securely employed are most likely to provide some kind of help in return. The source of such aid for the securely employed is overwhelmingly other employed people, and so there is no strong indication of the employed purchasing services from the unemployed. Differences are sharper in the pattern of return for aid in kind, with the long term unemployed very much more likely than other groups to give nothing. In contrast reports of repaying financial aid were fairly high, albeit highest for the securely employed and lowest for the long term unemployed.

IMPLICATIONS

The fact that informal exchange is generally fairly common throughout this overwhelmingly working class sample (80 per cent manual working class) militates against any argument that we might be detecting the development of a distinctive culture of the 'underclass' based on social exclusion and/or collective awareness. This is especially the case given the varied sources of aid to the unemployed. There is however, evidence to suggest that the density of informal support is highest among the long term unemployed, and that they are to a considerable degree mutually supportive. Much of this support, however, is based on kinship rather than friendship links, and there are signs that friendship, and hence the potential for 'collective' awareness, attenuates rather than strengthens with long term unemployment.

The data so far presented show a tendency towards mutual association by employment status, but stop short at any clear segregation of the long term unemployed, except perhaps in the case of the small proportion receiving aid only from other unemployed people. It is nevertheless the case that the concentration of unemployment in kinship and friendship networks will produce a propensity for patterns of support to show a density of exchange between people whose circumstances are similar. Whilst there is considerable support which flows from the employed to the unemployed, that which comes from other unemployed people is disproportionately high. Thus the unemployed depend to a considerable degree on those who are least able to offer support, and their social contacts also include a majority of other unemployed or non-employed people. This fact alone may have implications for their future employment prospects, a point which has been argued by Wilson (1991) with reference to the ghettoization process in American cities.

JOB SEARCH

One somewhat unsatisfactory aspect of the polarization thesis in the British literature is that it offers no means of explaining why some workers are more adept than others at finding employment. Work related contacts and informal methods of contact could provide one key to the difference. Data on job search from the labour force survey (*Employment Gazette*, March, 1988, Table 21) show that informal methods of jobs search, that is asking friends and relatives, and making direct application to employers, each account for less than ten per cent of reported methods. The *General Household Survey*, however, (1987, Table 6.41) showed information from friends and relatives to be by far the most successful means of search, accounting for about half of the jobs started in the 12 months prior to the research.

There are a number of reasons why such methods may suit employers (see Grieco, 1989; Jenkins et al., 1983), notably to enhance feelings of loyalty from existing workers by favouring their network, to avoid trouble makers by relying on existing workers to vouch for new recruits, to enhance discipline, to identify workers with a particular relevant skill, and to save the time and money involved in formal recruitment. The importance of informal access to employment is apparent in data from the job histories of respondents in the Hartlepool survey, which collected information both on the job search methods of the unemployed, and on the means of access to all jobs enumerated in respondents' histories. The main means of access to first job for both men and women was the careers service, accounting for about one third, and friends and relatives accounting for about one quarter. By the second job this relationship had reversed, with friends and relatives accounting for one third of jobs found. By totalling all jobs in the employment histories then we get some indication of the overall importance of informal contacts in job search; accounting for roughly one third of jobs among both men and women, with informal approach to an employer accounting for 18 per cent and the job centre only 13 per cent.

Looking at currently held jobs only, we find that women's access relied more heavily on friends etc. than men's (39 as compared with 31 per cent) and was much higher than unemployed women's reporting of sources of job information. Generally speaking women successfully gaining access to employment relied to a much higher degree on informal contacts than unemployed women currently seeking work. The contrast was much more marked than for men. One possible explanation could be related to the tendency for women not to define themselves as unemployed, and possibly therefore to be less involved in active job search, but inclined to take a job should it become available through informal means. The findings may also reflect a tendency for employers to favour particularly informal methods of recruiting women workers.

The most important sources of informal information for both men and women are old friends, close relatives, and friends and acquaintances; roughly equal in their significance. This seems to contradict Granovetter's argument (1982) that it is weak ties which are more important because they spread the net of job search more widely. This may be because in circumstances where competition for jobs is high then a preferential channelling of information may assert itself. The outcome of the search is, however, strongly affected by the employment status of the contact, such that information from someone themselves in employment is much more likely to produce success.

The reason for this seems to be that the most effective source of information is someone already employed where the vacancy is available. This was the case for 70 per cent of the informal sources which yielded employment, and only 50 per cent of those informal sources which did not. The pattern is repeated when we ask whether the informant put in a good word for the candidate, and the application was more likely to be successful where they did. It is fairly clear then that the concentration of unemployment in the kinship and friendship networks of the unemployed is likely to reduce their chances of finding work in relation to those with stronger contacts in the world of employment.

Accepting the influence of informal factors, however, does not over-rule the other long familiar association between long term unemployment and lack of a formal skill. This association is confirmed in the present study with unskilled workers making up 44 per cent of the long term unemployed, as compared with five per cent of the securely employed, and

11 per cent of the insecurely employed. We also find that the 'skilled' workers included among the long term unemployed were less far likely than those in the other two groups to have served an apprenticeship. Lack of a skill, combined with reduced contact with the world of work may explain the position of the long term unemployed, but what of those men with broken empoyment histories?

TYPE OF EMPLOYMENT

One of the research questions which informed the design of this research was whether there is evidence of a distinctive job history made up of broken employment and short term unemployment. This appears to be confirmed by the profiles of workers in group C, 70 per cent of whom had four or more jobs in the previous ten years, as compared with 22 per cent for those in group B. This pattern of broken employment is explained in part by vulnerability to redundancy, as a result of generalized economic decline, together with the apparently increasing incidence of temporary work, as a result of employment restructuring. These jobs show characteristic features of what would, in third world economies, be termed the informal sector.

Of the total jobs covered by the employment histories about one third were stated at the outset to be temporary. These jobs showed a somewhat higher incidence of recruitment by informal methods than did other jobs (58 as compared with 42 per cent). Although informal recruitment is generally high, especially in traditionally working class labour markets, it is particularly so for short term employment. One of the potential reasons for an employer seeking to recruit through informal means is the reduction in time and money in comparison with formal recruitment. This is of particular importance when the job is temporary. Does this offer some possible explanation of the sample groups with a distinctive broken employment history?

Further progress was made in analysis by focussing on the nature of job loss, and the fragmented pattern was revealed to be a result of a combination of redundancy with the experience of temporary work. There was also a tendency for this association to be sequential, that is for redundancy to be more often followed by temporary work than *vice versa*. Once out of work a person is likely to become prone to redundancy in firms which operate on a 'first in, last out' basis, and also to become likely candidates for temporary employment for which the competition is lower than for secure jobs. There are also some signs of an age related pattern; a result of the greater vulnerability to redundancy of those who entered the labour market close to the onset of recession.

There was also a difference between the sample groupings in terms of access to employment. The men who had started employment within the last 12 months had both had a history of broken employment, and showed a higher reliance on informal means of access to their current job than the securely employed (50 as compared with 39 per cent). This could be explained either by a recent increase in informal methods of recruitment, or by the fact that this particular group had a history of broken employment. The most marked finding, however, was the association for group C between informal access to employment and its temporary nature. It should be stressed that it was not simply means of access *per se* which explains the characteristic pattern of group C's work history, but the nature of the jobs which informal methods yield for them in particular. There was, after all, a high reliance on informal access to employment among the secure workers. In this case we are left with an explanation of the broken employment pattern which shows an age and skill related influence, but seems most strongly linked to the types of jobs which are available through the respondents' own particular social networks of information. In other words, the world of social contact which grows up around insecure employment does much to reproduce the pattern.

HOUSEHOLD STRATEGIES

The notion of household strategies, though first developed in the context of poverty and underdevelopment (eg. Lomnitz, 1977), was taken up in the UK in the early eighties as a vehicle for addressing questions about the impact of economic change at the level of the household. The appropriation of this term at a time of economic restructuring in the context of overall decline was partly prompted by the assumption that there could be innovative responses at the level of the household (Pahl, 1980). It was also thought that the informal sector of the economy – whether in the form of domestic labour, self-provisioning, or undeclared earning – could play a central role in these responses (Gershuny and Pahl, 1979). Household arrangements were to be viewed in terms of the harnessing of resources for labour, which would be dictated by the relative advantages and disadvantages of different household members with regard to different types of labour (Pahl, 1980; 1984).

The findings of these endeavours have been summarized and evaluated elsewhere (Morris, 1990), but one of the major criticisms has direct relevance to the data presented so far in this chapter. The idea of strategy implies a degree of voluntarism which is not supported by empirical results. In fact, household arrangements with respect to labour and resources fall into a fairly limited, albeit contrasting, range of possibilities. The most notable distinction is clearly the two-earner/no-earner division, or the distinction between long term unemployment, insecure, and secure employment outlined above. The strategies approach offers no means of explaining why it is that particular households fall into one category and while others do not.

STRATEGIES IN CONTEXT

Part of the contextualizing work necessary to remedy this defect will be the documentation of the types of economic change which households are facing, and the identification of the more vulnerable groups of workers. In the present study the obvious example is the disproportionate vulnerability of the unskilled worker (both male and female) to long term unemployment. Other elements in explanation, however, draw upon informal aspects of economic life, which in the present study do not so much offer the potential for innovative household change, but rather reinforce established patterns of disadvantage. The importance of contact with the world of work in securing access to employment was one example of this, though it was also the case that informal access to employment could in itself be disadvantaging; a particular network might tend to carry information about a particular kind of work, as seemed to be the case for the insecurely employed group in the data discussed above.

Spatial concentrations can play a part in this picture where the relationship between the housing market and the labour market produce concentrations in particular kinds of housing, though the most extreme example of this is the emergence of black inner city ghettoes of the 'underclass' in the US. We also saw informal networks play a role in the provision of support in cash or kind, though noted that to some extent the composition of a network replicated the labour market disadvantage of the respondent. One interesting aspect of these data was the particular pattern of mutual support between women, little affected by the employment status of the husband, but seemingly revolving around specifically female domestic obligations.

In fact, the internal organization of the household is another aspect of the context in which 'strategies' must be placed, for they are certainly constrained by different – gendered – sets of assumptions or requirements. These it seems have not been too amenable to renegotiation. The clearest example from the present study emerges from the analysis of female employment histories, and the attempt to arrive at a fuller explanation of the two-earner/no-earner pattern.

WOMEN'S EMPLOYMENT HISTORIES[2]

The explanation for such a pattern has normally assumed the benefit disincentive to be a powerful influence, albeit in association with other factors (Cooke, 1987; Joshi, 1984; Morris, 1990), and there is a related tendency to treat male employment status as the independent variable in explaining household patterns. If a substantial proportion of a woman's earnings are offset against the benefit claim this would logically seem to act as a disincentive to her employment. The data from the present study challenge an overly simple account of this process, revealing a complex interaction between male employment status, household composition and female occupational standing. Life course and domestic circumstances are typically controlled for in comparisons of working and non-working women (eg. Davies, 1991), but this standardization sacrifices important information about their interaction with economic structure. Only 12 per cent of the present sample of non-working women married to unemployed men said that they were not available for work because their spouse's benefit would be cut. Whilst the benefit regulations may have a more powerful latent influence than this result indicates, some further exploration of women's non-employment seems warranted.

In an examination of all jobs held since 1979 women's most common reason for leaving jobs were pregnancy, family or health reasons, and redundancy. For groups A, B and C respectively pregnancy accounted for 21, 15 and 13 per cent of jobs left, family and health for 17, 13 and 12 per cent, and redundancy for 15, 18, and 18 per cent. These results suggest two possibilities; that life course position and child rearing responsibilities are a factor in differential non-employment, and that women's own labour market disadvantage also plays a part. These two dynamics may of course be inter-related. 45 per cent of women married to long term unemployed men were aged under 30, in contrast with 22 per cent of women married to securely employed men. Correspondingly, the percentages of homes with children under five for groups A, B anc C respectively are 52 per cent, 28 per cent and 35.5 per cent. Thus women in the most disadvantaged households are more likely to be negotiating difficult domestic circumstances than the women in other groupings.

Vulnerability to unemployment for men is concentrated in the lower age ranges, because of the harsh impact of economic decline on younger workers. One result is that the wives of the long term unemployed are more likely to have young children to contend with, but they are also likely to cite child care as a reason for not working. Other women, with children at equivalent ages, are far more likely to be in paid employment. We therefore need to identify some additional factor, which may operate in interaction with the presence and age of children, to account for the differences between women in the sample. One possibility is their overall labour market strength or weakness. The distribution of female occupational class is strongly related to male employment status. 70 per cent of women married to long term unemployed men entered semi- or unskilled occupations, or were without employment on leaving school, in contrast with only 30 per cent of women married to securely employed men.

Considering current or recent occupations we also find a concentration of such women in the five lowest ranked occupations; 48 per cent of women whose husbands are currently employed and 82 per cent of women whose husband are currently unemployed. Furthermore, women married to securely employed men were consistently more likely than those married to long term unemployed men to either maintain or improve upon their starting position, whilst the latter group not only started in lower status and lower paying occupations but are also more vulnerable to losing their occupational position. This, of course is also linked to child bearing patterns, though there is a possibility that a positive view of motherhood is linked to a negative experience in employment.

Whilst evidence indicates that the presence of young children is strongly associated with weak male labour force status, so too is the concentration of women in low paying occupations. It is this combination of factors, rather than male employment status per se, or the direct and unitary effect of the benefit regulations, which offers the fullest explanation of the concentration of male and female unemployment within households. Employment demand, occupational status and the presence of young children are not simply the context of household level relationships and decision-making, or 'strategies'; they are part of their substance. The internal organization of domestic life is in constant interaction with the labour market behaviour and experience of household members.

DOMESTIC ORGANIZATION

One of the consistent findings to emerge from the flurry of household related research in the eighties was the apparently non-negotiable nature of basic domestic divisions. Although predictions of change were part of early thinking on 'strategies' the general consensus to emerge from research is that of resistance – particularly among unemployed men – to any fundamental reorganization of gendered tasks in the home. There have been slight shifts (see Wheelock, 1990; Gershuny et al., 1986) which involve a greater degree of domestic involvement by men but no fundamental change. This has highlighted another problem with the 'strategies' approach; if basic economic logic, that is labour market change, does not prompt domestic re-organization this must be because of constraints at the level of a culture or ideology concerning acceptable gender behaviour.

To investigate this question in the present study a classification of domestic orientation was devised based on the two most firmly 'female' tasks; cooking and cleaning. This decision was to avoid the possibility that contrasting scores on different tasks would offset each other. The choice made was therefore one which would be most readily indicative of flexible or rigid responses on the part of the man. Combinations of never and occasionally were termed rigid; occasionally and often, traditional; often and always, flexible; with a fourth, 'joint' category. The resulting classification was then validated against the women's responses.

Although almost one quarter of unemployed men in the sample fall into the rigid category this is lower than for the other sample groups of the securely and insecurely employed, and considerably lower than those out of the market (health may be an issue here). The majority response in all groupings was 'traditional', but was ten per cent higher in the working as opposed to non-working population (50 as compared with 40 per cent). Flexible responses on the part of the man, though generally rather low, are more common among the unemployed, followed by those out of the labour force. For unemployed men the flexible response is neverthless out-weighed by the rigid response (18 as compared with 23 per cent) and this finding suggests the possibility of contrasting reactions to unemployment.

One obvious possible source of variation in male responses is the situation of the woman. The rigid response among men is particularly high (40 per cent) with male unemployment whilst female part time work. This seems likely to be a defensive response on the part of the man, particularly if the arrangement is deemed temporary, and part time work is often undertaken with a view to accommodating the woman's domestic obligations. One might expect that resistance would be harder to sustain when the woman is employed full time, and this is certainly so for most couples. Flexible responses by the man are by far the highest in cases of male unemployment and women's full time employment (39 per cent), though numbers here are small (only 28 cases), for reasons discussed earlier. The rigid response is lowest for this category, closely followed by couples in which both are employed full time. One perhaps predictable circumstance which seems conducive to a rigid reponse on the part of the man is the male sole or main earner pattern (that is employed men with non-employed or part time employed spouse), in which about one third of the men fall into the 'rigid' category. It would seem then that it is women's employment circumstances rather than the man's which are most likely to influence the organization of domestic labour, albeit to a limited degree.

HOUSEHOLD FINANCE

It could be argued that particular arrangements for financial decision making are part of a strategy for coping, though the household strategies literature has not generally engaged with this issue. Thus one neglected aspect of 'informal work' has been the work which goes into the management of household resources, and the nature of the relationship between both power over financial arrangements, and position in the labour market. These issues have been one aspect of the research reported in the present paper. The models used will be familiar to anyone with an interest in this area, and may be briefly characterized as follows (see Jan Pahl, 1983; and see Morris, 1990 for review): female managed whole wage – in which the woman is solely responsible for all household income; allowance system – in which the woman receives a regular allowance from the man; male managed whole wage – in which the man is solely responsible for all household income; joint management; independent management; other.

It was possible from the data to construct a random sample for the labour market categories outlined, which showed the female whole wage and joint management system to be almost equal at 35 and 40 per cent respectively, followed by the allowance system at 16 per cent. The next most frequent was the independent management at just under five per cent. Analysed by sample groupings the female whole wage occurred in a majority of couples experiencing long term male unemployment, and a smaller majority of couples outside the labour market, findings roughly consistent with qualitative work suggesting that this management type occurs with male unemployment, benefit dependence, and/or low overall income. Analysis of finance type by level of income shows the whole wage type to fall and the shared management type to rise as income rises.

When we consider finance management alongside employment status for both members of the couple the common argument that male unemployment is a determinant of the female controlled whole wage system is slightly weakened by the finding that it is most likely, at 70 per cent, where both members of the couple are unemployed, and falls to 54 per cent when the woman works part time. In the admittedly few cases where the woman works full time with male unemployment the shared management system takes over as the majority pattern. In general the results suggest a tendency towards the shared system when there are two incomes, whatever the source. This system is at its highest incidence, at 50 per cent, among couples where both members are employed, with no significant difference between part time and full time work for the woman. The allowance system shows no clear pattern except in being particularly low in cases of both male and female unemployment.

There was relatively high agreement (80 per cent) between couples as to who had the final say in financial decisions, with the highest incidence of women's final say occurring in cases of male unemployment, where either the woman is also unemployed or works part time. In such cases the woman's final authority outnumbers both joint and male final authority. The next highest incidence of women's final say is where both members of the couple are employed, though here joint final authority is the most common. Male final authority is highest where the man is employed and the woman is not, but again the incidence is lower than joint authority. Joint final authority is also, surprisingly, highest for couples with an unemployed man and full time employed woman. Women's authority within the home would appear to be greatest in cases which require close monitoring of low income. Their position is also enhanced, albeit to a lesser extent, by dual employment, though here joint authority is the majority outcome.

With regard to personal spending money, overall we find a difference of about ten per cent between men and women, to men's advantage. The difference between men and women with regard to whether they have any access to personal spending is when the man is employed and the woman is not. The percentages are respectively 82 and 62 per cent. The gap generally widens if we asked about a fixed and regular amount. The most marked contrast is in cases of long term male unemployment where only eight per cent of women have specified spending money, in contrast with 25 per cent of men. Other data from the survey seem to undermine any suggestion that the principal motivation for women's labour force participation is the desire for personal spending, for the common use of the wife's wage, regardless of the husband's circumstances, is for the collective benefit of the whole household. Housekeeping and the payment of bills together accounted for 75 per cent of responses about the main use to which the woman's wage is put.

Despite the clearly limited claims by women to a fund for personal spending it would seem from the above findings that economic change in recent years has been such as to enhance women's financial influence in the households. Admittedly, a good part of this influence is a result of their budgeting responsibilities in cases of male unemployment, a situation from which they rarely derive any personal advantage. The other, more positive, influence however has been the increased presence of married women in the labour market. It is the traditional and declining situation of a sole male earner in which female authority over final decisions is least likely.

CONCLUSION

This paper has presented an argument for the examination of 'household strategies' and structured inequality not simply in the context of labour market change, but also through the investigation of the household's location in a web of social contacts. There is strong evidence of informal support, and some suggestion that this is gender specific, whilst the informal flow of information is an important dimension of job search in which the long term unemployed are disadvantaged. Another aspect of the household strategy must be its internal organization, and here, the direction of influence will be two-way, with domestic constraints affecting labour market activity, but with employment structures and status also acting back upon the internal dynamic of the household. Whilst there are some signs of adjustment as a result of married women's continuing presence in the labour market, there has by no means been a revolution of gender roles within the home.

Economic decline and the restructuring of employment in Hartlepool has been shown in this paper to be mediated by a number of factors, principally informal structures of association and support, social class as defined by skill, state provisions in both housing and welfare, and established practices in both domestic labour and the management of household finance. Whilst the interaction between these different influences is complex and varied, there is clear evidence of structural constraints which limit the potential range of 'strategies' available. Whilst much of the literature on this topic stresses variety and innovation, such a view should perhaps be offset by a consideration of the constraints derived both from the gendered practices of everyday life and the institutional arrangements of the state and the labour market.

NOTES

1.   This research was funded by the ESRC, whose support is gratefully acknowledged. The present paper first appeared as 'Informal aspects of social divisions' in the *International Journal of Urban and Regional Research*, Vol. 18, 1994.
2.   The argument in this section owes much to the work of Sarah Irwin, Senior Research Officer on the project (see Irwin and Morris, 1993).

8 The Culture of Ownership and the Ownership of Culture

INTRODUCTION

Over the past decade the rate of innovation of managerial theory has apparently been enormous. Buzz words and key phrases have proliferated, we have seen organizations adopt the tenets of flexibility, quality, human resource management, whilst structurally changes have variously involved: outsourcing, downsizing, delayering, strategic partnerships, and lean production. All of these changes are usually related in one way or another to a view of increasing competition in national and international product markets. The stress upon competitive efficiency has effectively rendered the division between private and public organizations redundant, with internal markets and market testing driving changes in the public sector at least as far and fast as, and arguably more so than, in private industry. We are all encouraged to see ourselves as shareholders in Great Britain PLC, where the permanent revolution of managerially inspired change is seen as in no way a process of conflict. Rather the final triumph of private ownership, the apparent collapse of socialism and the perceived irrelevance of trade unionism are seen to bear witness to the culture of ownership.

Thus objective organizational changes are accompanied by a concern at developing the relevant subjectivities in employees. Any scope for delegitimation of the coupling of strategies of downsizing and a concern with human resources is nullified by reference to the logic of ownership and the market. For those who lose out by way of unemployment they are assured that it's nothing personal, besides they should see not the problem but the opportunity that being able to take one's own human capital onto the market may afford. For those who remain they must assume responsibility for their own contribution, and quality thereof, to the collective enterprise of the organization. They must be encouraged to own their own jobs and to see the importance of the market by way of relationships with customers, be they purchaser of the final product or service, or workers in other departments. In all of this the legitimacy to define the situation has passed to management, and is embedded in their world view of the ubiquity and efficacy of the market.

As far as employees are concerned they need to contribute to the organization as an active and willing player. Their views will be sought by management through the channels of consultative machinery, they have a vital role to play but it must be in terms of the machinery provided. Once again the stress is on consensus, for those employed, who still have their place in the sun, management have provided mechanisms through which to contribute and to be informed. As others have suggested though, such machinery has often had the role of supplanting the autonomous instruments of workforce participation through trade unions with a unitary culture:

> There is a strong argument to suggest that employee involvement does pose a significant challenge to the traditional influence of trade unions in the workplace. Employee involvement programmes provide an alternative source of information, of ideas and interpretation of workplace experiences, an alternative to that provided by the union. EI programmes actively promote a new culture in competition with the traditional explanations and culture communicated by the union.
>
> (Beale, 1994, p. 120)

Whilst the union may be seen to have traditionally been the organized voice of the workforce it is not only at this level that the supplanting legitimacy of managerially structured process and discourse is apparent. In Japan where the strength of workplace consensus and harmony is often stressed individual expression of disagreement with management and unions is often severely sanctioned. A number of accounts of the repressive reaction to individual dissent in Japanese factories are recorded by Armstrong, Glyn and Harrison in their book, *Capitalism Since 1945*. The point about examples such as these is that viewed from a distance such organizations appear as the epitome of consensus and harmony, and, as long as no challenges to managerially defined reality are forthcoming or that what dissent is expressed is done so within accepted procedure, then such a view is indeed warranted. However the terms of membership of such organizations are increasingly prescribed by management as are the acceptable and unacceptable avenues of dissent. In this way as Susan Wright has observed meaning itself is increasingly defined by management where:

> Culture has turned from being something an organization is into being something an organization has, and from being a process embedded in context to an objectified tool of management control. The use of the term culture itself becomes ideological.

(Wright, 1994, p. 4)

In this way organizational culture becomes less the emergent property of all members of an organization and rather becomes the prescribed and policed representation of a managed form. Now all of this sounds very sinister and perhaps conspiratorial, the subsumption of the autonomous culture of workers under managerial control, the systematization of informal and non-formal cultures of the workplace to a centralized design. What I want to argue is that such developments are, from a particular point of view, sinister and often conspiratorial but that within any empirical situation they are also beset with inherent contradictions. Whilst management do aim to set agendas and define organizational culture, wherever such attempts are situated on a real terrain of an empirical situation they always confront limits not only of active, and more characteristically passive, resistance of employees but also express the unanticipated outcomes of social action to the extent that management are never totally omniscient.

In short management never have perfect information about either the internal or the external environment of the organization and even if they had there is no reason to believe that they will always make the correct decision even in their own terms.

The dilemmas that stem from never being completely in control will be illustrated in the rest of the paper through a consideration of the historically evolving nature of skill and its relationship to training with particular reference to the construction and engineering industries.

THE HISTORICAL LEGACY

The problem with attempting conscious organizational change, of managing a transformation in organizational culture or indeed any other form of social engineering, is that unless the historical context, past structures, meanings and cultures are understood imposed innovations risk having less than the desired effect. Nowhere is this more true than with respect to innovations in training in the construction and engineering industries, where in recent years we have seen, from employers and government alike, a denigration of the 'traditional' apprenticeship system which in the context of the structural collapse of this system of training, particularly in construction, looks rather like trying to make a virtue out of a necessity. In order to understand both the strengths and weaknesses of the 'traditional' apprenticeship form of training we need to look at its historical origins. To see that it never was solely imposed by strong trade unions against employers' wishes, but rather that it represented a form of training in which both labour and capital found benefits (Roberts, 1993; More, 1980). Given this, it also represented the form which could unite both formal and non-formal aspects of organizational culture in a way which implied active input from both workers and employers.

The origins of the 'traditional' apprenticeship system in Britain have deep roots which stretch back to the industrial revolution and beyond. The hallmark of the first industrial nation was clearly etched on the emergent form of labour regime. In spite of the technological determinism of many of the accounts of the industrial revolution in Britain, it is clear that of great importance were the changes in the supervision and control of labour that were possible with the agglomeration of workers under the roof of an employer (Marglin, 1980; Thompson, 1967). Whilst the control of time worked remained a perennial problem in some industries the traditions of craft work did much to ensure performance to quality, and a degree of responsible autonomy in both apprentices and journeymen. In Britain then the collective application of labour rather than massive capital investment was the key to the birth of the first industrial nation. The role of skilled labour, in the absence of large amounts of new industrial technology was of particular importance. The nature of the control of this workforce often owed much to internalized notions of standards and performance. Thus as Elbaum (1991) has argued the honouring of indentured apprenticeships which could be legally enforced under common law as a binding contract well into the twentieth century owed more to moral than juridical control:

> More important than the legal status of apprenticeship were its quasi-legal, moral legitimacy and associated social sanctions.
>
> (Elbaum, 1991, p. 197)

This should not be seen as an appeal to idealism as such moral legitimacy was clearly bound up with material advantages which accrued to both capital and labour:

> Custom...assured that a completed apprenticeship would have recognized market value and gave youths an incentive to honour their indenture obligation...Apprenticeship indenture also had definite and significant efficiency advantages over an unstructured market for job training.... In particular apprenticeship facilitated employer financing of investment in job training for skills that were transferable between firms.
>
> (Elbaum, 1991, p. 195)

The advantages that accrued to employers included paying apprentices below the journeyman rate even in the latter years of training when they were contributing substantially to productivity. Also changes in technology, such as those in the Engineering industry in the early years of the twentieth century could increase the value of apprentice labour where skills levels were downgraded and apprentices thereby became fully productive at an earlier point. As one Glasgow manufacturer explained to R. H. Tawney in 1909, apprentices became less of a 'learner' of a trade and more 'productive boy workers' where:

Boys are being employed for their present commercial utility to the detriment of skill training.

(quoted in McKinley, 1991, p. 96)

McKinley goes on to observe that in spite of such market pressures acting against the development of a stable training instinct amongst employers apprentice training remained very popular with young workers, the failure to complete the period of indenture being less than ten per cent for the period of his study, 1897–1939. Indeed such a relatively small wastage rate continued in some industries, such as construction, well into the 1960s (Phelps-Brown, 1968). What then were the reasons for the popularity of serving one's time, even up to the present period? Clearly within the British labour market, which historically has displayed a high level of occupational segmentation located directly into the class structure (Inui, 1993), the relative pecuniary value of skilled work has remained high. In this sense apprentices for skilled trades are far better candidates for displaying deferred gratification than are middle class youth attending higher education. However it is arguably not just the financial rewards that accrue to those who have experienced apprenticeship and skilled work. Rather both the training and the craft are productive of an identity which incorporates a moral order and a form of the performance principle (primarily qualitative rather than quantitative) which inculcates an ownership of an occupation arguably stronger than most job identifications that human resource managers are able to instil. To understand these aspects of skilled identity we will need to look at some of the defining processes of assuming a skilled identity.

ASSUMING A SKILLED IDENTITY

A first point to be made is that such identities are not just free floating labels to be appropriated by anyone. As Charles More and several other theorists have told us, historically the largest single source of apprentice recruits was the relatives of workmen in the same firm or occupation (More, 1980; Roberts, 1993; Sabel, 1984). The importance of this form of embeddedness (Granovetter, 1985) as Roger Penn (1986) has suggested is that it enables a form of anticipatory socialization into skilled identities which begins in the community. Thus in industries like engineering and shipbuilding the occupation is 'owned' by the occupational community itself. The expectations about what the work involves and about the value of skilled work are part of a culture which exists relatively autonomously of any managerial framing. Thus in a segmented working class skilled work is seen to testify to the intellectual liveliness of the skilled workers, as Braun and Furhman noted in their study of German craft workers when asking a respondent about the difference between white collar and blue collar work.

> Blue collar workers have to do a bit more manual labour, but I don't think there is any difference in the economic situation. And that's how it should be. And I can't think of any differences [of styles of life]. For that matter there are no differences in the way they think. At least not in respect to craftsmen. But a simple laborer, he hasn't developed himself intellectually, so naturally he thinks differently. He can't see how things are connected, and if someone tells him something, he parrots it. But the intellectually alive person thinks his own thoughts, independently of whether he is a blue or white collar worker.
>
> (quoted in Sabel, 1984, p. 86)

The sense of pride in trade and social distinction are intimately connected in first hand accounts of undergoing apprenticeship and skilled work. The account of a toolmaker is given in the volume edited by Ronald Fraser (1969):

> I was just fifteen when I left secondary modern school to start an apprenticeship in a heavy engineering factory. The vividness of the transfer left an indelible imprint. One day I was a boy among boys – and girls – the next I was a boy among men....[In the toolroom] The atmosphere, while still being informally friendly, had a faint air of professionalism about it. Right from my first day there, it was made clear to me that toolmakers were craftsmen, and as such inherently superior to all the other workers except for a few other small and highly skilled trades. The ethos which has been graphically described as the 'aristocracy of labour' was

very present. At the centre of this ethos lay a strict adherence to very high standards of workmanship. The chief demand of the job was the attainment of linear accuracy to one-thousandth of an inch....This meant that firm command over the use of many types of measuring instruments constituted the essential skill required of the toolmaker.

(quoted in Fraser, 1969, p. 26)

In this view the identity of skilled work is variously located in the work, the community and wider conceptions of gender, respectability and dignity, this is one of the reasons why such identities have exhibited such a force over those socialized into them. Moreover it is this self confident autonomy of occupational ownership that management have often found hard to bear. Yet as Sabel (1984) has noted such an ethos has both negative and positive implications for management. On the negative side any dispute that assumes the contours of quantity versus quality in the production process will usually see management supporting the former and skilled workers supporting the latter. However more positively from a management point of view the craft ethos often obviates the need for close supervision. Again the pride in taking responsibility for a job comes through in the testimony of a joiner interviewed as part of my current research project when talking about the best time he can remember when serving his apprenticeship in a shipyard.

[The best time was]...When the strike was on....The apprentices weren't on strike. And we were left to do – to get on with the work ourselves and I was nearly out of me time then....And you were left to do it yourself and you knew you had to fend....by...stand by your own skill, or the job went down. When you reckon the job I did was...five hundred desks...for the full ship from...the Captain...right down to the crew...from cheap plywood...up to the top mahogany and teak and oak, stuff like this. And if you made one mistake and set one – set the machine up wrong once and ...all these gone through, thousands of pounds worth of stuff.

(Geoff Watkins, joiner, tape 10, 1995)

This account is interesting for several reasons. Firstly it bears testimony to the anomalous position of apprentices with respect to the employment relationship. They are in the employment relationship but their status as trainees absolves them from participation in formalized conflict between capital and labour, that is they don't go on strike. However in this case it is exactly that anomalous situation that enables this apprentice to experience the responsibility of skilled work before completing his apprenticeship. The well of meaning springs from the exercise of adult skilled responsibility in non-standard circumstances, where the transition from apprentice to skilled journeyman was effectively short circuited. Another account of a plumber in the building trade emphasized that he didn't mind doing the 'fetching and carrying' that was at least part of an apprentices life:

> No 'cos I knew I had to. 'Cos I'd been told by my dad what you'd got to do. 'Cos my dad worked in the building trade all his life and he says 'you'll start at the bottom...and you'll work up'. Why the kids today want to start at the top, they don't want to carry the can (tea making) and carry your tools and...That's all you done...No, I knew I had to do it.....as you tried harder they let you do...things by yourself and when you were by yourself it was great, you know, oh you were producing something, you know, it was a great feeling....It was brilliant!
>
> (Peter Atkinson, Plumber, tape 9)

Again this account draws together several aspects of apprenticeship that we have already discussed. The socialization into a skilled identity through the embeddedness of the labour market is clearly an issue when 'dad' tells you 'what you've got to do', thus the expectations taken by the new trainee into the workplace are realistic. Moreover what has since been pilloried by employers and government as the negative aspects of apprenticeship, the stress upon 'serving one's time rather than an emphasis upon competencies'(Carr and Roberts, 1994; Everett and Leman, 1995) can be seen in this account to carry with it significant positive features. Namely the cultivation of competency at a rate defined by the individual learner in the context of his peer group, continual assessment and mentoring of the most direct kind. Moreover the repetition in such accounts of the way in which one is always learning one's trade even after many years of experience suggests that within this culture the concept of the 'learning society' was alive long before educationalists and business people alerted us to its possibilities (Ball, 1991; Ranson, 1992).

In accounts such as these then the value of traditional apprenticeships is well attested and includes an interpenetration of the technical and social aspects of learning located in a moral framework which overlays the development of competence with maturational aspects and the rituals of transition between childhood and adulthood.

The popularity of time served apprenticeships with working people represents not only the pecuniary advantage of being able to assume skilled status, but also is shot through with moral issues of self worth and respectability that come from having a high degree of ownership of a culture which is an emergent property of the inter-relationship of capital and labour. If the apprenticeship system of training was so valued then the question emerges as to why in the industries with which I am concerned has it become imperilled, and in construction in particular almost extinct?

THE COLLAPSE OF APPRENTICESHIP

It is possible to argue that because time served apprenticeships involve both technical competence and aspects of a peculiarly moral career the viability of such relatively prolonged periods of training depended upon stability, and within this perceived benefits accruing to both sides of the employment relationship. Stability was necessary in a number of spheres. Firstly, a stable labour market was required in order to ensure the orderly re-production of skilled workers. This means that both over and under recruitment of apprentices can threaten skilled status. Thus in the engineering and shipbuilding industry in the 1920s the over recruitment of apprentices, and their retention at a higher rate than journeymen in the face of a difficult trading conditions, produced a response from labour which in some sectors led to a ban on recruitment of such cheap labour. Stability of labour markets should be seen to imply stability of industrial sector as well as absolute levels of fluctuation in response to the economic cycle. Stable communities have also been associated with successful apprentice training where socialization into skilled identities implies generational reproduction. Finally, stability in technical processes, or at least a slow rate of change, are conducive to the efficacy of traditional apprentice training where the mysteries of the trade are not deemed irrelevant by technical change.

Even a cursory glance at the areas where stability facilitates the optimum application of apprentice training will lead us to begin to appreciate some of the reasons for its demise. The collapse of manufacturing industry has eliminated many of the occupations that traditionally demanded skilled workers. As Richard Brown has noted in relation to the northern region:

> The region's labour force used to be dominated by skilled male manual workers in manufacturing industry and in mining, with those skills being based either on apprenticeship (as in engineering, shipbuilding and construction) or, in the cases of production workers in industries such as iron and steel, chemicals and mining, on training and long experience on the job....In terms of occupation men are now more likely to be in a managerial, professional or quasi-professional occupation than in traditional skilled manual work.
>
> (Brown, 1995, p. 172)

These objective shifts in the pattern of employment have done much to eradicate apprentice training as in some cases, such as shipbuilding, whole industries are closed down. Clearly in such circumstances industrial cultures are lost in circumstances where the call to 'own one's own career' sounds like rubbing salt into open wounds. However the pressure for increased competitiveness in a context of tight product markets is not conducive to the efficacy of work based training where 'present commercial utility' is pursued 'to the detriment of skill training'. This is true not only in terms of new apprentices but, as one foreman in the building trade indicated, it remains true where craftsmen transfer from another industry (which is the way that much of the training deficit has been handled in the northern region):

> I started six electricians yesterday. Now I want somebody who's gonna be up and running straight away, Monday

morning....because we haven't got time...it's contract work...I started them and they were on their notice...the minute I started them...'cos they've got three month contracts and...now I would love to think that was gonna go on for a long time but I can't guarantee it because I don't know whether we're going to win work and this that and the other. So, I can't take somebody on to be a tradesman and think well....he's got potential, in six months time he'll have learnt the ropes and he's got to be up and running.

(David Thompson, Foreman, tape 12)

This view of the problems for training created by extreme market pressure was repeated by several respondents. Furthermore the necessity of work based experience was again a much mentioned item in the 'training' of young people on YTS schemes or of older dilutee workers trained on employment training schemes:

What they should do with these fellas is say right...put them on there with the instructors...actually on the conditions they're going to work in, not coming out of a classroom onto a building site. 'Cos I mean that's chalk and cheese...you know it's alright standing there with a bench and doing the plumbing or the piping that's there. But once you get into a house and you're underneath floorboards, you know....It would appear that you get trained on isolated things. You'll get trained on...how to wire a socket, how to wire a light...how to build a wall, how to build a corner...but your real experience is when you get on the job...and you're putting it together, and you're wiring the lights, the sockets, the cooker, de de, de de...

(Alan Thompson, Electrician, tape 12)

A similar account was forthcoming from a plumber:

They haven't got the confidence...still it's great working in a class in college on a nice flat bench...doing this and doing that, but when you're up in lofts, or under the floor, it's completely different, you know what I mean? Oh yeah, it's great wiping the joints on a flat bench like that. But when you're lying on the floor upside down wiping a one and the spiders are crawling over you, it's a different sort of thing you know...You know they just haven't done it, you know. Yet they've got to get experience somewhere...

somehow. So you try to help them on a little bit like you know.

(Peter Atkinson, Plumber, tape 9)

The same authority goes on to say that dilutee workers can be spotted on a building site immediately:

You can see them a mile off. 'Cos they're all carrying new gear. It's a fact, they've all got brand new bags with brand new gear. Our gear's all battered and chipped and they've all got brand new gear...

The same point is made forcibly in the literature:

The tools themselves, how they are used, when they are used, and how they are taken care of, are important indicators of skill and expertise. The tools of a craftsman...reflect something of the worker himself. Much can be determined about a construction worker by the tools he has, how he displays them and how he uses them. When a new craftsman arrives on a job, he is evaluated by other workers prior to beginning work. The tools he brings with him serve as an accurate indicator of his ability and experience. Worn, quality tools reflect experience. Specialized tools, in addition to the required set of hand tools, reflect ability. (quoted in Steiger, 1993, p. 538)

NEW FORMS OF TRAINING

Acquiring expertise under the real conditions of the work, gaining confidence and the socialization into the culture of the workplace all require time and are relatively expensive. Arguably it is these features of the traditional apprenticeship that most importantly lie behind employers' and government's advocacy of other forms of competence based training. Recent figures on relative costs of training in the construction industry show that traditional apprentice training produces a net cost to an individual employer of £6,826 over the first three years of training (that is when gross cost is offset against productivity benefits and training grants). The comparable net figure for an individual employer partaking in a YT

Foundation Training Scheme is a benefit of £1,665 over the first three years of training (JAGNET, 1994). Thus by 1992 only approximately 5 per cent of first year trainees entered the industry by way of the traditional apprenticeship system, whereas 68 per cent of first year trainees were accounted for by the youth training route. The report went on to note that whilst YT 'has had some success in meeting its objectives' it nevertheless 'has a low cost, low skill image' (JAGNET, 1994, p. 31). However, the actual aggregate cost benefit of YT schemes and more recently Employment Training schemes aimed at young workers may be rather less than the theoretical figures indicate once wastage rates are taken into account. As Mizen has suggested:

> of those who joined during its (ET) first 18 months, just over half who were actually referred to the scheme completed their initial assessment period and, among those who stayed, more than two thirds left early. The latest evidence shows that this ambivalence has persisted, and by March 1992 only 41 per cent of trainees were completing their agreed training programme.
>
> (Mizen, 1995, p. 17)

It would appear then that a concern with cost and desperation to provide some form of training rather than a concern with rising skill needs is what recent alternatives to the traditional apprenticeship have been driven by. It was then not the technical superiority of Youth Training that has led to its eclipse of traditional apprentice training but rather its cost (or rather benefit) appeal to individual employers in a period of recession: a conclusion that is now apparently accepted by both employers and the government, as evidenced in the revival of the title of the 'modern apprenticeship' to replace the discredited title of youth training. According to the regional director of the Engineering Employers Federation apprenticeship in the modern usage should be differentiated from earlier understandings:

> Trainee, we feel, has been devalued by the government – YTS. We need a new word really, but we're using the name 'modern apprentice' and what modern means is no longer time serving. It is competence based.

Thus in September 1994 we have witnessed the launch of the 'Modern Apprenticeship'. The juxtaposition of 'modern' and 'apprenticeship' is no coincidence and yet does initially jar the officially sanctioned view of what apprenticeship has been seen to involve:

> Tradition is the matrix in which apprenticeship, one of the corner-stones of skills definition is embedded.
>
> (Hall and Miller, 1975, p. 27)

There are then several respects in which these recent training schemes differ from previous systems in relation to both structures and processes of training and the way in which such training relates to the division of labour in the workplace. Firstly, consequent upon a conception of the progressive accumulation of competencies the structural divisions that have traditionally existed between skilled, semi-skilled and unskilled work are to be replaced by a gradation of competence accredited levels, for example, NVQ (National Vocational Qualification) levels. At the level of the workforce this represents a diminution of the collective labourer in so far as traditional collective divisions between skill levels become replaced by more individuated competence certification. The literature produced by the National Council for Vocational Qualifications makes it clear that the only legitimate collective body it is concerned with is the company itself, workers are seen merely as individuated units of human capital which can be progressively empowered within the firm or the labour market. Thus:

> Within companies, NVQ's can assist in improving business performance and results; create a more flexible and motivated workforce; and introduce a targeted and systemic approach to training, resulting in a more economic use of resources to meet business objectives. NVQ's are by their very nature relevant to companies' objectives and human resource development strategies. They work effectively within and support human resource development strategies.... For individuals, an NVQ provides the clearest possible evidence that the holder can make a contribution to effective business performance. NVQ's encourage not only more and better learning opportunities, but also higher levels of

participation and achievement. Certification can be progressive throughout the unit structure of an NVQ.

(NCVQ, 1995)

For whilst it must be recognized that there was some gradation of 'achievement' in the traditional apprenticeship system these were not reflected at the point of production where craftsman identity was the 'master status' and skill was seen to reside both at the level of individual competence but also at the level of the collective worker. Similarly where individual wage packets did vary this was usually as a result of special payments and bonuses which accrued to individual jobs rather than to differences within the basic rates for a particular class of labour. In so far as the new training schemes emphasize individual progression up the competence hierarchy, that is then mirrored in the division of labour at work, they represent an attenuation of collective structural division and thereby a weakening of the focus for collective identity. If the traditional divisions around the axis of skill were divisive (Lane, 1976) the newer forms of individuated 'achievement' are positively fragmentary.

Underlying such developments is a changing conception of what is implied in the notion of a skilled workforce. There is a move away from seeing the skills of the workforce as residing within the collective worker to a concern with measurable individual competence. Surely then there is a manifest concern to render the training process and the subsequent division of labour more instrumentally rational when viewed from the position of capital. There is also however a particular vision of education which underlies such developments and that is the notion of human capital theory, the idea that individuals invest in their own human capital in order to secure competitive advantage in a market. Especially in a situation where training does not take place within the employment relationship the view is that training is an individual investment in which 'deferred gratification' should be rewarded not only by labour market advantage but in some senses more directly:

Individuals need to be motivated to maintain their employability and to increase their contribution to the performance of the economy. Motivators include modular qualifications and credit transfer, training credits, and grants and career development loans. Further tax relief should be given for individuals' expenditure on training and self-development.

(EEF, 1992, p. 22)

What is being offered then is not only a change to the structure of training and the division of labour that is driven by technical and instrumental rationality but changes that also incorporate a specific form of substantive rationality. For both at the level of the philosophy of education and, more pragmatically, at the level of industry in the absence of collective statuses the structure of training assumes and formally incorporates an image of individual career progression that is very different from that implied in being a time served craftsman. Where such individuated progression is inserted onto the real terrain of the shop floor it often clashes with longer established notions of the collective equality of given skilled statuses. An example of such an occurrence was given by a joiner who worked with 'up-graded' electricians and plumbers on maintenance work in the health service:

> They were alright at their own skill, and eventually somehow or other they wangled theirselves onto dental – doing dental repair work – then they went to college for three month and they came back as dental technicians (sic)...But the lads still class them as an electrician and a plumber....But see when they were off sick or on holiday or there was too much work for them, Colin, the other plumber, went and did the same job, the plumber....[I had to go] to Hartlepool, and there's a unit to go in the top to be fit and cut. So we went through with him...he went up the stairs and I followed him up. I was a few seconds behind him. And I heard him say to the girl behind the reception, 'Oh I'm Mr ——, dental technician, I've come to fit...I've brought my joiner with me'. So I just turns straight round, I says 'Hey boy', 'cos he's only about 26, I says, 'Hey boy, don't class me as *your* joiner'. ...I said, 'You are a plumber, skilled...I'm a skilled joiner', I said, 'and I'm a lot older than you are, I've got more experience, show me respect'. I said, 'I've been sent to fix this unit because you can't do it'....(replies) – 'Oh I didn't meant it that way – Geoff'; I said, 'you did'. And I said, 'If you and I want to get on', I said, 'lose that attitude straight away with

me'. And he showed us where this thing wanted to be, so he
went somewhere...and the young girl come in, she says, 'I'm
pleased somebody brought him down'.

(Geoff Watkins, Joiner, tape 10)

A further change in the structural context of training ex-
acerbates these tendencies and that is the fact that, in spite of
the intention of those promoting the modern apprenticeship,
most initial training in these two industries now takes place
outside of the employment relationship (Everett and Leman,
1995). Clearly, this serves to encourage the individuated conception of human capital theory in an increasingly competitive market. Again we should be clear about the problematic
position of traditional apprentices in terms of the employment
relationship, especially those on block release to FE colleges,
often encouraged to join the student's union at college and
exempt from most industrial action at work. Nevertheless such
an anomalous position vis a vis the employment relationship
was seen as temporary and the 'preaching' of the training
officer on issues such as industrial relations was more than
counteracted by the less formal incorporation into collective
understanding via the socialization into skilled identities.

If the structure of initial training and increasingly its location outside the employment relationship militates against the
continuation of collective structural divisions of the workforce
then this tendency is reinforced by another tendency within
competence orientated training schemes. Specifically the
inclusion in most modular training programmes of the ability
to further train the competencies to others represents a
managerial codification and formalization of on the job training: a move away from being initiated into the tricks of the
trade to being trained in a managerially defined package of
competencies. Not only does this attempt to remove the normative aspects of being socialized into a skilled identity but it
also would appear to represent an arena in which a classic case
of the separation of conception and execution (Braverman,
1974) is being enacted. In other words the knowledge of craft
is no longer the possession of the collective worker but has
been codified into specific competencies by management, the
training of which is then also codified and subject to calcula-
tion and measurement.

However, it should not be assumed that these developments are without contradiction. Voices on both sides of industry are cautious of the possibility that competencies up to 'skilled status' can be taught without the trainee having shop floor experience. The clearest expression of the problems involved in this type of approach was suggested by a plasterer who when speaking of the deficiency of YT trained labour lamented not only their lack of rounded skills but more especially the fact that a high proportion of them lasted only a 'couple of weeks' on site. He explained that not only was it the case that they were ill equipped to practise their trade on the real terrain of a building site, but also that for many of these young lads they did not know how to respond to the practical jokes and 'wind ups' perpetrated on them on site. It is precisely these aspects of the socialization into skilled identities, both the ability to know and cope with what a job in its entirety actually demands and being able to deal with the culture of the shop floor that Roger Penn has directed our attention towards (Penn, 1986). It is these informal or non-formal aspects of shop floor based knowledge that the competence based approach is not only indifferent to, but is actively hostile toward. In short it is the embedded nature of the traditional apprenticeship system that is being exorcized in the move to substitute competencies for 'time served' knowledge. Most of those within the industries we are studying would agree that the 'traditional' apprenticeship did instil more real skills than recent attempts such as YT; its pitfalls however are variously seen, by management, to be those of prohibitive cost and/or the substantive content of the culture that was learnt alongside technical skills.

CONCLUSIONS

This look at some of the themes surrounding the issues of training and flexibility in the engineering and construction industries has suggested that the discourse developed around the issue of training has sought to do several things. Firstly it has sought to devalue the efficacy of the traditional forms of apprenticeship through mobilizing technocratic forms of discourse meant to render the image of the traditional apprenticeship as old fashioned, espousing the need to move from 'serving one's time to a more competence based approach'. However recent attempts at such new vocational training have faltered largely because the quality of training delivered is not generally perceived to have been as of as high a standard as that offered in the traditional form of apprenticeship. The objective environment in which YT was offered almost guaranteed that this should be the outcome. In particular the inability of the industries concerned to provide their own training schemes at a level sufficient to service their own requirements ensured that the support offered by state funding resolved the ambiguous status of training as either investment or cost firmly in the direction of the latter. Similarly, initial research into the pilot schemes of the modern apprenticeship report that employers retain reservations that the level of funding supplied from the public purse is insufficient to ensure a high level of training (Everett and Leman, 1995, p. 265). As has been shown in another context the definition of a process as a cost rather than an investment has a determined effect on the form of accounting deployed and thereby the material possibilities of the provision itself (Roberts and Wilkinson, 1991). In this way the perception of YT as being cheap if not cheerful was based on a material reality; the most potent driving force behind this provision was not the technical or instrumental rationality of the superiority of competence based training over traditional apprentice training but rather desperation to produce some training as cheaply as possible. Others have also noted the role of YT in keeping down the unemployment figures (Hollands, 1994).

The present examples of specific competence based training do not validate the thesis that what has occurred is the splitting of instrumental rationality from substantive rationality. Rather the present developments seem to speak of a change in the nature of the substantively rational basis of the training of occupations around the axis of skill. The language game being played attempts to eschew any notion of substantively rational criteria underlying current developments. What I am suggesting however is that rather than the dominance of instrumental rationality in a politically neutral form what we are witnessing is a fundamental shift in the educational basis of skills training, involving the purging of the non-formal and informal aspects of the socialization into skilled identities. The active input of the collective worker is being severely diluted as both training and its delivery are codified and formalized along lines dictated by management. In terms of the rationality underlying contemporary changes then we have not witnessed the eclipse of substantively rational forms by those of instrumental rationality, rather we have witnessed the interpenetration of substantive and instrumental elements (Munch, 1987) incorporated within a public discourse of instrumentality dressed up as common sense. Ironically, given that managers are not omniscient and that formal systems of communication are often subverted through their location on the contested terrain of the 'shop floor' (Garrahan and Stewart, 1992), the centralization of levels of competence attainment associated with the fragmentation of levels of attainment, if successful, could lead not to flexibility but to inflexibility. If unsuccessful, the potential for the divergence between accredited training and actual practice will continue and possibly further develop.

Whether the new initiatives, such as the modern apprenticeship, will eventually be judged as successfully delivering training or not will depend not only on the technical skills imparted but also on the way in which workers are socialized into their occupations. Are they to be seen merely as individuated and passive reflexes of managerially defined concerns or is the collective worker itself to be credited with an active and dynamic part in the creation and reproduction of workplace culture? A culture which is seen as something that organizations are, and thereby as an emergent property of all agents (Meek, 1988), real ownership, rather than seeing culture as something that is provided strictly by management design. The former speaks of the ownership of culture, the latter of the culture of ownership.

9 'Empowerment' or 'Degradation'? Total Quality Management and the Service Sector

INTRODUCTION

The aim of this chapter is to discuss the introduction of Total Quality Management (TQM) to paid employment within the service sector of the British economy. Following a brief review of existing literature on, and research into, the phenomenon of service sector TQM, the paper will draw upon original ethnographic research carried out by the author within the service sector of north-eastern England. An analysis will be undertaken of the nature and experience of work within two service sector organizations, where TQM had been introduced prior to the research process.

On the basis of our research findings, it will be argued that much of the existing literature which discusses the impact of TQM within the service sector has produced an overly-polarized debate. It will be suggested that the majority of writing on the subject can be divided between 'the optimistic' and 'the pessimistic'. It is claimed by a wide variety of authors that TQM enhances the work autonomy of service employees, thereby affecting their 'empowerment'. However, while arguing that TQM represents a sophisticated and ideological managerial *attempt* to actually *erode* service employee discretion and facilitate 'total' managerial control, it will be contended that authors who stress the 'degradation' of labour as an outcome of TQM also present an overly-simplistic portrayal.

'THE OPTIMISTIC PERSPECTIVE' – TOTAL QUALITY
MANAGEMENT AND 'THE DISCOURSE OF ENTERPRISE'

The phenomenon of TQM has rapidly and dramatically grown
within work organizational life during the late 1980s and into
the 1990s. Wilkinson and Willmott (1995) report that total
quality initiatives are currently present within 75 per cent of
all companies in the United Kingdom and the United States.
They also observe that 90 per cent of all chief executives
regard such initiatives as crucial to the financial success of
their organizations. Originally designed as a managerial
programme for implementation within manufacturing industry, via the pronouncements of the 'quality gurus' (for
example Juran, 1979; Crosby, 1980; Deming, 1986), TQM is
now increasingly applied to the expanding British service
sector. For example, McCabe et al. (1994) found that, within
financial services, 90 per cent of organizations have one or
more quality initiatives. Such developments can be linked to a
new generation of 'quality gurus' who prescribe the introduction of TQM to the service sector (for example Dale et al.,
1990; Howcroft, 1991; Boaden and Dale, 1993). It has been
suggested that TQM constitutes one of the most far-reaching
forms of organizational restructuring within the service sector
(Kerfoot, 1995; Walsh, 1995).

The writing of the 'quality gurus' constitute a part of what
Du Gay and Salaman (1992) have labelled 'the discourse of
enterprise'. This encapsulates a unique alliance of academic
(both managerially-orientated and sociological) and political
arguments which are all grounded in a *perception* of profound
contemporary social, economic and political change (for
example Piore and Sabel, 1984; CBI, 1988; Clegg, 1990;
Bauman, 1992). It is alleged within this discourse of enterprise
that, due to wider social change, the mass production of
standardized goods and services will no longer satisfy *consumer*
needs and expectations. It is widely accepted within the
discourse of enterprise and beyond that there has been a 'fragmentation and differentiation of demand for goods and
services...a change in consumer values and behaviour' (Du
Gay and Salaman, 1992, p. 617). We are apparently witnessing
the emergence of differentiated, discerning and quality-
conscious consumers (Clegg, 1990).

Acceptance of this argument involves accepting the necessity for radical transformation of work organizational structures and processes and the experience of paid work. The discourse of enterprise fundamentally contends that, due to external 'environmental' developments, we are witnessing the erosion of bureaucratic and hierarchical control and regulation both inside and outside of work organizational life. Furthermore, it is suggested that this is necessary to enable individual, organizational and nation-state development and prosperity within a rapidly changing global context. At the level of the work organization, it is asserted that the removal of bureaucratic forms of organization, hierarchical control of the workforce and Taylorist task specialization is vital to enable organizational survival within an ever-changing world (Sabel, 1982; CBI, 1988; Clegg, 1990). In short, if consumers are becoming more enterprising and 'quality conscious' – demanding differentiated goods and services, expressing everchanging needs and expectations – then work organizations must develop structures and processes which enable them to respond to this situation.

Radical organizational change has been charted as a response to the *perceived* changing economic, social and political environment. It would seem that the discourse of enterprise has been accepted as rational by those with work organizational power (Du Gay and Salaman, 1992). In particular, the implementation of TQM, as prescribed by much of the management-orientated literature within the discourse of enterprise, appears to have been authorized by senior management within the service sector as a response to the 'external' environment.

Central to quality-focused managerial initiatives within the service sector is an emphasis on 'the customer'. It is suggested that the only way in which organizations can survive within an increasingly competitive environment is to develop ways of working which enable the anticipation and satisfaction of the ever-changing needs and desires of the enterprising sovereign consumer. TQM supposedly constitutes one of these ways of working. TQM programmes seek to enhance the competitive position of work organizations through the establishment of qualitatively differentiated goods/services, in relation to the competition within the particular market and in line with customer expectations. This commits the entire enterprise to a philosophy of continual improvement in the quality of goods/services provided to customers:

> The real test of quality management is its ability to satisfy customers in the marketplace. TQM assumes that quality is the outcome of all activities that take place within an organization. Accordingly, all functions and all employees have to participate in the improvement process and, to ensure this, organizations need both quality systems and a quality culture. (Hill, 1995, p. 36)

Within the service sector, quality of service is increasingly perceived as *a*, if not *the*, key 'differentiation strategy' by management (Porter, 1990; Howcroft, 1991; Boaden and Dale, 1993). This means:

> The supplier of the service is attempting to establish his (sic) product as unique compared with those of his competitors by offering a better standard of service. (Howcroft, 1991, p. 12)

According to Howcroft, an essential characteristic of TQM is the realization by senior management of the need for *active management* of the quality improvement process, for example through monitoring the worker-customer relationship where the provision of a service involves worker/customer interaction, as in banking or telephone sales. The primary objective of this active management is to 'enhance customer perceptions of quality of service actually received and thereby equate them with customer expectations' (Howcroft, 1991, p. 13). Customer satisfaction is the overriding goal:

> In the...service industries...customer satisfaction is now defined as critical to competitive success, because of its importance in achieving high levels of customer retention. Quality is thus defined...in terms of giving customers what they want, yet at the same time traditional methods of control are too overtly oppressive, too alienating and too inflexible to encourage employees to behave in the subtle ways which customers define as indicating quality service, many of which – subtleties of facial expression, nuances of verbal tone, or type of eye contact – are difficult to enforce

through rules, particularly when the employee is out of sight of any supervisor. (Du Gay and Salaman, 1992, p. 621)

In relation to the service sector, one can distinguish between two types of quality. 'Technical' (Groonroos, 1984; Lewis, 1988) or 'hard' (Hill, 1991) quality includes product knowledge and knowledge of operational systems, while 'functional' or 'soft' quality comprises staff behaviour, attitude and appearance during interaction with internal or external customers. The delivery of the latter can often involve the performance of what Hochschild (1983) has termed 'emotional labour'. Clearly, the aim of TQM is to enhance both forms of quality in terms of the 'service' provided by employees to customers, by employees to work colleagues (the notion of the 'internal customer'), by management to employees and employees to management.

The discourse of enterprise, and in particular the prescriptive TQM literature, suggest that the delivery of both technical and functional quality can only be 'managed' by encouraging worker spontaneity, responsiveness and autonomy. Only service *employees*, who constantly interact with customers, are in a position to discern the needs and expectations of individual customers and thus define both technical and functional quality. It is suggested that both technical and functional quality are stifled by bureaucratic control. 'The "solution" is to seek to change behaviour, values and attitudes through culture change rather than structural change, and to measure the success of these programmes through customer feedback' (Du Gay and Salaman, 1992, p. 622).

For business success, the discourse of enterprise encourages the 'empowerment' of all organizational members in order to add 'value' – both to the company and themselves. It is claimed by the discourse of enterprise that managerial initiatives such as TQM 'empower' workers, offering them autonomy and responsibility. 'Control. That is what the "power" in "empowerment" is all about. The control of the activity we call work' (Price, 1993, p. 5). TQM has supposedly stimulated a process of making employees responsible and accountable for the content and quality of their own jobs. 'If TQM is applied as its proponents suggest, the focus for responsibility and quality is in the hands of those who do the work' (Wilkinson et al., 1991, p. 6).

'THE PESSIMISTIC PERSPECTIVE' – TOTAL QUALITY
MANAGEMENT AND 'TOTAL MANAGERIAL CONTROL'

The dominant representation of the impact of TQM upon
employment experience, through the discourse of enterprise,
has been challenged. Sewell and Wilkinson (1992) argue that
TQM is the most recent, and the most effective developed to
date, of managerial strategies to secure control of the labour
process.[1] Sewell and Wilkinson utilize a Foucauldian analyti-
cal framework to explain the implementation of TQM. In
particular, they focus upon the concept of the 'Panopticon'
(Foucault, 1977). The Panopticon engenders a particular surveillance process which effects total control over a subject population. Sewell and Wilkinson argue that the introduction of
TQM to work organizations is premised on 'direct and
detailed control, ideally "total" control...characterized by a
low degree of trust and strong management discipline...[and]
characterized by systems of surveillance which more closely
approximate the Panopticon than do those characteristic of
the traditional bureaucratic pyramid' (Sewell and Wilkinson,
1992, pp. 267–77).

This critical challenge to the discourse of enterprise notes
that employees, as a consequence of TQM, may be given some
discretion over the delivery of technical and functional quality.
However, simultaneous with such 'autonomy' or 'empowerment' is increased and detailed managerial supervision and
evaluation – that is surveillance – of, for example, em-
ployee/customer, employee/employee or employee/ management interaction. It is suggested that TQM embodies the most
complete form of workplace surveillance developed to date.
Consequently, service employees have little choice but to exercise discretion in ways which serve the interests of management (articulated around a particular definition of 'quality
service'). This will be labelled 'positive discretion'.[2]

The 'change in behaviour, values and attitudes' of employees which is supposedly a concomitant of TQM within the
service sector is, according to Sewell and Wilkinson, *enforced*
by *structures* of managerial surveillance and control within the
workplace, rather than being driven by worker autonomy.
Moreover, Sewell and Wilkinson are concerned that such
managerial control and degradation of labour, as it includes

cultural manipulation, can distort the very self-identity of TQM employees:

> In the same way that the Panopticon relied on the subjects of surveillance being aware that they were being watched...the knowledge that...basic work activity is subject to constant scrutiny...combined with the [possibility] of immediate public humiliation...[accompanying] the exposure of...[workers'] divergencies, invokes a powerful disciplinary force...the constant scrutiny of a Panoptic gaze which penetrates right to the very core of...[workers'] subjectivity creates a climate where self-management is assured...the controlling function of middle management has...been incorporated into the consciousness of [workers]...In Foucault's terms...[they] have become bound up in a power situation of which they are themselves the bearers. (Sewell and Wilkinson, 1992, pp. 283–4)

It can be argued that service employees are particularly vulnerable to the dangers outlined above. As already noted, the delivery of functional quality can involve the performance of emotional labour – the management of human feeling within paid employment in order to 'create a publicly observable facial and bodily display' (Hochschild, 1983, p. 7). Drawing upon Hochschild, we can suggest two main ways in which employees may attempt to manage feeling within the labour process: through *surface acting* and *deep acting.* 'Surface acting' involves 'pretending to feel what we do not...we deceive others about what we really feel, but we do not deceive ourselves' (Hochschild, 1983, p. 33). This involves changing how we outwardly appear within the workplace. 'Deep acting' involves 'deceiving oneself as much as deceiving others...we make feigning easy by making it unnecessary' (p. 33). In other words, one's feelings can be 'managed' in order to match any outward 'display' demanded by the labour process.

Increased managerial attention, via TQM, to the nature of social interaction within the service labour process clearly has implications for the emotional experience of the workers concerned. Hochschild suggests that such managerial programmes within the service sector often represent increased managerial demands for deep acting amongst employees. In short, in conditions of intense and increasing competition within the service sector, based upon the *quality* of service delivered, Hochschild argues that 'functional' quality of service becomes the differentiating factor. Not only is it notoriously difficult for service organizations to compete in terms of substantive services (technical quality) offered (Howcroft, 1991) but, as the 'quality competition' increases, consumers (either internal or external) become more adept at distinguishing between a 'genuine' quality service in functional terms (that is a service provider whose feeling matches the .appropriate attitude, tone of voice and appearance, and who is deep acting) and a 'feigned' quality service in functional terms (a service provider who is merely surface acting). Hochschild argues that the introduction of managerial programmes such as TQM, within the service sector, simultaneously demand deep acting rather than surface acting from employees. This opens up the *possibility* of such employees experiencing 'emotional alienation' – here it is suggested that it is possible to become estranged from the objects of emotional labour (our facial and bodily expressions, feelings and emotions) in the same way as it is possible to become estranged from the objects of physical labour (our bodily actions) and mental labour (our thoughts).

We shall now attempt to contribute to a rather polarized debate on the impact of TQM within the service sector on the basis of ethnographic research into two service organizations within north-eastern England.[3] Research was conducted into two particular labour processes. Both of these – the telephone sales operation of a major British airline ('Flightpath') and the work of branch bank clerks within two medium-sized branches of a major British clearing bank ('Friendlybank') – had been affected by the introduction of TQM prior to the research process. The research included: semi-structured, audio-taped interviews throughout both organizations; non-participant observation of both labour processes (including 'listening in' to, and sitting in on, employee-customer interactions); observation of training processes, team meetings and 'working group' meetings; and examination of relevant written documentation. All levels and grades of staff were represented within the interviewing and observation process. The gender mix of those interviewed and observed was as representative as possible.

This chapter can do no more than offer *indications* as to the impact of TQM upon employee experience of paid service work. It cannot be claimed that our findings are in any way representative of the experience of all service workers under the influence of TQM. However, it can be argued that an examination of these particular cases forms an important contribution towards understanding the changing nature of paid employment within Britain, and north-eastern England in particular. The latter, in a similar way to many other parts of the nation, but perhaps in a more dramatic manner, has undergone rapid economic and occupational transformation and is still struggling to come to terms with its new identity. The north-eastern economy was formerly dominated by coal, shipbuilding and heavy industry. Even in 1971, manufacturing and work in the primary industries still accounted for 40 per cent of employment in the region (Robinson, 1988). This situation has been transformed beyond all recognition. For example, on Tyneside, only 17 per cent of the labour force work in manufacturing. Over 70 per cent are employed within the service sector (Tyneside TEC, 1993). The last decade has also witnessed an increase in female employment within the north-east. Women now make up nearly half the labour force and are predominantly employed in the service sector. Banking and telephone sales, the latter is the fastest growing industry on Tyneside (Morrison, 1994), can be seen as emblematic of the changing shape of work in the north-east. As we have already noted, much of this employment has also been affected by the introduction of TQM.

THE RESEARCH SITES

Flightpath

Research at Flightpath focused upon the labour process of Telephone Sales Agents (TSAs). The labour process is concerned with the vast array of travel-related services provided by Flightpath. This primarily involves agents receiving, and dealing with, calls from people who are interested in purchasing or reserving a particular service or combination of services. TSAs work within a large 'open plan' office

(a 'community'). They are equipped with a headset, a telephone system and a computer system. TSAs themselves push a
button when they wish to receive a call. 'Dealing with' calls
usually involves placing the caller on hold and accessing particular information from the computer system. Full-time TSAs
work an eight hour shift constituted by constant call taking.
They are entitled to a ten minute 'machine break' every three
hours and a forty minute 'lunch break' within this shift. The
centre is open from 06.00 until 22.45 and shifts rotate within
this period. Many of the calls are from travel agents (acting on
behalf of individuals) as well as direct customers. According
to Flightpath Telephone Sales Worldwide management, the
overall aim of this work is to transform as many of the calls as
possible into actual bookings and sales. It is a worldwide operation with international calls received. Flightpath Telephone
Sales Worldwide has five regional centres throughout Britain.
There is also a centre in New York, USA.

Within the centre studied, Telephone Sales Agents are
divided into teams of nine. They are managed by one Sales
Team Supervisor (STS). In turn, a team of eight supervisors is
responsible to one Sales Team Leader (STL). STLs, as a team,
are responsible to the unit manager of the telephone sales
centre studied. S/he is then accountable to the head of
Telephone Sales UK. Everyone within the centre is rewarded
through performance-related pay. Each STL manages a community – one office of TSAs consisting of eight teams of nine
agents each managed by one STS. Of all TSAs, 81 per cent are
female while 52 per cent of STSs are female. Above this level,
only one STL is female. During the research period, the
telephone sales centre studied became the biggest of all
Flightpath Telephone Sales Worldwide centres.[4]

Friendlybank

Here, research was conducted into the labour process of
'personal banking' clerks within two regional branches of
Friendlybank. Due to a restructuring of banking operations,
which was integral to the introduction of a quality programme, personal banking clerks are largely responsible for
dealing with the *immediate* business and enquiries of personal
customers only. Bulk cash processing, the majority of customer

telephone calls, administrative work which arises from customer business and enquiries, the responsibility for branch security and the business and enquiries of branch commercial customers have all been transferred to other elements within the Friendlybank network. These tasks were all formerly undertaken within all branches.

Personal banking clerks are organized into 'Personal Sales Teams' within the branches. Each team is made up of 'Customer Service Officers' (CSOs – formerly known as 'Cashiers') and 'Personal Advisors' (PAs). The team is managed by a 'Customer Service Manager' (CSM). Each team is hierarchically structured. Following the CSM., there are: Senior Personal Advisors (SPAs); PAs; Senior Customer Service Officers (SCSOs); and CSOs. Clerks are remunerated according to their seniority. Two personal sales teams were studied. All personal clerks, excepting one CSM, one SPA and one CSO, were female.

TQM AND EMPLOYEE EMPOWERMENT

Flightpath as a whole has long recognized the importance of 'quality' customer service (Hamill and Davies, 1986; Lewis, 1988). They have been running customer care campaigns since 1983 'to enhance the quality of service and increase staff morale' (Lewis, 1988, p. 72). However, Telephone Sales Worldwide management argued that it was only during the 1990s that they were able to implement quality management 'throughout and as part of their structures and processes' (Unit Manager, Newcastle).

Telephone sales is one unique part of Flightpath where employee/customer interaction and the generation of revenue occur instantaneously. TSAs are often the first contact a prospective customer will have with the company. Speaking to the whole of Newcastle Telephone Sales, the head of Telephone Sales Worldwide commented:

> Your job is as important as any other in the company, the smile that you send down the phone can be vital...I cannot think of another part of the company where service and the generation of revenue come together. (1994)

The importance of quality customer service is recognized within the mission statement of TSW:

> We in telephone sales will together achieve profitable growth in sales through professional delivery of quality customer service. (TSW, 1994)

Importantly, *quality* and *professionalism* are defined by the customer. 'Quality is in the eye, and the *ear*, of the beholder' (Unit Manager, Newcastle, 1994). Providing quality customer service entails responding to customers' changing needs and expectations, thus ensuring satisfaction and loyalty:

> probably the most important goal that we have is that we have to establish a customer intimacy that goes beyond our competitors. Customer intimacy. That is, going beyond just reacting to what the customer is wanting, if we can take it that next step we are going to be ever so much better and if we do that then the difference is our competition is going to be fighting after us and not after our customers and that is really what we want to see. (Head of Telephone Sales Worldwide, 1994)

Customer satisfaction through the provision of continually improving quality service is a clear differentiation strategy of Flightpath Telephone Sales Worldwide.

Similarly, at Friendlybank, it was explicitly stated by all levels of management that the restructuring described above and the processes of recruitment and training for, and supervision and evaluation of, the personal banking labour process have been 'clearly based upon the principles of total quality management' (CSM, 1992). Bank management claimed that the major aim of the restructuring and banking operation as a whole was to continually improve the knowledge, meeting and anticipation of 'customers' needs' (CSM, 1992). Prior to the implementation of TQM, it was felt that the bank was insufficiently 'customer focussed'. The timing of the move 'from recognizing this...to actually doing something about it' (CSM, 1993) was shaped by the increasingly competitive nature of the banking and financial services industry (Howcroft, 1991; Cressey and Scott, 1992; Boaden and Dale, 1993; Dignan, 1995). Friendlybank management stressed that one vital element of this competitive environment is increasingly differentiated and sophisticated customer needs and expectations within a shrinking consumer market:

> I think banks generally, led by Friendlybank, are becoming clear that a relationship with customers is more important than perhaps volume of customers...I think what you are finding is that customers are becoming more sophisticated in their requirements and are generally starting to shop around...relationship management is now important. It's a lot harder for them to walk away from you if you've got a relationship. (CSM, 1993)

In line with the discourse of enterprise, management at both Flightpath and Friendlybank claim that TQM is enabling the delivery of quality service to customers through the 'empowerment' or autonomy of service employees, particularly within the worker/customer interface. This was seen as the main way in which Flightpath Telephone Sales could establish a 'competitive edge'. The perception of Newcastle Telephone Sales management is that 'genuine' quality service or 'customer intimacy' will only emerge from 'natural', 'spontaneous' employee-customer interaction – 'equal emotional exchanges' (Hochschild 1983) – and, by implication, the *non*-performance of emotional labour. According to management, the facilitation of agent autonomy or 'empowerment' is integral to delivering such quality:

> We must respect that agents know what they are doing, that is the bottom line, we must never forget that, they do know, they know exactly what passengers want, what they have been through, exactly how they are feeling and what is going to work...we do encourage people to be themselves on the phone. There is nothing worse than phoning up and listening to that awful spiel that you get with a lot of companies and I think that people (customers) do genuinely feel that they are speaking to another human being which is quite an advantage certainly in a selling context because they can identify with that person, we do give people room to build rapport and you know some people do want to talk at length whilst they are making a booking. There is no harm in that, it is still a very cost effective way for us to sell

our product, we are quite happy with that – our culture does support that. (STS, 1994)

Similar arguments were advanced by Friendlybank management. The following comments are representative:

officers' attitudes and feelings are crucial to what we are trying to achieve...we cannot supervise everything that they do, they have to be able to react to customers in the correct fashion and believe in the bank enough to constantly provide quality service...we cannot do it for them...we want our staff to develop a relationship with customers, build a rapport and get to know them...we want that interaction to be as natural as possible...we don't want people to have a forced smile or forced to be friendly...we want people who are naturally friendly...to be themselves so there is no front to see through. (CSM, 1993)

Both managements argued that the 'systems and techniques' (Boaden and Dale, 1993) of TQM – selection and training processes, a particular form of work organization (teamworking), communicative and participative structures and mechanisms for measuring the quality improvement process all 'empowered' agents/officers to take responsibility for the delivery of technical and functional quality. Thus, at Friendlybank:

Training involves talking about customers' perception of you personally and how you come over to customers. We do role play and go into body language, how you relate to customers and how you interpret how they are feeling...we see training as vital, as perhaps the most important thing that enables our staff to meet customers' needs...we provide constant training for established staff away from the branch as our products are always changing and so are our customers' needs. (CSM, 1993)

Teamworking at Flightpath means:

You're not just a number, because you're one of nine rather than 250, you get more autonomy. You get that feeling that you are close...you feel that 'I can make a decision more'...the teamworking system means that you know who your manager is...it facilitates communication...communication is absolutely essential. One day you can go on the phone with a customer and say this is the right thing, the next day it's not...if you get the information wrong, you're not delivering the expectations of the customer and you won't sell because of it. ...Teamworking here is about being recognized and knowing who you report to and who manages you well so that you have got constant dialogue with them. We call the supervisory role 'counselling and coaching'. (Unit Manager, 1993)

According to both managements, such systems and techniques have helped to shape, and have been shaped by, a change in the culture of the organization (whereby the norms, values and identities of employees become committed to delivering quality service to customers). They have also supposedly been instigated by important managerially-inspired infrastructural developments, such as the communication of what quality service is, why it is important and how it can be delivered.

Perhaps the most contentious of managerial claims at Flightpath and Friendlybank is that managerial evaluation of the TQM process also empowers employees to deliver quality through the exercise of workplace discretion.

At Flightpath, the work of TSAs is evaluated through 'hard' and 'soft' targets. Working to the former means that individual service providers have to meet targets in terms of revenue earned per month (the value of services sold) and productivity per month (number of calls taken, duration of calls, time spent in between calls). Soft targets include managerial evaluation of individual TSAs' 'teamwork, commitment and the nature of their interaction with customers' (STS, 1994). In addition to direct STS observation of TSAs within an open plan office, the main way in which these 'softer' aspects of the TSA labour process are monitored is through 'known' and 'remote' monitoring. The latter means that any member of the managerial hierarchy can 'listen in' to a TSA/customer telephone interaction, without the knowledge of either the employee or customer concerned. However, even this form of evaluation, which could be construed as the ultimate form of detailed supervision, the complete surveillance process, was seen by management as a way of empowering – increasing the autonomy and discretion – of TSAs:

> ...the point of listening in is not to say 'listen to that, you were pathetic!'. It's not for control, it's a development tool...you need to be careful as a manager not to use it as a 'big brother' tool and to use it as a quality assurance, performance management and employee development tool and I think we are careful here. (STL, 1994)

Every employee within Newcastle Telephone Sales is remunerated on the basis of their performance. TSA performance-related pay is shaped by an STS monthly report which results from weekly review and appraisal meetings. This is, in turn, based upon evaluation according to both hard and soft standards.

At Friendlybank, the delivery of quality is evaluated through customer feedback (established through customer surveys and informally asking customers how satisfied they are with the service received), direct managerial supervision of the personal banking labour process and branch targets. Each branch has targets for: the length of time within which telephone calls must be answered; that the sales desk be manned (sic) whenever staff are available; the length of time that customers are permitted to wait in a queue; the amount of complaints per branch per year; and a branch revenue target for the sale of branch products. The *branch* is evaluated according to these targets largely through the annual questionnaire sent to customers and through 'spot checks' from head office – what is known as 'mystery shopping'. Head office 'mystery shoppers' and the customer questionnaire also evaluate the 'softer' aspects of quality service such as staff attitudes, appearance, dialogue and teamwork. Friendlybank branch management argued that the above evaluation of service quality – in addition to the development of an appropriate organizational infrastructure, selection and training processes, a teamworking system and communicative and participative mechanisms – *empowers* personal branch clerks to deliver quality service to customers. A 'genuine' and 'natural' service is delivered through the spontaneous reactions and work autonomy of individual personal clerks. Thus, for example, when describing her direct observation of the personal banking labour process, one CSM stated:

> I'm not necessarily looking to catch them out when I observe. On the contrary, I am looking for things to praise them about...people can forget how important and motivating praise can be. If I do tell them things, I am only trying to help, improve their work...empower them to improve the service to customers. That is what we are all here for after all. (CSM, 1993)

WORK AUTONOMY OR 'TACTICAL RESPONSIBILITY'?

As we have seen, it is suggested through academic representation of the TQM labour process (via the discourse of enterprise) and by management at both of our research sites that the introduction of TQM has empowered service employees to take responsibility for the delivery of quality service. In fact, the empowerment of agents is seen as *vital* to the delivery of quality service. The remainder of this chapter will involve a critical analysis of the TSA and CSO labour process which suggests that the implementation of TQM, far from empowering employees, constitutes a managerial attempt to erode employee autonomy and effect total managerial control. In fact, TQM can be seen as the most sophisticated managerial initiative developed to date aimed at solving the enduring managerial 'control-engage dilemma' (Thompson 1989).

Positive Discretion

It was alleged by both managements that they, to a certain extent, and largely through selection and training, prescribe the delivery of both technical and functional aspects of quality service. They instruct, and expect clerks to display, certain product knowledge (for example, the range of tickets operated by Flightpath throughout the world or the various insurance products offered by Friendlybank). Management also prescribe how to utilize the respective computer systems in order to access such information and they outline certain ways of communicating product knowledge to customers.

However, it was fundamentally stressed by both managements that these are very *general* prescriptions. For example, Flightpath management prescribe that, following a greeting of the customer over the telephone and the gathering of relevant information through 'questioning and listening', TSAs should match customer requirements with appropriate product information. However, one can argue that TSAs ultimately decide how, when or whether to question the customer over the telephone and how, when or whether to match her/his requirements with relevant product information. Thus, it was suggested by the majority of agents that their decision over how to respond to customers was largely shaped by the nature of the particular customer and the nature of the communication. They argued that *they* decide *whether* to attempt to turn an enquiry into a sale in the fashion prescribed by management:

> You can tell really when the call comes through if you stand any chance with it, really 'cos the majority of them will say 'I only want the fare' and you say 'right, that's fine'...there's no possible way they're going to buy anything. There's no point in even trying to sell them something...if they know what date they want to travel, then you think 'they've already planned what date they want to go', give them the fare, if that seems okay for them then you can start to turn it round. (TSA, 1994)

Many agents argued that they exercise this discretion during the course of conversations with customers. It was frequently stated that one must 'go with the flow' of the conversation, and then instantly decide whether information and services should be offered and, if so, which ones.

As a result of the bank restructuring and implementation of TQM, CSOs at Friendlybank are required to develop in-depth product knowledge and to offer bank products (such as high interest accounts, foreign currency services or insurance services) to match particular customers' needs and requirements at every possible opportunity. Through a selling skills programme, management do prescribe particular ways in which employees can match particular products to particular customers. However, the majority of CSOs argued that they do *not* offer product information to customers at every possible opportunity. When to do so was left to the discretion of employees:

> Sometimes, in fact a lot of times, it's just not appropriate. People come into the bank sometimes in a real rush or in the middle of doing something else, they just want to deposit a cheque, make a withdrawal or whatever and get out, they don't want the salesman's (sic) bit from us. (CSO, 1993)

Both CSOs and PAs (including the senior grades) argued that they also exercise discretion over *when* product information should be offered, once the decision to do so has been made:

> You've got to wait 'till the right moment...it's difficult to say in words when that actually is but you can tell when you're in the course of a conversation...it's when they say they're going on holiday, or they mention they're retiring, or they give the impression that they're worried about their job...they might want insurance...I suppose what they say, how they look is the spark...I suppose you decide that you are going to go for it and when you're going...at the same time, at the same instant (CSO, 1993).

These can be seen as examples of positive discretion. Both managements, on the whole, encourage and value such employee 'empowerment' as part of the TQM process.

It can be argued that even greater service employee positive discretion is exercised over the delivery of functional quality. Thus, for example, when gathering information from customers, TSAs argued that they frequently, with the encouragement of management, interact with customers in their own personal or 'natural', rather than a tightly prescribed, manner. This is known as 'building rapport'. It was claimed by both agents and management that this is an effective way of gathering information and of appealing to potential customers – producing the experience of a quality service – and thus increasing the possibility of turning an enquiry into a sale. Furthermore, many agents argued that their own 'natural' technique for interacting with customers is directly influenced by their own particular personality:

> I'm naturally quite a chatty person and I'm chatty on the phone. I like to find a common link, so if someone has

gone to college in Brighton or they live in Brighton, I say 'ah, I went to college there, is such and such still there?' and they like that. I've had feedback on my phone technique and they say 'keep that in, it's good, it establishes a rapport' which I don't mind doing because that is the sort of person I am anyway whereas some other people who may be different, they just answer the question and that's it. (TSA, 1994)

'Building rapport' with customers was also encouraged by management at Friendlybank. In fact, it was suggested above that one of the prescriptions managerially issued at branch level is for clerks to develop a 'friendship' with customers, ensuring that employee-customer interaction is as 'natural' as possible. Despite prescribing certain techniques for the establishment of dialogue, inherent within this managerial instruction is that clerks exercise positive discretion. The majority of Friendlybank branch clerks confirmed that they *did* exercise discretion over the delivery of functional quality:

I've got my own techniques for getting to know, building a rapport the official term is, with customers...I suppose every person has...I'm sure they [customers] sometimes only come in for the patter...everyone reckons I'm the best at it here, especially with the blokes...it's great though because the boss loves it. I was wary at first 'cos in the old days you had to make sure the boss was out of sight or it was Friday afternoon and everyone had been to the pub, but she actually wanted me to do it the other day, I can't believe it really, I'm only being myself. (CSO, 1993)

These examples illustrate the way in which many TSAs and Friendlybank clerks exercise positive discretion – they devise and implement their own individual ways of delivering quality customer service. Under TQM, such discretion is deliberately encouraged, and positively rewarded by management. This is partly what the 'empowerment' which is intrinsic to TQM actually entails. Integral to TQM is a managerial strategy of 'identifying positive divergencies [from managerial prescriptions] and maximising their creative potential' (Sewell and Wilkinson, 1992, p. 271). TSAs are financially and symbolically rewarded for exercising such positive discretion.

Centralized Control

Despite the above, it can be argued that within both of our cases there is evidence of thoroughgoing and centralized managerial control mechanisms, many of which are attempted through surveillance processes, which are also simultaneous with the implementation of TQM to service work.[5]

Following Sewell and Wilkinson, the devolvement of responsibility and employee 'empowerment' which TQM enables is an important element in the 'total' managerial control which TQM constitutes. The decentralization of 'tactical responsibility' – or positive discretion – occurs at the same time as 'strategic' managerial control is centralized through sophisticated workplace surveillance. Thus, the forms of managerial supervision used to evaluate the work of TSAs and Friendlybank branch clerks – personal, direct managerial supervision, the use of targets and customer feedback – attempt to centralize managerial control of the labour process, encourage the deployment of employee positive discretion or tactical responsibility and minimize employee opportunities for negative discretion, *thus aiming to actually erode work autonomy within the employment relationship.*

Managerial attempts at 'total control' of the workforce through TQM are particularly pronounced at Flightpath. Here, the information technology utilized, in the form of highly sophisticated computer and telephone systems, enables individualized evaluation of TSAs work according to both 'hard' and 'soft' standards. Collectively, these systems could be seen as an 'electronic Panopticon' which 'can overcome the constraints of architecture' and facilitate 'a Panoptic gaze which can penetrate walls' (Sewell and Wilkinson, 1992, p. 283). The surveillance process engendered *could* mean that TSAs 'are totally seen [and heard], without ever seeing [or hearing]' while telephone sales management see (and hear) 'everything without being seen [or heard]' (Foucault, 1977, pp. 201–2).

Hard Targets and Disciplinary Force

Firstly, TSAs are *individually* measured according to hard revenue targets. The computer system records the result of every single call. Each 'direct sale' achieved by an individual is recorded against her/his personal name. Each booking which may be 'held', but not confirmed, by a customer is also recorded against the name of the agent who constructed the booking. It is thus impossible for agents to 'claim' sales which have not actually been achieved or those which have been achieved by others. TSAs have an obvious interest in surpassing hard revenue targets – consistent failure to reach these would eventually result in dismissal. Furthermore, given the existence of performance-related pay and the various rewards and prizes for surpassing monetary targets, agents have a clear motivation to implement managerial prescriptions and exercise positive discretion (that is deliver management's version of quality service) in order to sell as many Flightpath products as possible:

> You get a basic wage…and then everything you do on top of that is more money for you…what you do wrong, you don't get extra money for it, that's the way it works…it's really in all our favours to try and do well. (TSA, 1993)[6]

It must be noted that the majority of TSAs interviewed stressed that the 'basic wage' (without any performance-related pay) 'is hardly enough to live on…most people, I would say, like it here because of the perks and bonuses you can get' (TSA, 1994).

At Friendlybank, revenue targets are non-individualized – they are measured at branch level. Consequently, it can be argued that the 'disciplinary force' exerted here is not as 'complete' as that attempted at Flightpath. However, some constraints are experienced by branch clerks – particularly when it was communicated to staff that the branch was underachieving in terms of its revenue target or if the target had not been met during the previous month:

> Some people don't take any notice of the targets, but sometimes I do, especially if we've fallen behind. I take note, and I definitely offer more products and services during these periods…You never know what's coming next in this company…it used to be so stable…but because we are so sales-orientated now, the cashiering role could well disappear soon. With all the advances being made, people

will be able to do all this over the telephone or by computer, from home...we will be purely sellers...if branches cannot do this, I don't think head office would think twice about getting rid of the whole branch. You have seen how quickly things have changed only in the past three years or so. (CSO, 1993)

At certain times during the year, the bank 'promoted' certain products, such as payment protection insurance on personal loans, above all others. Clerks were given incentives, in the form of holiday prizes or cash bonuses, for selling a certain amount of these products:

> When there is a promotion on, you'll find that we do go all out to sell whatever is being promoted...last year they had a prize of a trip to Singapore and the Maldives for the person in each region who sold the most payment protection insurance...I was offering it left, right and centre, and the personal loans and stuff that make you able to offer it in the first place...but I didn't win...a lot of customers knew about it though, it got quite cringey actually. (PA, 1993)

This supports our argument that when service employees are individually measured according to revenue targets, and when this affects their remuneration, the exercise of autonomy is more likely to be constrained within the employment relationship. A further set of hard targets set by management at both Flightpath and Friendlybank constitute 'productivity' evaluation. Thus, at Flightpath, the 'electronic Panopticon' records and stores detailed information on the number of calls answered per week, the amount of time spent in conversation with passengers per week and the amount of time spent in 'wrap up' (the time between the termination of one conversation and the beginning of another), for each individual TSA. These statistics are immediately available to management for, and at, any point in time. They are also visible to TSAs, STSs and STLs as they are being recorded. Once again, each individual is targeted in relation to each of these statistics. A 'norm', below which every agent is not expected to fall, is devised by a Core Management Centre. Each agent's performance according to these measures is reviewed in detail during their monthly appraisal meeting. This can further constrain the behaviour of TSAs within the labour process, particularly their control over the pace of work.

Subjective Evaluation

Service employees within both of our cases are also supervised and monitored according to 'soft' standards – a subjective managerial evaluation of their attitude and teamwork within the employment relationship, their performance within the various participatory and representative mechanisms introduced as part of TQM, and their social interaction with customers. There is only space here to illustrate our argument with examples of managerial attempts to control the latter activity.

At Flightpath, employee-customer interaction is largely supervised and evaluated through remote and known monitoring of agent-customer telephone conversations. According to management, the results of such evaluation significantly shape agents' performance related pay. At Friendlybank, clerk-customer interaction is monitored through mystery shopping from head office and customer feedback. Some managerial staff at Flightpath suggested that the capability, represented by 'remote monitoring' (again enabled by the 'electronic Panopticon'), to 'listen-in' to the conduct of employee-customer interactions without their knowledge meant that 'total' control was exerted over all such interactions:

> They (agents) know that we can 'listen in' at any time, they don't know when…it is a good managerial, quality assurance and development tool 'cos it means they are always on their toes…they can't really be slap dash 'cos they know we can always pull them up…in many ways, because it's there we don't have to use it that often – it varies between supervisors. (STS, 1994).

Another STS argued that, as part of the surveillance process, remote monitoring encourages TSAs to exercise positive discretion/ empowerment:

> I suppose it does mean that we can catch things we wouldn't otherwise hear and we can put those things right, but I don't just use it for that. It's their chance to shine, to show

us what they can do. If they're doing good things, using their own initiative, if good practice comes from interacting with customers naturally, then we'll notice that as well and praise them for it, they'll get more money for it as well. (STS, 1994)

Many agents endorsed the existence of permanent surveillance, through remote monitoring, of their interaction with customers. However, it was often claimed that this *prevents* 'natural', 'genuine' and 'spontaneous' interaction.

They can listen in to your calls and that's the bit I don't like because you don't know they're doing it...it really does have an effect upon you because you know that if you don't do things by the book they could be listening and they could pull you up on it. You've got to be on your guard all the time...I suppose in some ways you can't just be yourself. (TSA, 1993)

Given the last comment, it can be argued that the mechanisms for subjective evaluation of the TSA labour process, an integral element of TQM implementation, simultaneously demand the performance of emotional labour – both surface acting and deep acting. However, given managerial demands for 'natural' and 'genuine' interaction between employees and customers as an indicator of functional quality, deep acting is increasingly produced and demanded through selection, training, supervision and evaluation. This opens up the *possibility* of emotional alienation:

You have to think about the customer really...it's all part of the job, appreciating the different types of person you get and how everyone is different with their own values and expectations...you've got to learn not to get angry with people just because they might be different...I suppose the targets are good in that way because they make you appreciate people more, have a different attitude. If you don't do it, you might not sell and hit target or you might get pulled up because of listening in, in your appraisal or whatever...a lot of people keep telling me I've actually mellowed since I came here so it's done something for me. (TSA, 1994)

There was some evidence of disciplinary force exerted by subjective evaluation at Friendlybank. However, due to the non-individualized nature of this evaluation and its irrelevance to the financial remuneration of branch clerks, many argued that such managerial demands could be resisted.

Thus, it can be suggested that the implementation of TQM to the labour process of TSAs and Friendlybank branch bank clerks encompasses a managerial attempt to erode the discretion which many have argued is intrinsic to all employment relationships within capitalist society (Jaques, 1961; Fox, 1974; Cressey and McInnes, 1980; Brown, 1992). It can be argued that this has been undertaken with particular vigour at Flightpath, when compared to Friendlybank, driven particularly by electronic forms of surveillance and individualized targeting systems which are not yet in evidence at Friendlybank.[7] There *is* evidence of TSA autonomy at Flightpath. However, this is often positive discretion or 'tactical responsibility'. The *choices* of employees are commonly restricted to choices which further the interests of managerially-defined 'quality service'. There appears very little opportunity for employees to 'choose' negative discretion, given the extent of managerial surveillance of the labour process. Choosing between alternatives of action, and accepting responsibility for the consequences, is the essence of workplace discretion. The choice is apparently narrowed to encompass only positive discretion as a result of TQM. However, throughout the chapter, we have stressed that TQM involves a managerial *attempt* to realize 'total control'. There is evidence, at both research sites, of 'space' for employee negotiation with, and resistance to managerial demands. This will be reviewed in our final section. There will only be space to consider TSA negotiation and resistance at Flightpath, the case where, as we have argued, centralized managerial control and surveillance is most complete.

A DIALECTIC OF CONTROL

It was established in the previous section that the hard revenue targets can exert a strong disciplinary force upon the employment experience of TSAs. However, this force did not *always* facilitate the performance of managerial prescription and the exercise of positive discretion. For example, many

TSAs argued that meeting revenue targets and winning awards for an outstanding sales performance is a result of 'luck' rather than the implementation of managerial prescription and positive discretion:

> You can be exactly the same with every caller during the day, saying the same things in the same order, some will book things, others will not...it depends on them (customers) not you. (TSA, 1993)

Many agents went on to suggest that customers decided to purchase products according to many different criteria. The service they received when interacting with TSAs was one, subordinate criterion amongst these. It is also important to point out that there was also division amongst *managerial* staff over the extent to which the attainment of revenue targets and the winning of prizes is the result of 'luck' or the implementation of managerial prescription and the exercise of positive discretion. The following comment was representative of a *minority* of STSs:

> Some of them (agents) will say 'yeah but some people are just lucky, some people just get these lucky bookings' and I say 'they can't always get the lucky bookings'...but I don't know if I fully believe it. There is a certain amount of skill involved but I have to admit that luck does play a big part. (STS, 1993)

It can also be argued that the mechanisms for managerial supervision and evaluation of TSA productivity performance do not entirely 'discipline' employee autonomy. In fact, TSAs suggested that this particular disciplinary force is largely experienced during 'exceptional' circumstances. The majority contended that most STSs only analyse individual productivity data when dramatic weaknesses are noticed or if TSAs struggle to meet revenue targets:

> It's only if something is really bad that she (an STS) would go into your 'phone stats and then you would get an objective to work on. I have never had any because my phone stats have been generally okay, pretty average I think...as long as you hit your targets, she doesn't hardly look at them or mention them. (TSA, 1993)

As for the influence of the productivity evaluation upon performance-related pay:

> There's hard and soft standards but I mean it's really whether you've actually consistently hit target, sales targets over the past few months. The other targets...on the phone stats, they keep an eye on those as well...in the end it's really decided by whether you've hit target and what you've sold, that's what they (STS) really decide it by. (TSA, 1994)

This does allow some employee negative discretion over: the number of calls taken; the pace of work; the length of time spent interacting with customers; the length of time spent in 'wrap up'. It must be noted, however, that the extent to which agents' discretion was eroded by the collection of productivity statistics appears to depend upon their particular STS. Some supervisors were accused of scrutinising productivity statistics to find fault with agents who had met, and surpassed, their revenue target.

Despite known and remote monitoring, there is also evidence of TSA negative discretion over the employee/customer interface and the performance of emotional labour. Firstly, it can be argued that, for a vast majority of TSAs, their interactions with customers were transformed during periods in which they experienced known monitoring. Many of them argued that such supervision frequently made them feel 'uncomfortable' and 'unnatural'. The fact that employees *change* their behaviour during periods of known monitoring clearly suggests that they exercise considerable autonomy during periods when such supervision is absent. There was actually much TSA resentment at having to change one's natural behaviour:

> They tell us to be as natural as possible all the time but it's only if you fit with what they want. If I was natural, they'd have me out that door in a flash...I hate it though, they tell us to use our personality, 'that is why you were employed', and then they do us for using it, or they would do us if they caught us. (TSA, 1994)

With regard to remote monitoring, many agents claimed that, with experience, they have learned to ascertain when their conversations are directly supervised. Being situated within an open plan office, this was recognized by the actions of the supervisor and regular gazes in their direction. One agent stated that:

> When I know she (the supervisor) is listening, I can't help but change my accent, what I actually say and the words I use. She would only pull me up for not talking the way that I'm supposed to in our supervision and counselling sessions. I had one really ignorant get on the phone once, I was seething, but I knew she was listening so I had to contain it. When she is not listening, I just prefer to be myself...when I am positive she is not listening, I have been really short with bad customers, it's a great feeling. (1994)

Thus, it can be argued that the above agent is engaging in surface acting, and *this* is only performed when he is aware of managerial supervision. Remote and known monitoring can, for some agents, also shape the feeling behind the display demanded by the labour process. However, when other TSAs are able to interact 'naturally' with customers, using their own feelings, personality and 'self', they seize the opportunity:

> I prefer just to talk to people naturally, I think they (customers) prefer it as well...I talk to people as I would talk to any friendly person outside of here...it doesn't really get any more sales but it doesn't get any less. (TSA, 1993)

There were numerous examples of TSAs expressing their 'true' feelings and selves through overt resistance to managerial prescription of the employee/customer interaction.[8] For example, some agents were observed, and many stated that, they simply disconnect calls from customers that are particularly rude or ignorant. Such practices are undertaken when TSAs are sure they are not being observed by management, either physically or electronically. When questioned whether they are overtly rude or dismissive with a caller, the common response is summarized by the following agent:

> Oh god yeah! Of course we are, we're just like everyone else you know, that's when you turn round and make sure nobody's listening in, you *can* tell if there's anybody listening in. (TSA, 1993)

The workplace discretion which *is* open to TSAs during much interaction with customers is demonstrated by instances where workers *choose* to exercise negative discretion. Agents developed an intuitive knowledge of calls that were definite enquiries and not sales. One agent explained how such calls are sometimes handled:

> It really annoys me when it's obvious people are just ringing up for information...when I am sure that my supervisor is not listening I love to fuck about with them. If it is someone from outside the area, I lay the accent on really thick. You can hear them getting embarrassed when they have to say 'pardon' all the time. (TSA, 1993)

A popular TSA practice involves limiting the information given to a rude, ignorant or offensive caller. Many revealed that they would immediately withhold relevant, sometimes important, information on products from customers who provoked feelings of anger, irritation or dislike within them. Some TSAs further suggested that such autonomous, and some might say resistant, practices are to some extent condoned by *some* STSs. There is evidence that some managerial staff tolerated the exercise of such 'negative discretion' provided that the agent concerned was a 'good performer'.

CONCLUSION

On the basis of the empirical research upon which this chapter is based, it could be argued that the increasing implementation of TQM to the service sector constitutes a managerial attempt to eliminate the autonomy of employees and 'the dual nature of the labour process' (Cressey and McInnes, 1980) which has been central to all employment relationships within capitalist societies – this is, then, the ultimate degradation of labour. The claims of the discourse of enterprise, that TQM 'empowers' employees, are ideological in that they conceal the erosion of employee autonomy and the subordination of labour which TQM *can* facilitate.

However, whilst recognising that the 'pessimistic' perspective appears closer to the lived experience of TSAs at Flightpath and personal branch clerks at Friendlybank, than the optimistic perspective presented by the discourse of enterprise, it has also been suggested that this representation is over-simplistic.[9] Even when it appears that service sector management have 'achieved' 'total control' through the 'complete' electronic and individualized surveillance system (as at Flightpath), there is evidence of spaces for employee involvement in the 'negotiated order' (Brown, 1993) of the (TQM) service organization. This space includes scope for overt employee resistance to managerial demands and the exercise of negative discretion.

Our findings demonstrate that, within the TQM service labour process, the irremediable dependence of capital upon labour (Cressey and McInnes, 1980) would appear to remain. This is partly a result of the integrally incoherent, fragmentary and contradictory nature of 'management' (Hyman, 1987; Watson, 1994). It also results from the fact that managerial attempts to 'totally control' the delivery of (functional) quality within the service sector simultaneously involve attempts to control and commercialize the very feelings, identities and personalities of service personnel. This can provoke particular indignation and strong resistance amongst the workforce (Filby, 1992).

NOTES

1. Despite drawing empirical evidence from manufacturing industry, Sewell and Wilkinson do point out that their argument can be similarly applied to understand TQM within the service sector.
2. 'Positive discretion' refers to the exercise of discretion in the interests of the organization and management. 'Negative discretion' implies the opposite. The rather simplistic nature of this distinction is recognised. Much employee practice can actually be seen as ambiguous in relation to these definitions. This was clearly evidenced by our ethnographic research (see Taylor, 1995).
3. The research upon which this paper is based was financed by the Economic and Social Research Council (ESRC), Award No. R00429134273. The author acknowledges this support with gratitude.
4. Research at Flightpath took place in the context of corporate development and success for the company as a whole. This was attributed, by both management and many academics, to the implementation of

TQM and an associated 'culture change'. The particular telephone sales centre studied had contributed to this success. It was viewed, throughout the company and beyond, as the most profitable of all centres, as a 'centre of excellence'. The unit was often visited by representatives of other Flightpath units and telephone sales operations from different service industries.

5. I have argued elsewhere (Taylor, 1995) that this simultaneously con-stitutes sophisticated mechanisms for *patriarchal* control of the service labour process. Due to spatial constraints, I am unable to develop this argument further.

6. It can be noted that, in addition to individualized performance-related pay, many TSAs are also motivated by a regular 'league table' of top performers where the winners are awarded prizes such as free holidays. Further, teams are set a monthly revenue target. When surpassed, this results in the award of a sum of money to the whole team. This was commonly used to fund team social activities. 'Top performing teams' were awarded collective holidays as prizes.

7. Friendlybank management claimed that they were in the process of attempting to develop individualized targeting systems. However, at the time of the research, they were discussing this possibility with trade unions who were resisting the initiative. The very low level of trade union membership and participation at Flightpath may explain why these initiatives were introduced with relative ease here.

8. This paper assumes the existence of a 'true self', an assumption which is disputed by many. We do not have the space to engage in this debate. For a full discussion (see Taylor, 1995).

9. In this vein, we are contributing to an *emerging* critical literature on the implementation of TQM to the service sector (for example Knights and McCabe, 1994; Kerfoot & Knights, 1994; Tuckman, 1995).

Bibliography

Adler, S., Laney, J. and Packer, M. (1993) *Managing Women*. Milton Keynes: Open University Press.

Allen, J. and Henry, N. (1996) 'Fragments of industry and employment. Contract service work and the shift towards precarious employment' in R. Crompton, D. Gallie and K. Purcell (eds) *Changing Forms of Employment. Organisations, skills and gender*. London: Routledge, 65–82.

Allen, J. and Massey, D. (eds) (1988) *The Economy in Question*. London: Sage.

Allen, S. (1989a) 'Flexibility of work and working time: a gendered approach' in J. Buber Agassi and S. Heycock (eds) *The Redesign of Working Time: Promise or Threat?* Berlin: Sigma, 238–48.

Allen, S. (1989b) 'Economic recession and gender divisions' in R. Scase (ed.) *Industrial Societies*. London: Unwin Hyman, 120–145.

Allen, S. (1992) 'Counting Women's Labour', paper presented to the Vth International Interdisciplinary Congress on Women, University of Costa Rica.

Allen, S. and Truman, C. (1992) 'Women, business and self-employment: a conceptual minefield' in S. Arber and N. Gilbert (eds) *Women and Working Lives. Divisions and Change*. Basingstoke: Macmillan, 162–174.

Allen, S. and Truman, C. (1993) 'Women and men entrepreneurs: life strategies, business strategies' in S. Allen and C. Truman (eds) *Women in Business Perspectives on Women Entrepreneurs*. London: Routledge, 1–13.

Allen, S. and Waton, A. (1986) 'The effects of unemployment: experience and response' in S. Allen, A. Waton, K. Purcell and S. Wood (eds) *The Experience of Unemployment*. Basingstoke: Macmillan, 1–16.

Allen, S. and Wolkowitz, C. (1987) *Homeworking: Myths and Realities*. Basingstoke: Macmillan.

Anthony, P. D. (1990) 'The paradox of the management of culture or "He Who Leads is Lost"', *Personnel Review*, 19, 4.

Anthony, P. D. (1994) *Managing Culture*. Buckingham: Open University Press.

Armstrong, P., Glyn, A. and Harrison, J. (1991) *Capitalism Since 1945*. Oxford: Blackwell.

Ashton, D. N. (1986) *Unemployment under Capitalism. The Sociology of British and American Labour Markets*. Brighton: Wheatsheaf.

AUT (1994) 'Members' workloads', *Manchester AUT Newsletter*, 4, October.

AUT (1996) 'Lessen the load', *AUT Bulletin*.

Bagguley, P. and Mann, K. (1992) 'Idle, thieving, bastards: scholarly representations of the "Underclass"', *Work, Employment and Society*, 6, 113–26.

Ball, C. (1991) *Learning Pays: the role of post-compulsory education and training*. RSA.

Bauman, Z. (1989) *Modernity and the Holocaust*. Cambridge: Polity Press.

Bauman, Z. (1992) *Intimations of Postmodernity*, London: Routledge.

Beale, D. (1994) *Driven By Nissan*. London: Lawrence and Wishart.

Beatson, M. (1995) *Labour Market Flexibility*. Research Series No. 48, Sheffield: Employment Department.

Bell, D. (1973) *The Coming of Post Industrial Society*. New York: Basic Books.

Beveridge, W. H. (1944) *Full Employment in a Free Society*. London: Allen and Unwin.

Bevins, A. (1993) 'Benefits supplement pay at supermarkets', *The Independent*, 27 January.

Beynon, H. (1984) *Working for Ford*. Harmondsworth: Penguin, second edition.

Beynon, H. (1992) 'The end of the industrial worker?' in N. Abercrombie and A. Warde (eds) *Social Change in Contemporary Britain*. Cambridge: Polity.

Beynon, H., Hudson, R., and Sadler, D. (1994) *A Place Called Teesside: A Locality in a Global Economy*, Edinburgh: Edinburgh University Press.

Boaden, R. J. and Dale, B. G. (1993) 'Managing quality improvement in financial services: a framework and case study', *The Service Industries Journal*, 13, 1, 17–39.

Boris, E. and Daniels, C. (eds) *Homework: Historical and Contemporary Perspectives on Paid Labour at Home*. Illinois: University of Illinois Press.

Bradley, H. (1996) *Fractured Identities*. Cambridge: Polity.

Bradshaw, A. and Holmes, H. (1989) *Living on the Edge*. Tyneside: Tyneside Child Poverty Action Group.

Brannen, J. and Moss, P. (1991) *Managing Mothers*. London: Unwin Hyman.

Braverman, H. (1974) *Labor and Monopoly Capital*. New York: Monthly Review Press.

Bright, G. et al. (1988) *Small Business and the Rebirth of Enterprise in Britain*. London: Conservative Political Centre.

Brindle, D. (1993) 'Care role preparation blighted', *The Guardian*, 30 March.

Brown, P. and Scase, R. (1991) (eds) *Poor Work: Disadvantage and the Division of Labour*. Milton Keynes: Open University Press.

Brown, R. K. (1984) 'Work' in P. Abrams and R. K. Brown (eds) *UK Society: Work, Urbanism and Inequality*. London: Weidenfeld and Nicolson, 129–197.

Brown, R. K. (1988) 'The employment relationship in sociological theory' in D. Gallie (ed.) *Employment in Britain*. Oxford: Basil Blackwell, 33–66.

Brown, R. K. (1992) *Understanding Industrial Organisations. Theoretical perspectives in industrial sociology*. London: Routledge.

Brown, R. K. (1993) 'The negotiated order of the industrial enterprise' in H. Martins (ed.) *Knowledge and Passion: Essays in honour of John Rex*. London: I. B. Taurus, 51–78.

Brown, R. K. (1995) 'The Changing Nature of Work and Employment' in L. Evans, P. Johnson and B. Thomas (ed.) *The Northern Region Economy*. London: Mansell, 171–189.

Brown, R. K., Curran, M. and Cousins, J. (1983) *Changing Attitudes to Employment?* London: Department of Employment, Research Paper No. 40.

Bryson, A. and Jacobs, J. (1992) *Policing the Workshy*. Aldershot: Avebury.

Burchell, B. and Rubery, J. (1992) 'Categorising self-employment: some evidence from the Social Change and Economic Life Initiative in the UK' in P. Leighton and A. Felstead (eds) (1992) *The New Entrepreneurs: Self Employment and Small Business in Europe*. London: Kogan Page, 101–22.

Burrows, R. (ed.) (1991) *Deciphering the Enterprise Culture: Entrepreneurship, Petty Capitalism and the Restructuring of Britain*. London: Routledge.

Burrows, R. and Curran, J. (1991) 'Not such a small business: reflections on the rhetoric, the reality and the future of the enterprise culture' in M. Cross and G. Payne (eds.) *Work and the Enterprise Culture*. Basingstoke: Falmer.

Byrne, D. (1995) 'Deindustrialisation and dispossession: an examination of social division in the Industrial City', *Sociology*, 29, 1, 95–117.

Campbell, B. (1993) *Goliath*. London: Methuen.

Campbell, M. and Daly, M. (1992) 'Self-employment: into the 1990s', *Employment Gazette*, June, 269–291.

Carr, M. and Roberts, I. (1994) 'Centralisation and Fragmentation: The Changing Nature of Training and Work', paper at JETS conference, 'Social Change in Tyne and Wear', University of Sunderland, 1994.

Casey, B. and Creigh, S. (1988) 'Self-employment in Great Britain: its definitions in the labour force survey, in tax and social security law and in labour law', *Work, Employment and Society*, 2, 3, 381–91.

CEC (Commission of the European Communities) (1993) *Growth, Competitiveness, Employment. The challenges and ways forward into the 21st century*. Bulletin Supplement 6/93, Luxembourg: CEC.

Central Statistical Office (1995) *Social Focus on Women*. London: HMSO.

Charles, L. (1994) *Gender Segregation in the Contemporary Hotel Industry*, Ph.D. Thesis, University of Bradford.

Chittenden, F. and Caley, K. (1992) 'Current policy issues and recommendations' in K. Caley et al. (eds) *Small Enterprise Development*. London: Paul Chapman Publishing.

Christensen, K. (1989) 'Homebased clerical work: no simple truth, no simple reality' in N. Cooper (1995) 'Two nations divided by their walls', *The Guardian*, 21 June.

Citizens Advice Bureaux (1992) *Job Insecurity: CAB Evidence on Employment Problems in the Recession*. London: National Association of Citizens Advice Bureaux.

Clegg, S. (1990) *Modern Organizations: Organization studies in the postmodern world*. London: Sage.

Cleveland County Council (1986) *Cleveland Structure Plan: People and Jobs*. Middlesbrough: Economic Development and Planning Department.

Cleveland County Council (1992) 'Review of the Assisted Areas of Great Britain: A Response to the DTI Consultation Paper', Middlesbrough: the Local Authorities and Organisations of Cleveland County.

Cleveland County Council (1993) *Cleveland's Economic Prospects 1993–2006*. Middlesbrough: Department of Environment, Development and Transport.

Cleveland County Council, (1994) *Unemployment in Cleveland*. Middlesbrough: Department of Environment, Development and Planning, September.

Cleveland County Council (1995) *Cleveland Factsheet 2/95*. Middlesbrough: Environment and Planning Department.

Cleveland Council for Voluntary Service (1990) *Community Opportunities in Cleveland: A programme for the 1990s*. Middlesbrough: CCVS.

Cockburn, C. (1991) *In the Way of Women*. London: Macmillan.

Commission for Social Justice (1995) *Social Justice: Strategies for National Renewal*. London: Viking.

Confederation of British Industry (1988) *People – The Cutting Edge*. London: CBI.

Cooke, K. (1987) 'The withdrawal from paid work of the wives of unemployed men', *Journal of Social Policy*, 16, 371–48.

Coombes, M., Atkins, D., Dorling, D. and Wong, C. (1994) 'Unemployment in the North: recession or recovery in the regions?', *Northern Economic Review*, 21, 80–89.

Cooper, N. (1995) 'Two nations divided by their walls', *The Guardian*, 21 June.

Coward, R. (1992) *Our Treacherous Hearts*. London: Fontana.

Craine, S. and Coles, B. (1995) 'Alternative careers: youth transitions and young people's involvement in crime', *Youth and Policy*, 48, 6–27.

Cressey, P. and MacInnes, J. (1980) 'Voting for Ford: industrial democracy and the control of labour', *Capital and Class*, 11, 5–33.

Cressey, P. and Scott, P. (1992) 'Employment, technology and industrial relations in the UK clearing banks: is the honeymoon over?', *New Technology, Work and Employment*, 7, 2.

Crompton, R. and Sanderson, K. (1990) *Gendered Jobs and Social Change*. London: Unwin Hyman.

Crosby, P. B. (1980) *Quality is Free*, London: Mentor.

Cross, M. and Payne, G. (1991) (eds) *Work and the Enterprise Culture*. London: The Falmer Press.

Dahrendorf, R. (1987) 'The Underclass and the Future of Britain', Tenth Annual Lecture, St. George's House, Windsor Castle.

Dale, B. G., Lascelles, D. M. and Plunkett, J. J. (1990) 'The process of Total Quality Management' in B. G. Dale and J. J. Plunkett (eds) *Managing Quality*. London: Philip Allan.

Davies, R. B. et al. (1991) 'The relationship between a husband's unemployment and his wife's participation in the labour force', mimeo, University. of Lancaster.

Dean, H. (1995) 'Underclass or Undermined? Young People and Social Citizenship', paper given to Youth 2000 conference, University of Teesside, July.

Deming, W. C. (1986) *Out of the Crisis*. Cambridge: Cambridge University Press.

Dennis, N. and Erdos, G. (1992) *Families Without Fatherhood*. London: Institute of Economic Affairs.

Department of Employment (1985) *Employment. The Challenge for the Nation*. Cmnd 9474, London: HMSO.

Department of Employment (1991) *Small Firms in Britain*. London: HMSO.

Devine, F. (1992) *Affluent Workers Revisited*. Edinburgh: Edinburgh University Press.

DfEE (Department for Education and Employment) (1996) *Labour Market and Skill Trends 1996/1997*. Nottingham: Skills and Enterprise Network.

Dignan, W. (1995) 'Business Process Re-engineering at The Co-operative Bank: improving personal customer service', *The T.Q.M. Magazine*, 7, 1.

Drake Bean Morin (1995) *The Positive Management Of Redundancy Survivors*. London: Drake Bean Morin.

Du Gay, P. (1995) *Consumption and Identity at Work*. London: Sage.

Du Gay, P. and Salaman, G. (1992) 'The cult(ure) of the customer', *Journal of Management Studies*, 29, 5, 615–33.

Durkheim, E. (1960) *The Division of Labour in Society*. Illinois: The Free Press of Glencoe (translated by G. Simpson).

Elbaum, B. (1991) 'The persistence of apprenticeship in Britain and its decline in the United States' in H. Gospel (ed.) *Industrial Training and Technological Innovation*. London: Routledge.

Elger, T. (1990) 'Technical innovation and work reorganization in British manufacturing in the 1980s: continuity, intensification or transformation?', *Work, Employment and Society*, Additional Special Issue, 67–101.

Employment Department (1994a) *Employment Department Group: Departmental Report*. Cm. 2505, London: HMSO.

Employment Department (1994b) *Labour Market and Skill Trends 1995/96*. Nottingham: Employment Department Group, Skill and Enterprise Network.

Employment Gazette (1988) Department of Employment, London: HMSO.

Employment Gazette (1989) 'Identifying fast small growth firms', 97, 1, Department of Employment, London: HMSO, 29–41.

Employment Gazette (1994) Department of Employment, London: HMSO, June.

Employment Gazette (1995) Department of Employment, London: HMSO, March.

Engineering Employers Federation (EEF) (1992) *Industrial Strategy*. London: EEF.

Esping-Andersen, G. (1993) *Changing Classes*. London: Sage.

European Commission (1993) 'Bulletin on women and employment in the EC', no. 2, DGV, *Network of Experts on the Situation of Women in the Labour Market*, Brussels.

Evans, L., Johnson, P. and Thomas, B. (eds) (1995) *The Northern Region Economy. Progress and prospects in the North of England*. London: Mansell.

Everett, M. and Leman, S. (1995) 'Modern Apprenticeships: the experience so far', *Employment Gazette*, June.

Fairbrother, P. (1995) 'The management of benefits' in T. Butler and M. Savage (eds) *Social Change and the Middle Classes*. London: UCL Press.

Felstead, A. (1992) 'Franchising, self-employment and the "Enterprise Culture": a UK perspective' in P. Leighton and A. Felstead (eds) *The New Entrepreneurs: Self Employment and Small Business in Europe*. London: Kogan Page, 237–66.

Fevre, R. (1986) 'Contract work in the recession' in K. Purcell et al. (eds) *The Changing Experience of Employment*. London: Macmillan.

Field, F. (1989) *Losing Out*. Oxford: Blackwell.

Filby, M. (1992) 'The figures, the personality and the bums: service work and sexuality', *Work, Employment and Society*, 6, 1, 23–42.

Finch, J. (1989) *Family Obligations and Social Change*. Cambridge: Polity.

Foucault, M. (1977) *Discipline and Punish: The birth of the prison*. London: Allen Lane.

Fox, A. (1974) *Beyond Contract: Work, Power and Trust Relations*. London: Faber and Faber.

Fraser, R. (1969) *Work: 2*. Harmondsworth: Penguin.

Froebel, F., Heinrichs, J. and Kreye, O. (1981) *The New International Division of Labour*. Cambridge: Cambridge University Press.

Froud, J., Johal, S., Haslea, C., Shaoul, J. and Williams, K. (1996) The Right Arguments: Refocusing the Debate of Privatization', *Working Paper 12*, Manchester: International Centre of Labour Studies.

Fukuyama, F. (1995) *Trust: the social virtues and the creation of prosperity*. London: Hamish Hamilton.

Furedi, F. (1995) 'Is it a girl's world?', *Living Marxism*, 79, 10–13.

Gabriel, Y. (1988) *Working Lives in Catering*. London: Routledge.

Gallie, D. (ed.) (1988) *Employment in Britain*. Oxford: Blackwell.

Gallie, D. (1990) 'Unemployment, the Household and Social Networks', paper presented at ISA (International Sociological Association) conference, Madrid.

Gallie, D. (1994) 'Are the unemployed an underclass? Some evidence from the Social and Economic Life Initiative', *Sociology*, 28, 3, 737–759.

Gallie, D. and White, M. (1993) *Employee Commitment and the Skills Revolution*. London: PSI Publishing.

Garrahan, P. and Stewart, P. (1992) *The Nissan Enigma*. London: Mansell.

General Household Survey (GHS) (1987) London: Office of Population Censuses and Surveys.

Gershuny, J. I., Miles, I., Jones, S., Thomas, G., and Wyatt, S. M. E. (1986) 'The preliminary analysis of the 1983/4 ESRC time budget data', *Quarterly Journal of Social Affairs*, 2, 13–39.

Gershuny, J. I. and Pahl, R. E. (1979) 'Work outside employment: some preliminary speculations', *New University Quarterly*, 34, 120–35.

Giddens, A. (1973) *The Class Structure of the Advanced Societies*. London: Hutchinson.

Gladstone, F. (1979) *Voluntary Action in a Changing World*. London: Bedford Square Press.

Gorz, A. (1982) *Farewell to the Working Class. An essay on post-industrial socialism*. London: Pluto Press.

Gorz, A. (1985) *Paths to Paradise*. London: Pluto Press.

Granovetter, M. (1982) 'The strength of weak ties' in P. V. Marsden, and N. Lin, (eds) *Social Structure and Network Analysis*. London: Sage.

Granovetter, M. (1985) 'Economic action and social structure: the problem of embeddedness', *American Journal of Sociology*, 91, 3, Nov.

Grey, R. (1994) 'Career as a project of the self and labour process discipline', *Sociology*, 28, 2, 479–498.

Grieco, M. (1989) *Keeping it in the Family*. London: Tavistock.

Groonroos, C. (1984) *Strategic Management and Marketing in the Service Sector*. London: Chartwell-Bratt.

Grunwald, J. and Flamm, K. (1985) *The Global Factory*. Washington, D.C.: Brookings Institution.

Guest, D. (1990) 'Have British workers been working harder in Thatcher's Britain? – a re-consideration of the concept of effort', *British Journal of Industrial Relations*, 28, 3, 293–312.

Hakim, C. (1987) 'Trends in the Flexible Workforce', *Employment Gazette*, 95, 11, 549–60.

Hakim, C. (1989a) 'Workforce restructuring, social insurance coverage and the black economy', *Journal of Social Policy*, 28, 4, 471–503.

Hakim, C. (1989b) 'New recruits to self-employment in the 1980s', *Employment Gazette*, June, 286–297.

Hakim, C. (1990) 'Core and periphery in employers' workforce strategies: evidence from the 1987 E.L.U.S. survey', *Work, Employment and Society*, 4, 2, 157–188.

Hakim, C. (1991) 'Grateful slaves and self-made women: fact and fantasy in women's work orientations', *European Sociological Review*, 7, 2, 101–121.

Hakim, C. (1993) 'The myth of rising female employment', *Work, Employment and Society*, 7, 1, 97–120.

Hall, K. and Miller, I. (1975) *Retraining and Tradition: The Skilled Worker in an Era of Change*. London: Allen and Unwin.

Hamill, B. and Davies, R. (1986) 'Quality in "Flightpath"' in B. Moores (ed.) *Are They Being Served?*. Oxford: Philip Allan.

Handy, C. (1994) *The Empty Raincoat. Making sense of the future*. London: Hutchinson.

Harding, P. and Jenkins, R. (1989) *The Myth of the Hidden Economy*. Milton Keynes: Open University Press.

Harkness, S. (1996) *The Gender Earnings Gap*. London: Institute of Fiscal Studies.

Harley, S. and Lee, F. (1995) 'The Academic Labour Process and the Research Assessment Exercise: academic diversity and the future of non-mainstream Economics', *Occasional Paper 24*, Leicester Business School.

Harris, C. C. (1987) *Redundancy and Recession in South Wales*. Oxford: Blackwell.

Harris, M. (1990) 'Working in the UK voluntary sector', *Work, Employment and Society*, 4, 1, 125–140.

Harrop, A. and Moss, P. (1995) 'Trends in parental employment', *Work, Employment and Society*, 9, 3, 421–444.

Harvey, M. (1995) *Towards the Insecure Society:the tax trap of self employment*. London: Institute of Employment Rights.

Hedley, R. and Davis Smith, J. (eds) (1992) *Volunteering and Society: Principles and Practice*. London: Bedford Square Press.

Henry, S. (1978) *The Hidden Economy*. London: Martin Robertson.

Hepple, B. A. (1986) 'Re-structuring employment rights', *Industrial Law Journal*, 15, 2, 69–83.

Hewitt, P. (1993) *About Time: The Revolution in Work and Family Life*. London: Rivers Oram Press

Hill, S. (1991) 'How do you manage a flexible firm? The total quality model', *Work, Employment and Society*, 5, 3, 397–415.

Hill, S. (1995) 'From Quality Circles to Total Quality Management' in A. Wilkinson and H. Willmott (eds) *Making Quality Critical: New perspectives on organizational change*. London: Routledge.

HMSO (Her Majesty's Stationery Office) (1994) *Regional Trends 29*. London: HMSO.

HMSO (1996) *Regional Trends 31*. London: HMSO.

Hochschild, A. R. (1983) *The Managed Heart: The commercialization of human feeling*. Berkeley: University of California Press.

Hollands, B. (1994) 'Back to the future? Preparing young adults for the post-industrial Wearside economy' in P. Garrahan, and P. Stewart (eds) *Urban Change and Renewal: The Paradox of Place*. Aldershot: Avebury.

Howcroft, J. B. (1991) 'Customer satisfaction in retail banking', *The Service Industries Journal*, 11, 1, 11–17.

Hudson, R. (1989) 'Labour market changes and new forms of work in old industrial regions', *Environment and Planning*, 7, 5–30.

Hunter L., McGregor A., MacInnes, I. and Sproull, A. (1993) 'The "flexible firm": strategy and segmentation', *British Journal of Industrial Relations*, 31, 3, 383–407.

Hutton, W. (1995) *The State We're In*. London: Jonathan Cape.

Hutton, W. (1996) 'Fool's gold in a fool's paradise', *The Observer*, Review, 2 June 1996, 1–2.

Hyman, R. (1987) 'Strategy or structure? Capital, labour and control', *Work, Employment and Society*, 1, 1, 25–55.

IM (Institute of Management) (1995) *Survival of the Fittest*. Bristol: Burston Distribution Services.

Inui, A. (1993) 'The competitive structure of school and the labour market: Japan and Britain', *The British Journal of the Sociology of Education*, 14, 3.

Irwin, S. and Morris, L. D. (1993) 'Social security or economic insecurity', *Journal of Social Policy*, 349–72.

JAGNET (1994) *Proposals for the Construction Industry Training Scheme for Craft and Operative New Entrants*. London: CITB (Construction Industry Training Board).

Jahoda, M. (1982) *Employment and Unemployment: a Social Psychological Analysis*. Cambridge: Cambridge University Press.

Jaques, E. (1961) *Equitable Payment*. London: Heinemann.

Jencks, C. (1996) *Visual Culture*. London: Routledge.

Jenkins, R., Bryman, A., Ford, J. and Keil, T. (1983) 'Information in the labour market: the impact of recession', *Sociology*, 17, 260–7.

Jenson, J., Hagen, E., and Reddy, C. (eds) (1988) *The Feminization of the Labour Force*. Cambridge: Polity.

Jones, G. R. (1993) *Organizational Compliance in a Region of Low Job Availability*, M. Phil. Thesis, University of Wales.

Jordan, B. et al. (1992) *Trapped in Poverty?* London: Routledge.

Jordan, B. and Redley, M. (1994) 'Polarization, the "underclass" and the Welfare State', *Work, Employment and Society*, 8, 2, 153–176.

Joseph Rowntree Foundation (1991) *National Survey of Volunteering*. Social Policy Research Findings, no. 22, York: JRF, December.

Joshi, H. (1984) *Women's Participation in Paid Work*. Research Paper No. 45, London: Department of Employment.

Jowell, R., Brook, L. and Taylor, B. (eds) (1991) *British Social Attitudes. The 8th report*. Aldershot: Dartmouth.

Jowell, R., Brook, L., Prior, G. and Taylor, B. (eds) (1992) *British Social Attitudes. The 9th Report*. Aldershot: Dartmouth.

Juran, J. M. (1979) *The Total Quality Control Handbook*. New York: McGraw Hill.

Kerfoot, D. (1995) 'The "value" of social skill ?: A case from centralised administration in a UK bank', paper to *The 13th Annual International Labour Process Conference*, University of Central Lancashire, Blackpool.

Kerfoot, D. and Knights, D. (1994) 'Empowering the "quality" worker? The seduction and contradiction of the total quality phenomenon', paper to *The 12th Annual International Labour Process Conference*, University of Aston, Birmingham.

Knights, D. and McCabe, D. (1994) 'Total Quality Management and organizational "grey" matter', paper to *Work, Employment and Society in the 1990s: Changing boundaries, changing experiences*, Conference at Rutherford College, University of Kent at Canterbury.

Kovalainen, A. (1993) *At The Margins Of The Economy: Women's Self-Employment in Finland 1960–1990*. Turku: School of Economics and Business Administration (Avebury forthcoming).

La Fargue, P. (1937) *Le Droit à la Paresse (The Right to be Idle)*. Paris: Librairie Populaire.

Lane, T. (1976) *The Union Makes Us Strong*. London: Arrow Books.

Leighton, P. and Felstead, A. (eds) (1992) *The New Entrepreneurs: Self Employment and Small Business in Europe*. London: Kogan Page.

Lewis, B. R. (1988) 'Customer care in service organizations', *International Journal of Operations and Production Management*, 8, 3.

Leys, C. (1996) 'On top of the world', *Red Pepper*, 25, June, 5.

Lilley, P. (1992) 'The Something for Nothing Society', Speech to the Conservative Party Conference, Blackpool.

Lomnitz, L. (1977) *Life in a Mexican Shanty Town*. London: Academic Press.

Luttwack, E. (1994) 'Why Fascism is the wave of the future', *London Review of Books*, 7 April.

Lyon, D. (1986) 'From "Post-Industrialism" to "Information Society": a new social transformation', *Sociology*, 20, 4, 577–88.

Lyotard, J. F. (1984) *The Postmodern Condition*. Manchester: Manchester University Press.

MacDonald, R. (1994) 'Fiddly jobs, undeclared working and the "Something for Nothing Society"', *Work, Employment and Society*, 8, 4, 507–530.

MacDonald, R. (1996a) 'Labours of love: voluntary working in a depressed local economy', *Journal of Social Policy*, 25, 1, 19–38.

MacDonald, R. (1996b, forthcoming) 'Welfare dependency, the enterprise culture and self-employed survival', *Work, Employment and Society*, 10.

MacDonald, R. and Coffield, F. (1991) *Risky Business? Youth and the Enterprise Culture*. Basingstoke: Falmer Press.

MacDonald, R. and Coffield, F. (1993) *Adults, Enterprise and New Forms of Work in a Depressed Local Economy*. Final Report to the ESRC, University of Durham.

MacKenzie, D. and Wajcman, J. (1985) *The Social Shaping of Technology*. Milton Keynes: Open University Press.

MacNicol, J. (1994) 'Is there an Underclass? The Lessons From America' in M. White (ed.) *Unemployment and Public Policy in a Changing Labour Market*. London: Policy Studies Institute.

McCabe, D., Knights, D. and Wilkinson, A. (1994) *Quality Initiatives in Financial Services*, Research Report, Financial Services Research Centre, Manchester School of Management, UMIST.

McKinley, A. (1991) 'A certain short-sightedness: metalworking, innovation and apprenticeship, 1897–1939' in H. Gospel (ed.) *Industrial Training and Technological Innovation*. London: Routledge.

McLaughlin, E. (1994) 'Flexibility or Polarisation?' in M. White (ed.) *Unemployment and Public Policy in a Changing Labour Market*. London: Policy Studies Institute.

Maddox, S. (1996) 'Rhetoric and reality: the business case for equality and why it's resisted', *Women in Management Review*, 10, 1, 14–20.

Manwaring, T. and Wood, S. (1985) 'The ghost in the labour process', in D. Knights, H. Willmot and D. Collinson (eds) *Job Redesign: critical perspectives on the labour process*. Aldershot: Gower, 171–96.

Marglin, S. (1980) 'The origins and functions of hierarchy in capitalist production', in T. Nichols (ed.) *Capital and Labour*. Glasgow: Fontana.

Marshall, T. H. (1950) *Citizenship and Social Class*. Cambridge: Cambridge University Press.

Meadows, P. (1996) (ed.) *Work Out – or Work In? Contributions to the debate on the future of work*. York: Rowntree Foundation.

Meager, N. (1992) 'The characteristics of the self-employed: some Anglo-German comparisons' in P. Leighton and A. Felstead (eds) (1992) *The New Entrepreneurs: Self Employment and Small Business in Europe*. London: Kogan Page, 69–99.

Meek, V. L. (1988) 'Organizational culture: origins and weaknesses', *Organization Studies*, 9, 4.

Metcalf, D. (1989) 'Water notes dry up: the impact of the Donovan reform proposals and Thatcherism at work on labour productivity in British manufacturing industry', *British Journal of Industrial Relations*, 27, 1, 1–31.

Millward, N. (1994) *The New Industrial Relations*. London: Policy Studies Institute.

Millward, N., Stevens, M., Smart, D. and Hawes, W. R. (1992) *Workplace Industrial Relations in Transition*. Aldershot: Dartmouth.

Minkin, L. (1996) *Exits and Entrances: political research as a creative act*. Sheffield: University of Sheffield Hallam Press.

Mintel (1995) *Leisure Time*. London.

Mintel (1995a) *Marketing to 45–64s*. London: Mintel.

Mizen, P. (1995) *The State, Young People and Youth Training*. London: Mansell.

More, C. (1980) *Skill and the English Working Class, 1870–1914*. London: Croom Helm.

Morgan, C. and Murgatroyd, S. (1994) *Total Quality Management in the Public Sector*. Buckingham: Open University Press.

Morgan, D. (1990) *Discovering Men*. London: Routledge.

Morgan, K. (1986) 'Reindustrialisation in peripheral Britain: state policy, the space economy and industrial innovation' in R. Martin and B. Rowthorne (eds) *The Geography of Deindustrialisation*. London: Macmillan.

Morris, L. D. (1987) 'Local social polarization: a case study of Hartlepool', *International Journal of Urban and Regional Research*, 11, 331–52.

Morris, L. D. (1988) 'Employment, the household and social networks' in D. Gallie (ed.) *Employment in Britain*. Oxford: Blackwell, 376–405.

Morris, L. D. (1990) *The Workings of the Household*. Cambridge: Polity Press.

Morris, L. D. (1992) 'The social segregation of the long-term unemployed in Hartlepool', *Sociological Review*, 40, 2, 344–369.

Morris, L. D. (1994) *Dangerous Classes. The underclass and social citizenship*. London: Routledge.

Morris, L. D. (1995) *Social Divisions*. London: UCL Press.

Morris, L. D. and Irwin, S. (1992) 'Employment histories and the concept of the underclass', *Sociology*, 26, 3, 401–420.

Morrison, B. (1994) 'Brave New World on the Tyne', *The Independent on Sunday Review*, December.

Munch, R. (1987) *Theory of Action*. London: Routledge and Kegan Paul.

Murdoch, L. (1995) 'Danger: women's work ahead', *Living Marxism*, 79, 14–16.

Murray, C. (1990) *The Emerging British Underclass*. London: Institute of Economic Affairs.

Murray, C. (1994) *The Underclass: The Crisis Deepens*, London: Institute of Economic Affairs.

Nash, J. and Fernandez-Kelly, M. P. (1983) (eds) *Women, Men, and the International Division of Labour*. Albany: State University of New York Press.

National Association of Citizens Advice Bureaux (1992) *Job Insecurity: CAB evidence on employment problems in the recession*. London: CAB.

National Audit Office (1988) *Department of Employment/Training Commission: Assistance to Small Firms*. Report 655, London: HMSO.

National Council for Vocational Qualifications (NCVQ) (1995) *NVQ criteria and guidance*. London: Employment Department.

NEDO (National Economic Development Office) (1986) *Changing Working Patterns. How companies achieve flexibility to meet new needs*. London: NEDO.

Nichols, T. (1986) *The British Worker Question. A New Look at Workers and Productivity in Manufacturing*. London: Routledge and Kegan Paul.

Nolan, P. and Marginson, P. (1990) 'Skating on thin ice? David Metcalf on trade unions and productivity', *British Journal of Industrial Relations*, 28, 2, 227–247.

OPCS/GROS (Office of Population Censuses and Surveys; General Registrar Office, Scotland) (1993) *1991 Census. Report for Great Britain (Part 2)*. London: HMSO.

OPCS/GROS (1994) *1991 Census. Economic Activity, Great Britain. Vol. 2*. London: HMSO.

Pahl, J. (1983) 'The allocation of money and the structuring of inequality within marriage', *Sociological Review*, 31, 235–62.

Pahl, R. E. (1980) 'Employment, work and the domestic division of labour', *International Journal of Urban and Regional Research*, 4, 1–20.

Pahl, R. E. (1984) *Divisions of Labour*. Oxford: Blackwell.

Pahl, R. E. (ed.) (1988) *On Work*. Oxford: Blackwell.

Payne, J. (1987) 'Does unemployment run in families?', *Sociology*, 21, 2, 199–214.

Payne, J., and Payne, C. (1994) 'Recession, restructuring and the fate of the unemployed: evidence in the underclass debate', *Sociology*, 28, 1, 1-21.

Penn, R. D. (1986) 'Socialisation into skilled identities', paper at 'Organisation and Control of the Labour Process' conference, April 1986.

Peters, T. and Austin, N. (1985) *A Passion for Excellence*, New York: Random House.

Phelps-Brown, E. H. (1968) *Report of the Committee of Inquiry under Professor E. H.Phelps-Brown into Certain Matters Concerning Labour in Building and Civil Engineering*. London: HMSO, Cd. 3714.

Phizacklea, A. (1990) *Unpacking the Fashion Industry: Gender, Racism and Class in Production*. London: Routledge.

Phizacklea, A. and Wolkowitz, C. (1995) *Homeworking Women*. London: Sage.

Piore, M. J. and Sabel, C. F. (1984) *The Second Industrial Divide*. New York: Basic Books.

Pixley, J. (1993) *Citizenship and Employment*. Cambridge: Cambridge University Press.

Pollert, A. (1988a) 'The "flexible firm": fixation or fact', *Work, Employment and Society*, 2, 3, 281–316.

Pollert, A. (1988b) 'Dismantling flexibility', *Capital and Class*, 34, 42–75.

Pollert, A. (1991) *Farewell to Flexibility?* Oxford: Blackwell.

Porter, M. (1990) *Competitive Strategy: Techniques for analysing industries and competitors*, London: Free Press.

Price, F. (1993) 'Educated power', *TQM Magazine*, 5, 3.

Proctor, S. J., Rowlinson, M., McArdle, L., Hassard, J. and Forrester, P. (1994) 'Flexibility, Politics and Strategy: in defence of the model of the flexible firm', *Work, Employment and Society*, 8, 2, 221–242.

Pulkingham, J. (1992) 'Employment restructuring in the health service: efficiency initiatives, working patterns and workforce composition', *Work, Employment and Society*, 8, 2, 221–242.

Rainbird, H. (1990) *Training Matters*. Oxford: Blackwell.

Rainnie, A. (1992) 'Flexibility and small firms: prospects for the 1990s' in P. Leighton and A. Felstead (eds) (1992) *The New Entrepreneurs: Self Employment and Small Business in Europe*. London: Kogan Page, 217–36.

Ranson, S. (1992) 'Towards the Learning Society', *Educational Management and Administration*, 20, 2.

Rees, G. and Fielder, S. (1992)'The services economy, subcontracting and the new employment relations: contract catering and cleaning', *Work, Employment and Society*, 6, 3, 347–368.

Rees, T. (1992) *Women and the Labour Market*. London: Routledge.

Regional Trends (1996) London: HMSO.

Reich, R. (1991) *The Work of Nations*. New York: Knopf.

Reynolds, J. (1983) *The Great Paternalist. Titus Salt and The Growth of Nineteenth Century Bradford*. London: Temple Smith.

Rifkin, J. (1996) *The End of Work*. London: Tarcher/Pitman.

Ritzer, G. (1993) *The Macdonaldization of Society: An Investigation into the Changing Character of Contemporary Social Life*. Thousand Oaks, Calif.: Pine Forge Press.

Roberts, B., Finnegan, R. and Gallie, D. (eds) (1985) *New Approaches to Economic Life*. Manchester: Manchester University Press.

Roberts, I. (1993) *Craft, Class and Control*. Edinburgh: Edinburgh University Press.

Roberts, I. and Wilkinson, A. (1991) 'Participation and purpose: boilermakers to bankers', *Critical Perspectives on Accounting*, 2.

Robinson, F. (ed.) (1988) *Post-Industrial Tyneside: An economic and social survey of Tyneside in the 1980s.* Newcastle: Newcastle upon Tyne City Libraries and Arts.

Rowbotham, S. and Mitter, S. (1994) *Dignity and Daily Bread: new forms of economic organising among poor women in the third world and the first.* London: Routledge.

Rubery, J. (1988) 'Women and recession: a comparative perspective' in J.Rubery (ed.) *Women and Recession.* London: Routledge and Kegan Paul.

Runciman, W. G. (1990) 'How many classes are there in contemporary British society?', *Sociology,* 24, 377–396.

Sabel, C. F. (1982) *Work and Politics.* Cambridge: Cambridge University Press.

Sadler, D. (1992) *The Global Region.* Oxford: Pergamon.

Sayer, A. and Walker, R. (1992) *The New Social Economy. Reworking the Division of Labour.* Oxford: Blackwell.

Scase, R and Goffee (1989) *Reluctant Managers: their Work and Lifestyles.* London: Unwin Hyman.

Schmitt, J. and Wadsworth, J. (1994) 'Unemployment, inequality and efficiency: the rise of economic inactivity' in A. Glyn and D. Miliband (eds) *Paying For Inequality: The Economic Costs of Social Injustice.* London: Rivers Oram Press.

Schor, J. (1992) *The Overworked American.* New York: Basic Books.

Sewell, G. and Wilkinson, B. (1992) '"Someone to watch over me": Surveillance, discipline and the just-in-time labour process', *Sociology,* 26, 2, 271–289.

Sheard, J. (1992) 'Volunteering and society; 1960 to 1990' in R.Hedley and J.Davis Smith (eds), *Volunteering and Society: Principles and Practice.* London: Bedford Square Press.

Showler, B. and Sinfield, A. (eds) (1981) *The Workless State.* Oxford: Martin Robertson.

Smith, D. J. (ed.) (1991) *Understanding the Underclass.* London: Policy Studies Institute (PSI).

Social and Community Planning Research (1992) *British Social Attitudes Cumulative Sourcebook. The first six surveys.* Aldershot: Gower (compiled by L. Brook, S. Hedges, R. Jowell, J. Lewis, G. Prior, G. Sebastian, B. Taylor and S. Witherspoon).

Social Trends (1996) London: HMSO.

Speakers Commission (1990) *Encouraging Citizenship.* London: HMSO.

Spencer, L. and Taylor, S. (1994) *Participation and Progress in the Labour Market: Key issues for women.* Sheffield: Department of Employment Research Series no. 35.

Stanworth, J. and Gray, C. (eds) (1991) *Bolton Twenty Years On: The Small Firm in the 1990s.* London: Paul Chapman Publishing.

Steiger, T. L. (1993) 'Construction skill and skill construction', *Work, Employment and Society,* 7, 4.

Stonier, T. (1983) *The Wealth of Information.* London: Thames and Hudson.

Storey, D. and Strange, A. (1992) 'New Players in the "Enterprise Culture"?' in K. Caley et al., (eds) *Small Enterprise Development.* London: Paul Chapman Publishing.

Streeck, W. (1987) 'The uncertainties of management in the management of uncertainty', *Work, Employment and Society*, 1, 3, 281–308.

Taylor, S. (1995) *Work and Autonomy: Case studies of clerical work*, unpublished Ph.D. thesis, Department of Sociology and Social Policy, University of Durham.

Teesside T. E. C. (1995a) *Labour Market Assessment*. Middlesbrough.

Teesside T. E. C. (1995b) *Annual Report 1994*. Middlesbrough.

Thompson, E. P. (1967) 'Time, work-discipline and industrial capitalism', *Past and Present*, 38, December.

Thompson, P. (1983) *The Nature of Work: An introduction to debates on the labour process*. London: Macmillan, 2nd edition 1989.

Toffler, A. (1981) *The Third Wave*. London: Collins/Pan Books.

Tomlinson, M. (1994) 'Employment stability in work histories', paper presented to European Science Foundation conference 'European Society or European Societies', Espinho, Portugal.

Touraine, A. (1974) *The Post-Industrial Society*. London: Wildwood House.

Trinder, C. and Worsley, R. (1996) *The Third Age: The Continuing Challenge*. London: Carnegie UK Trust.

Trotman, C. (1993) *Attitudinal and Behavioural Responses to Changing Patterns of Technological and Organizational Innovation*. Ph.D. Thesis, University of Wales.

Tuckman, A. (1995) 'Ideology, quality and TQM' in A. Wilkinson and H. Willmott (eds) *Making Quality Critical: New perspectives on organizational change*. London: Routledge.

Turnbull, P. (1991) 'Labour market deregulation and economic performance: the case of Britain's docks', *Work, Employment and Society*, 5, 1, 17–35.

Tyneside TEC (1993) *Training People...Developing Business: Labour market report 1992–3*. Newcastle: Tyneside TEC.

Walsh, K. (1995) 'Quality through markets: The new public service management' in A. Wilkinson and H. Willmott (eds) *Making Quality Critical: New perspectives on organizational change*. London: Routledge.

Walter, N. (1996) 'Bringing out the woman in New Labour', *The Guardian*, 29 February 1996.

Watson, T. (1994) *In Search of Management: Culture, chaos and control in managerial work*. London: Routledge.

Warde, A. (1996) 'The effects of the 1992 Research Assessment Exercise', *Network*, British Sociological Association newsletter, 64.

Webb, J. (1992) 'The mismanagment of innovation', *Sociology*, 26, 3, 471–92.

Webb, S. and B. (1913) *Industrial Democracy*. London: Longmans, Green & Co.

Wheelock, J. (1990) *Husbands at Home*. London: Routledge.

Whitston, C. and Waddington, J. (1994) 'Why join a union', *New Statesman and Society*, 19 November.

Wilkinson, A., Allen, P. and Snape, E. (1991) 'TQM and the management of labour', *Employee Relations*, 13, 2.

Wilkinson, A. and Willmott, H. (1995) 'Introduction' in A. Wilkinson and H. Willmott (eds) *Making Quality Critical: New perspectives on organizational change*. London: Routledge.

Willmott, H. (1993) 'Strength is Ignorance; Slavery is Freedom: managing culture in modern organizations', *Journal of Management Studies*, 30, 4.

Wilson, W. J. (1991) 'Studying inner-city dislocation', *American Sociological Review*, 56, 1–14.

Winterton, J. (1993) 'The end of a way of life: coal communities since the end of the 1984–85 miners' strike', *Work, Employment and Society*, 7, 1, 135–146.

Wood, S. (ed.) (1989) *The Transformation of Work? Skill, Flexibility and the Labour Process*. London: Unwin Hyman.

Wray, D. (1993) *Changing Employment Relations in a Local Labour Market: Consett after the Closure*. M. A. Thesis, University of Durham.

Wright, S. (ed.) (1994) *Anthropology of Organisations*. London: Routledge.

Young, M. and Halsey, A. H. (1995) 'Family and community socialism'. Institute for Public Policy Research.

Subject Index

apprenticeship, 15, 20, 139, 153–5, 163–5
  collapse of, 159–62
  cost of, 162–3, 169
  and employers/management, 153, 157
  and identity, 155–9
  modern, 163–4, 169, 170
  and skill, 155–9
  see also training
Association of University Teachers (AUT), 41
Australia, 73

British Association for the Advancement of Science, vii, 2
British Gas, 39
British Social Attitudes Survey, 47, 76, 77
British Sociological Association, 41
British Steel, 104

chemical industry, 91
  see also ICI
child care, 89, 95–6, 97, 99, 143–4
Civil Service, 40, 91
  see also employment, public sector
class, *see* inequality; workers
Cleveland, *see* Teesside
coal mining, 20, 22, 37, 79
collective worker, 164–5, 167, 170
Community Care, 114
Community Opportunities, 114
construction, 32, 33, 104, 125, 153–5, 158, 160–2, 166–7
consumption, 2, 80
crime, 103, 120
customers, 26, 80, 172–4
  and banking, 182–3, 188–90, 196
  satisfaction, 174, 182, 186
  and telephone sales, 181–2, 187–8, 194–5

Department of Employment (DE), 36–7, 70–1, 72, 73, 86, 105, 106, 107, 116, 118, 122
Department of Health, 49
Department of Social Security (DSS), 40, 116, 118, 122
discretion, 176, 187–96
  negative, 198–200, 201
  positive, 187–90, 201
distribution, *see* retailing
division of labour, 3–6, 54, 165–6
  gender, 5–6, 25, 62, 87, 92, 98–9, 100–1, 144–6
  see also labour force
domestic labour, 3, 55, 64, 89–90
  and gender, 144–6
  see also employment and household organization
downsizing, *see* employment, reductions in; redundancy
dual earning couples, *see* employment and household organization

economic inactivity, 43–5, 52
  see also unemployment
Economic and Social Research Council (ESRC) 102, 123, 201
emotional labour, 15, 175, 177–8, 183, 195, 199
employed population, *see* labour force
employment, 58–60
  changes in, 13, 16, 20–30, 76–7
  conditions of, 59, 64–5; in 'fiddly' jobs, 117
  core and periphery, 74
  feminization of, 5–6, 14, 16, 60, 87–92, 101–2
  future of, 18
  and household organization, 15, 17, 88–9, 96–7, 101–2, 144–6

informal, 103, 105–11, 132–3, 141
insecurity of, 8–9, 38, 43–53,
  74–6, 77–8, 83, 88, 97
instability in, 16, 18, 139–40
and job histories, 139; *see also*
  women, work histories
in multiple jobs, 34
non-standard, 8, 36, 37, 45, 75,
  88, 104–5
part-time, 8, 16, 33–7, 46, 59, 88,
  90
public sector, 7, 38–43, 71, 79
reductions in, 21–5, 46–8, 53,
  75–6, 79, 104
of women, 33–5, 59–60; *see also*
  women, employment
  opportunities for
and work, 1–3, 57–8
see also division of labour; self-
  employment;
  unemployment; work
employment relations, 5, 8, 64–5,
  81
changes in, 28–9, 49
deregulation of, 9–10, 53, 70, 74,
  82
employment relationship, 58, 82–3
and apprenticeship, 158–9, 165,
  167
and trust, 29, 38
Employment Training (ET),
  114–15, 161, 163
engineering, 153–6, 159, 160
enterprise, 7, 33, 121
culture, 62, 67, 106, 110–11, 121
and Total Quality Management,
  172–3, 183
see also self-employment; small
  firms
Enterprise Allowance Scheme, 106
entrepreneurship, *see* enterprise;
  self-employment
European Union, 11, 59, 64, 71, 73,
  85

family labour, 63
'fiddly' jobs, 115–19, 121–2
financial services, 25, 33, 87, 91
  see also Friendlybank

flexibility, 12, 17, 28, 34–5, 70, 71–3,
  88, 170
in numbers/numerical, 72, 74,
  79
in pay, 72
in tasks/functional, 72, 73, 74, 79
see also employment, non-
  standard
flexible firm, 12, 73–5
flexible labour market, 9, 34, 70–3,
  113
flexible specialization, *see* flexibility,
  functional
flexible work organization, 58
Flightpath, 179–88, 191–2,
  194–202
Fordism, 11–12, 21
fraud, 118
Friendlybank, 180–6, 188–9, 192–3,
  195–6, 200–2

Gateshead, 93
gender segregation, *see* division of
  labour, gender
General Agreement on Tariffs and
  Trade (GATT), 10
Germany, 61
government policy
  economic, 9, 21, 56, 70–1, 82,
    119
  employment, 64–5, 84
  welfare, 114
  see also privatization
globalization, 2, 9–11, 55–6, 150

Hartlepool, 14–15, 111, 125–49
hidden economy, 118–9
homeworkers, 37, 59, 62
hotels and catering, 26, 34, 35, 36,
  87
household strategies, 126, 140–2,
  148–9
household finances
  and employment status, 147
  and gender, 147–8
  typology of, 146
housing
  allocation and tenure, 128–9
  market, 80, 126

ICI, 23, 104
idleness
    right to be idle, 54, 66–7
incentives, *see* pay, performance
    related
industrial disputes, 40, 49, 157
industrialization, 62–3
    and changes in employment,
        3–6
    and training, apprenticeship,
        153–5
inequality, 16–17, 27, 60, 65, 88
    gender, 100–1
    and knowledge and information,
        66
    and social networks, 125–6
informal activity
    exchanges, 132–6
    see also employment, informal
International Labour Office (ILO),
    90
inward investment, 23

Japan, 23, 151
job search, 137–9
    see also employment; women,
        employment opportunities
        for
job security, 77–81
    see also employment, insecurity of

labour force
    changes in, 31
    industrial distribution of, 4,
        21–38
    occupational distribution of, 4–5,
        21–38
    women in, 5, 44, 87–90
    see also division of labour
Labour Force Survey, 31, 46, 75, 88
labour markets, 14, 69–86
    and apprenticeship, 154–5,
        159–60
    flexible, 34, 84
    local, 2, 126
Labour Party, 51
leisure, 14, 19
    see also idleness
Liverpool, 52

Macdonaldism, 26
management
    and the discourse of enterprise,
        172–5
    failings of, 28–9
    thought, 15, 29–30, 150–3
    women in, 30
    see also Total Quality Management
        (TQM)
manufacturing, 4–5, 21–5, 46, 47,
    60, 61, 79, 87, 104, 106, 125,
    160, 179
    foreign companies, 23
    see also specific industries,
        chemicals, engineering, etc.
Merseyside, 22–3
multi-national corporations, *see*
    transnational corporations

National Health Service (NHS), 42,
    91
National Union of Teachers, 41–2
National Vocational Qualifications
    (NVQs), 164–5
nationalized industries, *see*
    employment, public sector, *and
    specific industries*
Newcastle upon Tyne, 2, 91, 93
Nissan, 24, 26
North East of England, 2, 24, 91,
    101, 171, 178–9
North Wales, 28–9

occupational segregation, *see*
    division of labour
organizational change, 150–3,
    173–5
organizational culture, *see* work
    cultures
outsourcing, *see* sub-contracting

Panopticon, 176–7, 191, 193, 194
pay, 27–8, 50
    of apprentices, 154–5
    determination, 73, 83
    family wage, 37
    in 'fiddly' jobs, 117
    performance related, 73, 78, 192–4
    of self-employed, 109

post-Fordism, 11–13, 21, 28, 87
post-industrial society, 21, 46, 66, 87, 102
Post Office, 39
privatization, 7, 38–43, 71
    see also employment, public sector
public utilities, *see* employment, public sector, *and specific industries*

rationality
    and acquisition of skills, 166–70
redundancy, 46–7, 75, 125, 140
    see also employment, reductions in; unemployment
Redundancy Payments Act, 84
research methods
    economic change and domestic life, 126–8, 129
    gender and change, 91
    informal working, 105, 116, 123–4
    Total Quality Management, 176
restriction of output, 79
restructuring, 55–6, 60
    on Teesside, 103–4, 110–11, 125
    see also employment, reductions in; redundancy
retailing, 25, 33, 36, 52, 87, 91

salaries, *see* pay
Saltaire, 58–9, 67–8
Scotland, 25
Second World War, 2, 18, 59
    the post-war period, 6–9, 11, 18, 20–1, 56, 69–70, 84
self-employment, 7, 8, 31–3, 62–4, 105–11, 121, 124
    see also enterprise; small firms
service sector, 4, 22, 25–8, 46, 59, 87–8, 171, 178–9
    and self-employment, 63, 109–10
    workers, 26, 27, 178–200
shipbuilding, 79, 125, 156, 159–60, 179
small firms, 62–3, 68, 105–11
    on Teesside, 107–9
    see also enterprise; self-employment

Social Change and Economic Life Initiative (SCELI), 72, 76, 132
social networks, 130–1, 148–9
    friendship, 131
    and job search, 137–8
    kinship, 130–1
    and unemployment, 130–1, 134–6, 140
South East of England, 46
South Wales, 20–1, 24, 29
South West of England, 116, 117
steel industry, 20, 24–5, 38, 104, 125
stress, 13, 16–17, 31, 40, 43–52, 89, 101–2
strikes, *see* industrial disputes
sub-contracting, 24, 117, 122–3, 125
survival strategies, 49–51, 78–9, 103, 119–23

technology
    changes in, 13, 19, 65–6, 154, 160
    information, 32, 66
    new, 56, 60, 65, 67
Teesside, 14, 23, 103–24
Teesside Training and Enterprise Council (TEC), 104, 107, 124
television, *see* Yorkshire Tyne Tees TV
textiles, 22–3, 58–9
Total Quality Management (TQM), 15, 29, 171–202
    and managerial control, 191–200
    resistance to, 196–201
tourism, 25, 47–8
    see also hotels and catering
trade unions, 51–2, 59, 82, 150–1
    and apprenticeship, 153
    membership, 7–8, 51
Trades Union Congress (TUC), 40
training, 70, 162–8, 168–70
    see also apprenticeship
transnational corporations, 10–11
    see also ICI; Nissan
Tyneside, 91, 116, 179

underclass, 14, 103, 119–23, 136
unemployment, 6–7, 17, 31, 43–5, 47, 60–2, 69–71, 75–6, 79, 85–7, 103–4, 119–25, 150

unemployment – *continued*
  and benefits, 130, 142–3
  and crime, 120–1
  and deprivation, 60–1, 119–20
  deregulation, 70
  and exchanges of aid, 133–4
  and 'fiddly' jobs, 115–6, 121–2
  geographical concentration,
    128–30
  in households, 129–30
  and Keynesianism, 70, 85
  long-term, 120, 126, 130
  male, 61–2, 87
  and self-employment, 31, 108,
    110–11
  and skill, 138–9, 141
  and voluntary work, 111–13, 123
  of women, 61–2
  of young people, 7
universities, 41
USA, 27, 53, 73, 89

wages, *see* pay
West Yorkshire, 54
women
  attitudes/commitment to paid
    work, 35, 90–1, 93–5, 98–9,
    101
  in employment, 5–6, 25, 33–4,
    44–5; married women, 5–6,
    45
  employment opportunities for, 6,
    16, 20–1, 26, 30, 33–5, 45,
    59–60, 88–90, 100–1
  work histories, 95–6, 142–4
  see also division of labour, gender;
    unemployment, women
work, 57–8, 64–7

attitudes/orientations to, 77–8,
    98–9, 112–13, 121, 175–8; in
    'fiddly' jobs, 118, 122; in
    voluntary work, 112–13, 122
autonomy, 187–96, 198–200
cultures, 104–5, 150–70, 175, 185,
    202
and employment, 1–3, 57–8
hours of, 37, 50
and identity, 13, 20, 54–5, 61, 112,
    155–9
intensity of, 37, 40–3, 48, 78–9
manual, 4–5, 20–1
non-manual, 4–5, 21, 27
unpaid, 64, 113–14
voluntary, 3, 14, 111–15
see also domestic labour;
    employment; workers
workers
  clerical, 87, 171–202
  'hyphenated', 30–7
  managerial, 46, 49, 60, 78
  manual, 27–8, 33, 78
  non-manual, 27–8
  non-skilled, 156, 162, 164
  professional, 33, 40–2, 60, 63, 78
  skilled, 154–9, 160–2, 164–6
  white collar, 33, 46, 78, 156
work ethic, 14, 19, 40, 57, 118–19,
    121
work organization, 15, 36, 39, 40,
    42, 173
Workplace Industrial Relations
    Surveys (WIRS), 51, 72, 75, 78

Yorkshire Tyne Tees TV, 38
Youth Training (YT), 161, 162–3,
    168–9

Author Index

Adler, S., 90
Allen J., 8, 12, 21
Allen, S., 1, 58, 61, 62, 63, 68, 90
Anthony, P. D., 30
Armstrong, P., 151
Ashton, D. N., 7
Atkinson, J., 72

Bagguley, P., 120
Ball, C., 159
Bauman, Z., 67, 172
Beale, D., 151
Beatson, M., 8, 71, 72, 75
Bell, D., 65
Beveridge, W. H., 6, 60, 61, 89
Bevins, A., 117
Beynon, H., 23, 26, 42
Boaden, R. J., 172, 174, 182, 184
Bradley, H., 87
Bradshaw, A., 116
Brannen, J., 102
Braverman, H., 167
Bright, G., 106
Brindle, D., 114
Brown, P., 60, 88
Brown, R. K., 4, 5, 6, 8, 77, 83, 160,
    196, 201
Burchell, B., 59, 62
Burrows, R., 62, 106
Byrne, D., 120

Caley, K., 109
Campbell, B., 89
Campbell, M., 105, 106
Carr, M., 158
Casey, B., 62
Charles, L., 35, 36
Chittenden, F., 109
Christensen, K., 58
Citizens Advice Bureaux, 117
Clegg, S., 172, 173
Cleveland Council for Voluntary
    Service, 114

Cleveland County Council, 104,
    120
Cockburn, C., 89
Coffield, F., 106, 107, 108, 112
Coles, B., 121
Confederation of British Industry
    (CBI), 172, 173
Cooke, K., 142
Coombes, M., 87
Cooper, G., 30, 49, 50
Cooper, N., 61
Coward, R., 92, 98
Craine, S., 121
Creigh, S., 62
Cressey, P., 83, 182, 196, 200, 201
Crompton, R., 6, 35, 89
Crosby, P. B., 172
Cross, M., 56
Curran, J., 106

Dahrendorf, R., 119
Dale, B. G., 172, 174, 182, 184
Daly, M., 105, 106
Davidson, M., 30
Davies, R., 181
Davies, R. B., 143
Davis Smith, J., 114
Dean, H., 122
Deming, W. C. 172
Department for Education and
    Employment (DfEE), 4, 5
Dennis, N., 119, 122
Devine, F., 102
Dignan, W., 182
The Director, 39
Drake Bean Morin, 49
Du Gay, P., 26, 172, 173, 175
Durkheim, E., 54

Economic Trends, 39
Elbaum, B., 154
Elger, T., 79

Employment Gazette, 22, 25, 34, 62, 137
Engineering Employers Federation (EEF), 166
Erdos, G., 119, 122
Esping-Andersen, G., 88
European Commission, 64
Evans, L., 2
Everett, M., 158, 167, 169

Fairbrother, P., 40
Felstead, A., 62, 68
Fernandez-Kelly, M. P., 56
Fevre, R., 117
Field, F., 119
Fielder, S., 79
Filby, M., 201
Financial Times, 36, 37, 38, 46, 47, 48, 53
Finch, J., 132, 135
Flamm, K., 56
Foucault, M., 176, 191
Fox, A., 196
Fraser, R., 156–7
Froebel, F., 56
Froud, J., 39
Fukuyama, F., 38
Furedi, F., 89, 90, 100

Gallie, D., 76, 77, 119, 124, 133
Garrahan, P., 56, 170
General Household Survey (GHS), 44–5, 129, 137
General Registrar Office for Scotland (GROS), 5, 6
Gershuny, J. I., 141, 145
Giddens, A., 119
Gladstone, F., 114
Glyn, A., 151
Goffee, R., 28
Gorz, A., 67
Granovetter, M., 138, 155
Gray, C., 105, 106, 110
Grey, R., 98
Grieco, M., 137
Groonroos, C., 175
Grunwald, J., 56
The Guardian, 30, 77, 80, 102
Guest, D., 78

Hakim, C., 8, 34, 90, 92–3, 98, 104, 106
Hall, K., 164
Halsey, A. H., 89
Hamill, B., 181
Handy, C., 76
Harding, P., 118
Harkness, S., 28
Harley, S., 41
Harris, C. C., 128, 129
Harris, M., 111
Harrison, J., 151
Harrop, A., 96
Harvey, M., 33
Hedley, R., 114
Henry, N., 8
Henry, S., 118
Hepple, B. A., 65
Hewitt, P., 34
Hill, S., 174, 175
Hochschild, A. R., 175, 177–8, 183
Hollands, B., 169
Holmes, H., 116
Howcroft, J. B., 172, 174, 178, 182
Hudson, R., 23
Hunter L., 74
Hutton, W., 8, 18, 27, 76, 88
Hyman, R., 201

Institute of Management, 49
Inui, A., 155
Irwin, S., 149

JAGNET, 163
Jahoda, M., 112
Jaques, E., 196
Jencks, C., 27
Jenkins, R., 118, 137
Jenson, J., 60, 88
Jones, G. R., 29
Jordan, B., 103, 116, 117, 121
Joseph Rowntree Foundation, 111, 112
Joshi, H., 142
Jowell, R., 76
Juran, J. M., 172

Kerfoot, D., 172, 202
Knights, D., 202
Kovalainen, A., 63

La Fargue, P., 54
Lane, T., 165
Lee, F., 41
Leighton, P., 62, 68
Leman, S., 158, 167, 169
Lewis, B. R., 175, 181
Leys, C., 11
Lilley, P., 119
Lomnitz, L., 140
Luttwack, E., 53
Lyon, D., 66
Lyotard, J. F., 67

MacDonald, R., 106, 107, 108, 112,
    115, 116, 124
MacEarlean, N., 50
MacInnes, J., 83, 196, 200, 201
MacKenzie, D., 66
MacNicol, J., 120
McCabe, D., 172, 202
McKinley, A., 155
McLaughlin, E., 104
Maddox, S., 30
Mann, K., 120
Manwaring, T., 83
Marginson, P., 78
Marglin, S., 153
Marshall, T. H., 60
Massey, D., 12, 21
Meadows, P., 45
Meager, N., 63, 72
Meek, V. L., 170
Metcalf, D., 78
Miller, I., 164
Millward, N., 8, 51, 75, 78, 88
Minkin, L., 41
Mintel, 48, 101
Mitter, S., 37
Mizen, P., 163
More, C., 153, 155
Morgan, D., 89
Morgan, K., 56
Morris, L. D., vii, 88, 118, 120, 127,
    132, 141, 142, 146, 149

Morrison, B., 179
Moss, P., 96, 102
Munch, R., 170
Murdoch, L., 88, 90
Murray, C., 89, 103, 119, 120, 123

Nash, J., 56
National Audit Office, 106, 110
National Council for Vocational
    Qualifications, 165
New Earnings Survey, 28
Nichols, T., 28, 78
Nolan, P., 78

The Observer, 29, 35, 50, 51
Office of Population Censuses and
    Surveys (OPCS), 5, 6

Pahl, J., 146
Pahl, R. E., 57, 89, 116, 117, 129,
    132, 135, 141
Payne, C., 124
Payne, G., 56
Payne, J., 124, 130
Penn, R. D., 155, 168
Phelps-Brown, E. H., 155
Phizacklea, A., 37, 62
Piore, M. J., 21, 172
Pixley, J., 61
Pollert, A., 12, 58, 75, 88
Porter, M., 174
Price, F., 175
Proctor, S. J., 74
Pulkingham, J., 79

Rainnie, A., 58
Ranson, S., 159
Redley, M., 103, 121
Rees, G., 79
Rees, T., 95
Regional Trends, 91
Reich, R., 27
Reynolds, J., 58, 67
Rifkin, J., 23
Ritzer, G., 26
Roach, S., 53
Roberts, B., 103
Roberts, I., 153, 155, 158, 169

Robinson, F., 88, 91, 179
Rowbotham, S., 37
Rubery, J., 58, 59, 62
Runciman, W. G., 119

Sabel, C. F., 21, 155, 156, 157, 172,
    173
Sadler, D., 23, 56
Salaman, G., 172, 173, 175
Sanderson, K., 6, 35, 89
Sayer, A., 54
Scase, R., 28, 60, 88
Schmitt, J., 43
Schor, J., 37
Scott, P., 182
Sewell, G., 176–7, 190, 191, 201
Sheard, J., 114
Showler, B., 7
Sinfield, A., 7
Smith, D. J., 120
Social and Community Planning
    Research, 76, 77
Social Trends, 96
Speaker's Commission on
    Citizenship, 114
Spencer, L., 93
Stanworth, J., 105, 106, 110
Steiger, T. L., 162
Stewart, P., 56, 170
Stonier, T., 65
Storey, D., 106, 110
Strange, A., 106, 110
Streeck, W., 28

Taylor, S., 93
Taylor, S(tephen), 201, 202
Thompson, E. P., 153
Thompson, P., 57, 187

The Times, 22, 47, 50
Toffler, A., 67
Tomlinson, M., 96
Touraine, A., 66
Trinder, C., 46
Trotman, C., 29
Truman, C., 62
Tuckman, A., 202
Turnbull, P., 79
Tyneside Training and Enterprise
    Council, 179

Waddington, J., 47, 52
Wadsworth, J., 43
Wajcman, J., 66
Walker, R., 54
Walsh, K., 172
Walter, N., 93
Warde, A., 41
Waton, A., 61
Watson, T., 201
Webb, J., 28
Webb, S. & B., 81–2
Wheelock, J., 145
White, M., 76, 77
Whitston, C., 47, 53
Wilkinson, A., 169, 172, 175
Wilkinson, B., 176–7, 190, 191, 201
Willmott, H., 30, 172
Wilson, W. J., 136
Winterton, J., 79
Wolkowitz, C., 58, 59, 62
Wood, S., 24, 83
Worsley, R., 46
Wray, D., 36
Wright, S., 152

Young, M., 89